Health, Mental Health, and Safety Guidelines for Schools

NASN

National
Association of
School Nurses

American Academy
of Pediatrics

DEDICATED TO THE HEALTH OF ALL CHILDREN™

Library of Congress Control Number: 2005922062
ISBN: 1-58110-167-8
MA0309

The recommendations in this publication do not indicate an exclusive course of treatment or serve as a standard of medical care. Variations, taking into account individual circumstances, may be appropriate.

3-124/0505

OVERVIEW

These guidelines were developed by more than 300 health, education, and safety professionals from more than 30 different national organizations as well as by parents and other supporters.

Lead organizations:

American Academy of Pediatrics
http://www.aap.org

National Association of School Nurses
http://www.nasn.org

Resources and funding to develop *Health, Mental Health, and Safety Guidelines for Schools* provided by:

Maternal and Child Health Bureau
http://www.mchb.hrsa.gov
Health Resources and Services Administration
Department of Health and Human Services
Project Officer: Stephanie Bryn, MPH
Consultant: Trina Anglin, MD, PhD

For more information on participating organizations, steering committee, and expert panels, refer to the About the Authors section.

Editor-in-Chief:

Howard Taras, MD

Co-editors:

Paula Duncan, MD
Doris Luckenbill, MS, RN, CRNP
Judy Robinson, PhD, RN, CAE
Lani Wheeler, MD
Susan Wooley, PhD, CHES

Suggested citation:

Taras H, Duncan P, Luckenbill D, Robinson J, Wheeler L, Wooley S, eds. *Health, Mental Health, and Safety Guidelines for Schools.* Elk Grove Village, IL: American Academy of Pediatrics; 2004

The editors extend their gratitude to the following individuals for their assistance in the preparation of this publication: Alison Baker, Rachael Hagan, Sandi King, Wanda Miller, Rachael Widom, Theresa Wiener, Kyle Wolfe, and Jennifer Pane. The editors acknowledge the invaluable assistance provided by individuals who participated in the internal and public review process. Thank you!

ABOUT THE AUTHORS

Who Developed the Guidelines

The editors extend their acknowledgement and appreciation to the many hundreds of professional association members and members of the public who took time to read these guidelines when they were posted on the Internet in draft form. Comments, suggestions, additions, and corrections that were sent to us as a result of these efforts were essential to both the quality and utility of these guidelines.

Central Steering Committee

American Academy of Child and Adolescent
   Psychiatry
http://www.aacap.org
Graeme Hanson
Michelle D. Morse

American Academy of Family Physicians
http://www.aafp.org
Jeannette South-Paul
Barbara Widmar

American Academy of Pediatrics
http://www.aap.org
Paula Duncan
Howard L. Taras
Lani S. M. Wheeler
Lydia E. Bologna
Mary Pat Frintner
Su Li
Darcy Steinberg

American Association of School
   Administrators
http://www.aasa.org
Karl V. Hertz
Sharon Adams-Taylor

American Medical Association
http://www.ama-assn.org
Missy Fleming

American Psychological Association
http://www.apa.org
Jan N. Hughes
Angela M. Oddone

American Public Health Association
http://www.apha.org
Susan H. Pollack
Barbara J. Hatcher

American School Health Association
http://www.ashaweb.org
Laurie Jensen-Wunder
Susan F. Wooley

Association of Maternal and Child Health
   Programs
http://www.amchp.org
Deborah Klein Walker
Sarah Pfau
Sarah Roschwalb

Association of State and Territorial Health
   Officials
http://www.astho.org
Jimmy Guidry
Jennifer Henry

Centers for Disease Control and Prevention/
   Division of Adolescent and School Health
http://www.cdc.gov/nccdphp/dash/SHI/
   index.htm
Lisa Barrios
Howell Wechsler

Council of Chief State School Officers
http://www.ccsso.org
Nora Howley

National Assembly on School-Based
   Health Care
http://www.nasbhc.org
John Schlitt

National Association of School Nurses, Inc
http://www.nasn.org
Doris H. Luckenbill
Judy Robinson

National Association of Social Workers
http://www.naswdc.org
Millicent M. Williams

National Education Association
http://www.nea.org
Rena Large
Vicki Harrison

National PTA
http://www.pta.org
Gabriella Hayes
Linda Parkinson
Mary Anne Roll

National School Boards Association
http://www.nsba.org/site/index.asp
Margie T. Bradford
Brenda Z. Greene

Office of School Health, University of Colorado
http://www.uchsc.edu/schoolhealth
Judith B. Igoe

Society of State Directors of Health, Physical
    Education and Recreation
http://www.thesociety.org
Fran Anthony Meyer
Bill Datema

The final edited version of this document
was not reviewed by all members of the
Central Steering Committee.

Expert Panel Chairpersons

Howard Adelman
Claire D. Brindis
Ron Brown
Oscar G. Bukstein
Jack Campana
Paul S. Casamassimo
Sue Catchings
Linda Grossman
Eric G. Handler
Leslie A. Lytle
Patsy Maloney
Alice R. McCarthy

Ellen R. Schmidt
Stephen Silverman
Howard Spivak
Joyce N. Thomas
Franklin L. Till, Jr.
Carlos A. Vega-Matos
Genie L. Wessel
Katherine Wilbur
Judith Young

The final edited version of this document was
not reviewed by expert panel chairpersons.

Expert Panel Members

Clyde Alexander
Darryl Alexander
Betty Alford
John P. Allegrante
Clinton W. Anderson
Sue Anderson
Kristy Arbogast
Kari Arfstrom
Janice Bacon
Claire Barnett
Renee C. Barrett
Laurie Bechhofer

Jeanette N. Bennett
Marilyn Benoit
Nancy E. Berger
David Birch
Michael Black
Martin J. Blank
Lynda Boyer-Chuanroong
Beverly Bradley
Marilyn Briggs
Marilyn J. Bull
Harriet Burge
Caroline Butler

Marcia Bynoe
Dorothy Reddell Caldwell
Donna Callaway
Frank Campana
Mary Campbell
Fredric Cantor
David Chadwick
John Cheek
Mark Chenven
Priscilla Clarkson
Tami J. Cline
Jean Sheerin Coffe
Susan M. Colburn
Judy Comoletti
Jose Fernando Cordero
Petter Cortese
Carol Costante
Cindy L. Clark Craig
Linda Crawford
Erin Cruise
Tom Davis
Deborah Deas
Harriet Deel
Karen DePauw
Robert Dingman
Steve Michael Dorman
Judith Lomakin Dodd
Janice Doyle
Juan Dumois
David Fassler
Gerald A. Feretti
Andrea Ferreira
Linda M. Finke
Barbara Flis
Hector Flores
Brian S. Flynn
Tracy Fox
Steve Freedman
Stan Friedman
Linda D. Frizzell
Glen Gilbert
Benjamin Gitterman
Alvin Goldfarb
Leslie Goldman
Lani Graham
Linda Grant

Wendy Graves
Mark Greenberg
R. Terry Grubb
Patricia Guthrie
Deborah Haber
Karen Hacker
Richard Hanks
Shirley Hawkins
John Heeney
Charlotte Hendricks
Russel G. Henke
Terry Henry
Hope Hill
Molly D. Holland
Katrina Holt
Shirley Ann Holt-Hale
Jan Hootman
Janet W. Horsley
Andrea Hricko
Betty Hubbard
Oscie Huff
Robert Isman
Mary Grenz Jalloh
Renee Jenkins
Thomas Jeschke
Gail Johnson
Barbara Jones
Linda J. Juszczak
Constance Killian
Michele Kern
Joe Kimbrell
Douglas Kirby
Sandy Klarenbeek
Jay Kravitz
Tamara Kreinin
John Kulig
Charlene Lakhdar
Sandy Landry
Louise Lapeze
Curtis S. Lavarello
Barbara L. Leach
Julia Lear
Daniel Jay Levy
William H. Lieberman
Karen Liller
RoseMarie Lofgren

David Lohrmann

Bill Loshbough

Bobbie Boyd Lubker

Avi Madan-Swain

Theresa Madden

Delores Malvitz

Wanda Marshall

Eva Marx

Paul Melinkovich

Betsy McAllister Groves

Beverly McCarty

Beverly McCoun

Thomas McKenzie

Hector Mendez

Ricardo Mendoza

Deborah Milan-Niler

Brent Miller

Ted Miller

Wesley Mitchell

Juan Diego Montemayor

Luis Montes

Sharon Morrill

Linda Morse

Judy Mountjoy

Deborah Mulligan-Smith

Linda Murphy

Diane Neumark-Stzainer

Faye New

Lily Ning

Arthur J. Nowak

Beverly O'Bryant

Amy Okamura

Larry Olsen

Tom O'Rourke

Elizabeth Ortiz do Valdez

Angela Osterhuber

Joanna Owens-Nauslar

Jim Paavola

Carole Paladino

Linda Parkinson

Linn Parsons

Glen T. Pearson, Jr

Sylvia Pease

Cheryl Perry

David M. Perry

Yasenka Peterson

Susan Philliber

Robert Morgan Pigg, Jr

Scott Poland

Arif Quraishi

Barbara A. Ram

Brooke Randell

Robin Rasco

Robert Reece

Frances Riley

Dora Rivas

Robert Robinson

Mary Anne Roll

Barry Rosenberg

Susan Rosenthal

Marcia Rubin

Michael Sandner

Robin Sawyer

Diana Scalise

Steven P. Schinke

Manuel Schydlower

Esther Sciammarella

Karen Sedlacek

Herbert H. Severson

Wanda L. Shockey

David Marc Shore

Renee E. Sieving

Susanne Tropez Sims

Karen Slay

Eric Small

Becky Smith

Debbie Smith

Bonnie Alston Spear

Debbie Stasiw

Patricia M. Steele-Kefgen

Jane E. M. Steffensen

Marguerite M. Stevens

Mary Story

Larry Sullivan

James Sutherland

Kathleen Sutton

Jacqueline Tallman

Marlene K. Tappe

Linda Taylor

Lora Taylor

Susan Kay Telljohann

Ann Kelsey Thacher

Kathy Tipirneni
Penelope K. Tippy
Sandy Treager
Jane Tustin
Lee Ann Tyson Martin
Valerie A. Ubbes
Elizabeth Valdez
Richard Verdugo
Murray Vincent
Robert B. Voas
Mark Wagner
Lorrie Walker
Dorie Watkins
Stan Weed
Duane Weik
Fred Weintrauk

Mark Weist
Conni Wells
Chudley E. Werch
Barbara Westwater
Anita Wheeler
Debra Whitcomb
Sue Will
Janet Willis
Mary Margaret Windsor
Marleen Wong
Clay Yeager
Lenore Zedosky
Jean Zimmerman

The final edited version of this document was not reviewed by members of the expert panel.

Federal Advisors

Mark Anderson
Centers for Disease Control and Prevention
http://www.cdc.gov

Trina M. Anglin
Health Resources and Services Administration
Maternal and Child Health Bureau
http://www.mchb.hrsa.gov

Gail Beaumont
Office of Safe and Drug Free Schools
US Department of Education
http://www.ed.gov/about/offices/list/osdfs/
  index.html

Stephanie Bryn
Health Resources and Services Administration
Maternal and Child Health Bureau
http://www.mchb.hrsa.gov

Charlene Burgeson
Centers for Disease Control and Prevention
http://www.cdc.gov

Betty Chemers
Office of Juvenile Justice and Delinquency
  Prevention
Department of Justice
http://ojjdp.ncjrs.org

Linda Crossett
Centers for Disease Control and Prevention
http://www.cdc.gov

Diana Denboba
Health Resources and Services Administration
Maternal and Child Health Bureau
http://www.mchb.hrsa.gov

Connie Deshpande
Office of Safe and Drug Free Schools
US Department of Education
http://www.nationalguidelines.org/Office of
  Safe and Drug Free Schools

Patricia J. Dittus
Division of Adolescent and School Health
Centers for Disease Control and Prevention
http://www.cdc.gov/nccdphp/dash/SHI/
  index.htm

Kellie Dressler Tetrick
Office of Juvenile Justice and Delinquency
  Prevention
Department of Justice
http://ojjdp.ncjrs.org

Ann Drum
Health Resources and Services Administration
Maternal and Child Health Bureau
http://www.mchb.hrsa.gov

Michelle Edwards
Substance Abuse and Mental Health Services
    Administration
Center for Mental Health Services
http://www.samhsa.gov/index.aspx

Dena Green
Health Resources and Services Administration
Maternal and Child Health Bureau
http://www.mchb.hrsa.gov

Laverne Green
Health Resources and Services Administration
Maternal and Child Health Bureau
http://www.mchb.hrsa.gov

Isadora Hare
Health Resources and Services Administration
Maternal and Child Health Bureau
http://www.mchb.hrsa.gov

Delores Malvitz
Centers for Disease Control and Prevention
http://www.cdc.gov

Jen Medearis
Office of Safe and Drug Free Schools
US Department of Education
http://www.ed.gov/about/offices/list/osdfs/
    index.html

Cheryl Neverman
National Highway Traffic Safety
    Administration
Department of Transportation
http://www.nhtsa.dot.gov

Erica Odom
Centers for Disease Control and Prevention
http://www.cdc.gov

Elena Page
National Institute for Occupational Safety
    and Health
Centers for Disease Control and Prevention
http://www.cdc.gov/niosh/homepage.html

Jane Pritzl
Centers for Disease Control and Prevention
http://www.cdc.gov

Kim Smith
US Environment Protection Agency
http://www.epa.gov

Denise Sofka
Health Resources and Services Administration
Maternal and Child Health Bureau
http://www.mchb.hrsa.gov

Janet S. St. Lawrence
Centers for Disease Control and Prevention
http://www.cdc.gov

Bonnie Strickland
Health Resources and Services Administration
Maternal and Child Health Bureau
http://www.mchb.hrsa.gov

Ralph Swisher
Federal Emergency Management Agency
http://www.fema.gov

Howell Wechsler
Centers for Disease Control and Prevention
http://www.cdc.gov

Audrey M. Yowell
Health Resources and Services Administration
Maternal and Child Health Bureau

The final edited version of this document was
not reviewed by all federal advisors.

TABLE OF CONTENTS

◀ Introduction ▶

PURPOSE OF GUIDELINES

The purpose of *Health, Mental Health, and Safety Guidelines for Schools* is to help those who influence the health and safety of students and school staff while they are in school, on school grounds, on their way to or from school, and involved in school-sponsored activities. The guidelines recognize that the primary mission of schools is to educate students. Schools also have a responsibility for students' health and safety while they are at school. By addressing health, mental health, and safety issues (including transportation and motor vehicle safety), schools can improve students' academic performance today and contribute to their increased longevity and productivity long after they leave school.

Health, mental health, and safety, as defined here, are inextricably linked to student achievement. Poor nutrition, impaired vision or hearing, dental pain, sleep deficiency, substance abuse, anxiety about home life, anxiety about relations with peers, exposure to violence, and any unaddressed symptoms are examples of health and safety issues associated with less than optimal achievement in school. Sometimes the association between achievement and health, mental health, and safety is obvious (eg, an injury or illness that causes a low school attendance rate). At other times the association between student achievement and health, mental health, and safety is not easily observed (eg, when a teacher's health or mental health affects teaching and relationships with students or when a student's anxiety about a real or perceived threat of violence affects his/her attention to class work). Complementary to benefits of optimizing health and safety to improve student achievement is the understanding that an educated populace is a beneficial factor for the health and safety of the population.

Healthy People 2010 is the prevention agenda for the nation. It is designed to identify the most significant preventable threats to health and to establish national goals to reduce these threats. It should not be surprising that Healthy People 2010 includes many school-specific health objectives. There are 20 Healthy People 2010 objectives that are school specific, and these are listed in Appendix A. Increasing the number of students who complete high school is a Healthy People 2010 goal, as are increasing the number of schools with sound environmental policies and reducing school days missed as a result of asthma. The interwoven quality of educational achievement with health, mental health, and safety is one reason that the prevention, detection, and resolution of health and safety problems require cooperative efforts of students, their families, community agencies, and school personnel.

TARGET AUDIENCE

The primary target audience for these guidelines is the school administrator responsible for overall school or district policies or responsible for one or more components of school health and safety at the school site or district level. Undoubtedly, many others who play a role in the assessment, planning, or improvement of school health and safety programs or in advocacy efforts related to school health and safety programs will also find these guidelines helpful. These include school health professionals, educators, school board members, parents, other community members (including transportation officials and child advocates), legislators at all levels, professionals in government departments (eg, education, health, safety, transportation, justice, and labor), and students themselves.

FEASIBILITY

Many schools and districts have practices and policies in place that are consistent with guidelines recommended in this collection. Most schools will find many of the remaining guidelines easy to adopt. For some guidelines, however, a school or district might not find the guidelines feasible in the short-term, given resource limitations, but will include them in their planning.

GUIDELINES, NOT STANDARDS

Often, documents designed as recommendations are misused as standards or measures of basic quality, particularly when no other written standards exist. Some guidelines represent minimum standards for safety and health while others represent the optimum. Each community, with the help of its own health, safety, mental health, and educational experts and community members, can and should decide which guidelines are basic, which do not apply, and which to work toward. This collection of guidelines can help community and school leaders determine the breadth of school health, mental health, and safety issues and set priorities for future actions. The *Health, Mental Health, and Safety Guidelines* should not be used as a tool for punitive measures or legal threats.

NOT A "STAND-ALONE" DOCUMENT

This compendium of guidelines draws on other published guidelines on specific components of school health and safety programs as well as on overall coordination of these programs. It provides references to these other sources, most of which provide more description and detail than are included in this document. Interested readers should refer to the referenced guidelines and standards for additional information and details.

It is hoped that these guidelines will stimulate and invigorate discussions of methods that schools and districts can use to operationalize health and safety objectives outlined here. It is not unreasonable to expect that this compendium will inspire further publications that describe model programs, provide technical assistance, and uncover best practices so that schools and school districts can attain the intended purpose of each guideline.

THE FORMAT

The overarching guidelines serve as a starting point because they provide a context for all guidelines that follow. In practice, any one guideline in isolation is not truly meaningful unless it is considered in the broader context of a school health program. For example, a guideline that promotes the inclusion of healthy food items in the cafeteria may not address that students also require education on how to make healthy food choices—the latter point to be found in another guideline in another chapter. To help readers see connections, each guideline (other than the overarching guidelines) contains a section at the end titled "Related Guidelines." Here, there is a list of guidelines that the reader should read in order to learn other pertinent information related to that topic. As even this list is limited in scope, readers are encouraged to make use of the subject index.

USE OF TERMS

In order to describe health, mental health, and safety issues, use of some technical terms from these fields is sometimes necessary. Wherever a word, phrase, or term is used and not defined, a description is available for readers in the Glossary.

Schools work and interact with parents, guardians of students who are not their parents, and families in general. "Parent," "guardian," and "family" are all words that are used in this document. Sometimes when only one term is used, inference to one or both of the other terms must be made by the reader.

The terms "health" and "mental health" in the title of this document and in the content of each guideline refer to oral, physical, biologic, and psychological health. "Health" does not mean simply freedom from physical disease or pain; it describes a condition of being sound in mind and in spirit, a state of feeling vigorous, the ability to deal with physical and social stresses, and the ability to perform work (including school work) and engage in constructive family and community roles. In this document, the term "health" always connotes this full meaning and so it always includes mental health. Nevertheless, "mental health" is stated explicitly in addition to "health" in some circumstances in order to remind readers of the importance of this component of health.

The term "safety" is used throughout the document and means more than simply the absence of danger. Safety is used to describe a freedom from risk of injury and, not least, a feeling on behalf of each individual that he or she (or one's child) is free from both real and perceived danger.

REFERENCES AND RESOURCES

Referenced documents are listed at the end of each chapter. References that are pertinent to each guideline are cited by number next to the guideline's title. Internet sites that are recommended as useful resources for readers are also listed alphabetically in the "Related Links" section after each guideline.

The accuracy of all Internet addresses (URLs) for references and resources was verified at the time this document was submitted for publication. These addresses sometimes change. If an Internet address is no longer correct, a recommended action is to find the referenced Internet page by typing keywords (eg, subject, author, title, name of organization) into a general search engine or a search engine that lies within an organization's own Internet site.

◀ **Overarching Guidelines** ▶

GENERAL

0-01–AN INCLUSIVE, RESPECTFUL SCHOOL CLIMATE[1-13]

Create and maintain a school climate and learning environment that is safe for, respectful of, friendly toward, and responsive to persons of all racial, cultural, ethnic, and socioeconomic groups; of all faiths, family structures, and sexual orientations and identities; and with any special health need, developmental delay, or disability. Such a climate and environment must apply to students, staff, and families.

▶ RATIONALE

Schools that respect and promote the acceptance of diversities create environments that enhance the physical, emotional, and social health of students, faculty, and staff and ultimately contribute to a better learning environment for students. Staff training is usually necessary to create such an inclusive environment.

▶ COMMENTARY

Schools reflect the diversity of communities and their families. They have a unique opportunity to model tolerance, promote acceptance, and celebrate the contributions made by people from a variety of family structures; faiths; racial, ethnic, linguistic, and socioeconomic backgrounds; and sexual orientations and identities.

Families from diverse backgrounds sometimes do not feel included or engaged in school activities and in decision-making processes that influence all health and safety issues affecting their children. Efforts must be made to address language, economic, accessibility, and social barriers that inhibit full participation of students and their families in school activities.

Schools can work to accommodate different family situations in a variety of ways. Schools may:

- identify policies, practices, and curricula that promote acceptance of diversity. Any that may be interpreted as offensive or may be misunderstood by some groups must be addressed in a culturally competent and sensitive manner;
- hire staff who are culturally competent and speak languages of populations served by the school in order to interact with families of diverse backgrounds and increase their involvement with school matters;
- schedule parent-teacher meetings after work hours or via telephone and devise similar strategies to eliminate barriers to family involvement; and
- censure derogatory comments made to anyone else by students, staff, or family members at school and do so consistently and immediately.

Appropriate training can help school staff increase communication between families and school personnel and create a family-friendly environment that will encourage family involvement. To accomplish this, provide staff and volunteers with training opportunities to develop cultural competency (see Appendix B).

▶ RELATED LINKS

http://www.casel.org
http://www.no-bully.com
http://www.glsen.org
http://www.nameorg.org

0-02—SCHOOL POLICIES CONSISTENT WITH LAWS[14,15]

Ensure that district health, mental health, food service, and safety policies and procedures are congruent with federal, state, and local regulations as well as with current case law concerning school health and safety.

▶ **RATIONALE**

The magnitude of case law concerning school health and safety provides evidence of the importance of policies and procedures that are consistent with laws and regulations. Keeping school health- and safety-related policies congruent with the law is one important way for schools to maintain a high standard of quality for matters related to the safety and health of students and staff.

▶ **COMMENTARY**

State departments of health and education have a responsibility to ensure that local jurisdictions are aware of federal, state, and local laws, regulations, and legal actions that shape and modify local school health and safety policies and practices. Resources are available to schools and school districts that are designed to help identify areas of legal concern. Organizations sponsoring such resources include the National Association of State Boards of Education (http://www.nasbe.org), Council of Chief State School Officers (http://www.ccsso.org), National School Boards Association (http://www.nsba.org), and state and federal departments of education.

Up-to-date information about changes in federal law and regulations relevant to school health and safety are often available from federal agencies. These include the Department of Education (http://www.ed.gov; eg, Office of Special Education and Rehabilitative Services, Office of Safe and Drug-Free Schools [http://www.ed.gov/about/offices/list/osdfs/index.html], Office for Civil Rights [http://www.ed.gov/about/offices/list/ocr/504faq.html]), Department of Health and Human Services (eg, Centers for Disease Control and Prevention [http://www.cdc.gov], Centers for Medicare and Medicaid Services [http://cms.hhs.gov]), Department of Justice (http://www.ada.gov), Department of Agriculture (http://www.usda.gov; eg, National School Lunch Program; School Breakfast Program regulations), Consumer Product Safety Commission (http://www.cpsc.gov), Department of Transportation (http://www.nhtsa.dot.gov), Environmental Protection Agency (http://www.epa.gov), and Department of Labor (http://www.dol.gov/elaws/fmla.htm, including the Occupational Safety and Health Administration [http://www.osha.gov]).

▶ **RELATED LINKS**

http://www.cdc.gov
http://cms.hhs.gov
http://www.cpsc.gov
http://www.ccsso.org
http://www.epa.gov
http://www.mchb.hrsa.gov
http://www.nasbe.org
http://www.nhtsa.dot.gov
http://www.nsba.org
http://www.osha.gov
http://www.usda.gov

http://www.ed.gov
http://www.ed.gov/offices/OM/fpco/ferpa
http://www.ed.gov/offices/OSERS/Policy/IDEA
http://www.ed.gov/about/offices/list/ocr/504faq.html
http://www.ed.gov/about/offices/list/osdfs/index.html
http://www.ed.gov/pubs/whoweare/title.html
http://www.hhs.gov/ocr
http://www.ada.gov
http://www.dol.gov/elaws/fmla.htm

0-03—PROTECTION OF STUDENT AND STAFF CONFIDENTIALITY[10,16–20]

Maintain confidentiality of students' and staff members' health and mental health information including both personal and family health data.

▶ *RATIONALE*

Students and members of the staff must believe that their right to confidentiality and privacy will be respected. Maintaining confidentiality is mandated by many states' laws and regulations.

▶ *COMMENTARY*

Schools must have written policies that define when and how often signed consent is required to exchange information, the limits of information to be exchanged, and terms of notification when this information is exchanged. In the course of classroom discussions, private conversations with nurses, counselors, coaches, and others, students often reveal personal information they do not want others to know. Unless this information jeopardizes their safety or that of others (eg, suicidal thoughts, disclosure of sexual assault, expressions of harming others), students should have the right to control whom at school is informed. Confidentiality should include information about a pregnancy. The Code of Ethics of the National Education Association (http://www.nea.org) stipulates that educators "shall not disclose information about students obtained in the course of professional service unless disclosure serves a compelling purpose or is required by law."

Health agencies must handle personal health information under stipulations outlined under a federal law known as the Health Insurance Portability and Accountability Act (HIPAA) (http://cms.hhs.gov). Although only some school health records (eg, records that derive from school-based health centers) fall directly under HIPAA jurisdiction, all schools need to exchange information with health providers, clinics, hospitals, and other entities required to adhere to HIPAA. As such, "release of information" forms used by schools to notify health agencies that student information is being sought must now comply with HIPAA regulations if they are to serve their purpose. For example, parents' consent to have their children's health information disclosed to schools from a health agency should be revocable, explicitly limited to a defined duration of time, and limited in its scope and range of use.

The handling of private information described in HIPAA can be very instructive for schools. The flow of protected health information within the school system needs to be carefully analyzed. School administrators and the school health and safety team must review how items such as phone logs, records of students visiting the school nurse, students visiting the school psychologist or counselor, and lists of students with health problems are utilized and who has access to them. This confidentiality applies to written, oral, and electronic forms of information. Modifications to record-keeping may need to be made in order to be sure that those who require information have access to it and that the information is available only to those persons.

Under the Family Education Rights and Privacy Act (FERPA),[16] parents have the right to access all the records a school has on their children. In addition, with a few exceptions, the school may not release student information outside the school without consent of the parents. In cases where a student's safety is at risk (eg, an abusive family situation), school staff must inform external authorities (eg, child protective services). Schools that maintain health information about staff should seek guidelines for maintaining confidentiality of this information, through the National School Boards Association (http://www.nsba.org).

The training of health professionals often includes maintaining confidentiality of clients' personal information. However, educators and other school staff are often unaware of their responsibility to maintain confidentiality. Schools need to train school staff and volunteers who have regular contact with students or with student and staff records so that school policies are explicitly known.

▶ *RELATED LINKS*

http://www.ashaweb.org
http://cms.hhs.gov
http://www.ed.gov/offices/OM/fpco/ferpa
http://www.nea.org
http://www.nsba.org
http://www.ed.gov

◀ **Overarching Guidelines** ▶

HEALTH AND SAFETY INFRASTRUCTURE

0-04—HEALTH AND SAFETY COORDINATOR FOR SCHOOL, FOR DISTRICT [21-25]

Designate a "school health and safety coordinator" position at each school and at the district level. Individuals holding these positions should have the knowledge and skills necessary to integrate schools' health, mental health, and safety programs; to reach out to and involve families; and to collaborate with community agencies.

▶ *RATIONALE*

Having coordinators for health and safety at the district and school levels helps to coordinate and sustain activities that support students' health, safety, and academic achievement. Without a coordinator, situations may occur in which no one feels responsible for coordinating health and safety programs, or perhaps several people will do so independently. Administrative support and recognition are necessary to influence staff, change systems, and implement programs.

▶ *COMMENTARY*

School and district health and safety coordinators develop and coordinate activities that support the health, mental health, and safety of students and their families. The role should enhance and complement the school health and safety team, as well as the roles of its members (eg, school nurse, counselor, principal). At the district level and in large schools, coordination may be a full-time function. In small schools, coordination may only require release time from one class period. The salary should reflect the position's supervisory responsibilities. Delineate expected activities in a job description and assess them using performance evaluations. Define the scope of authority of the position. Activities differ in scope at the district and school levels. They may include:

- developing community resource listings (eg, medical, dental, vision-related, mental health, and social services);
- ensuring that offers from community agencies and professionals to provide schools with products or services are assessed and, if accepted, applied appropriately to school programs;
- helping teachers develop health- and safety-related activities that involve students' families and the community;
- acting as a liaison or representative to school and community partnerships;
- coordinating school health and safety teams and serving as a resource for school and district health and safety advisory councils;
- coordinating efforts of school nurses, counselors and other staff members to identify and address primary causes of student absences, student injuries, and disease outbreaks;
- coordinating efforts to assess the school environment for contradictory health- and safety-related messages;
- identifying potential funding sources for supporting programs; and,
- evaluating and revising components of school health and safety programs, including coordination itself.

Highly motivated, well-informed individuals who have the confidence of the school and community-at-large are most effective. A small number of colleges, as well as the American Cancer Society, offer training programs designed to build coordinators' skills and to train them to take on leadership roles within their schools and districts.

▶ *RELATED LINKS*

http://www.cancer.org
http://www.ashaweb.org

0-05—HEALTH AND SAFETY ADVISORY COUNCIL[22,26-30]

Establish a school and/or district health and safety advisory council that is composed of diverse members of the school and community, including family members of students and student representatives.

▶ *RATIONALE*

Working jointly with stakeholders (of children's education, health, and safety) helps to promote a safe school environment that best nurtures the health and mental health of students. Community partners are more likely to assume responsibility for meeting goals and objectives that they help identify jointly and that reflect the community's concerns and issues than they will for goals and objectives determined independently by schools who subsequently seek community help.

▶ *COMMENTARY*

In some school districts, each school may have an advisory council. In others, both schools and district or only the district will have an advisory council. Councils can be designed to address all components of a coordinated school health and safety program such as health and safety instruction, a healthful and safe school environment, health and mental health services, physical education, school counseling, food services, school site health promotion for faculty and staff, and integration of school and community programs. A council should advise staff members who are in positions to develop school health- and safety-related policies (eg, school principal at the school level; superintendent and/or school board at the district level).

Councils can provide advice on a variety of health and safety issues. They can operate as advocates for students and families, provide support and advice concerning controversial health issues, and advise on fiscal planning as well as on evaluation, accountability, and quality control. They can help school administrators and the school health and safety coordinator determine community needs, identify resources in the community, coordinate activities at school with those of other community agencies and organizations, improve communications between schools and the communities they serve, and recommend policy changes.

Family representatives and students on the advisory councils can help ensure that families and students are valued and that their interests are protected by school health and safety decisions. Seek diverse membership so that both genders are represented, there is geographic diversity, and the racial and ethnic groups of the community are well-represented. Welcome community representatives from youth organizations, government, service agencies (health-related and social services), justice and safety-related agencies (eg, emergency medical services, fire, police), faith-based institutions, media, and business/industry. In addition to community members, a school health and safety council should include the school health and safety coordinator (Guideline 0-04) as well as school personnel who represent components of the school's (or district's) health and safety programs.

▶ *RELATED LINKS*

http://www.cancer.org

0-06—SCHOOL HEALTH AND SAFETY TEAM[22,31]

Establish and maintain a school health and safety team composed of selected school-employed staff and contractors responsible for planning and implementing various components of a school health and safety program.

▶ *RATIONALE*

The school health and safety team is a component of a systematic process that encourages collaboration, joint planning, and training among school staff who share responsibility for implementing general health and safety programs as well as students' individualized health and safety plans.

▶ *COMMENTARY*

The school health and safety team is separate and different from an advisory council (see Guideline 0-05), although many staff may be members of both. Whereas the school or district advisory council recommends policy and programmatic issues to school or district administrators, it cannot determine the day-to-day processes required to implement programs at the school level. This is the role of the school health and safety team along with the school's health and safety coordinator (Guideline 0-04). Working with site administrators, team members can also ensure that everyone in the school community knows about the coordination and how to contribute. In addition to coordinating all components of health and safety programs at a school, the school's health and safety team coordinates how health- and safety-related accommodations for each student with special needs will be implemented once the individualized education program (IEP) team or other multidisciplinary student assistance team (Guideline 4-01) has determined necessary measures to take.

Members of a school health and safety team should include people with responsibility for a wide variety of health- and safety-related school services. Members may be representatives of school administration, nursing, social services, mental health and counseling assessment and services, physical education, health education, substance abuse prevention and intervention, food services, audiology, oral health, special education and special services (including personnel responsible for compliance with Individuals with Disabilities Education Act [http://www.ed.gov/offices/OSERS/Policy/IDEA] and with Section 504 of the Rehabilitation Act), occupational therapy, physical therapy, speech and language therapy, medical consultation, school based health centers (where applicable), staff wellness, health promotion programs, transportation, security, and building maintenance.

▶ *RELATED LINKS*

http://www.ashaweb.org
http://www.ed.gov

0-07—STAFF TRAINING FOR HEALTH/SAFETY EMERGENCIES[32-35]

Train all school staff on health and safety procedures so that they know what to do and whom to call at the outbreak of an urgent situation or emergency. Include training that prepares staff for urgent situations that may occur when there are students or staff with diabetes, asthma, seizures, and allergic disorders.

▶ RATIONALE

When a physical, mental health, or safety-related emergency occurs, quick action by those on the scene can often prevent further harm and avoid panic among students and staff witnessing the event. School health professionals and other school personnel who are designated as providers of first aid are often not on the scene when such events initially occur. Therefore, all school staff, including administrators, educators, support staff (eg, secretaries, custodial staff, bus drivers, cafeteria staff), and regular volunteers need to know how to respond to a variety of situations until professional help arrives.

▶ COMMENTARY

Each school requires a minimum number of trained personnel who know how to provide rescue breathing, render first aid, and take other special precautions, such as immobilizing a victim's head and neck after an injury (Guideline 4-07). These people are often called "first responders." All staff members need to be trained so that they know who these designated staff are and how to summon their help.

Train all new employees and regular volunteers who have contact with students and then retrain them at least annually thereafter. In addition to being able to identify designated school-based first responders and how to summon them, teach immediate response techniques that can be applied until this help arrives. Develop this training in consultation with the school's health and safety coordinator and the health and safety team. Also consult with local emergency services providers (eg, fire and emergency medical services, police). Immediate responses to a witnessed injury, mental health or emotional crisis (eg, an immediate threat of physical violence), severe allergic reaction, fire, explosion, poisoning, and exposure to a hazardous material should be covered. All employees need to know how to handle body fluids safely and be aware of basic procedures to protect students and staff.

▶ RELATED LINKS

http://www.aaaai.org
http://www.diabetes.org
http://www.americanheart.org
http://www.redcross.org
http://www.ems-c.org
http://www.nhlbi.nih.gov/about/naepp

0-08—PARTNERSHIPS WITH COMMUNITY SERVICE PROVIDERS[28,36-38]

Develop collaborative relationships with service providers in the community, including providers of health, mental health, and dental services; emergency services; hospitals; rehabilitation services; local health departments; social service agencies; youth service providers; and child care and after-school programs. Written agreements should be established for specific contract-related services to schools.

▶ *RATIONALE*

Development of partnerships between schools and community service providers helps improve access to needed services, coordination of care, and consistency of programmatic approaches. Coordination helps to reduce duplication of services and miscommunication. A contract, a memorandum of agreement or a memorandum of understanding clarifies the nature of the collaborative relationship.

▶ *COMMENTARY*

Schools exist within a community context, which can be of great support to the school's responsibility to provide a safe and healthy learning environment for students and to educate students. Schools should establish partnerships with community services that can provide health, mental health, and safety expertise as well as other support services. Schools are confronted with and need to address many complex issues (eg, violence, suicide, complex health conditions, addictive behaviors) that require multifaceted skills that are not necessarily within the purview of teaching professionals or that can be dealt with comprehensively by school health professionals. As such, schools need to develop outside partnerships with agencies that can provide quality services for students, families, and staff. In addition to community service providers listed above, many communities have other agencies (eg, universities) that provide services to students and families.

Individual health, dental, and mental health care providers; hospitals; state and local health departments; community agencies; and school-based health centers often contract or establish agreements with schools to provide services and consultation on health and safety. A written contract or memorandum of agreement clarifies roles, responsibilities, and lines of authority. Written descriptions of the relationship help to reduce confusion and the potential for misunderstanding and conflict.

▶ *RELATED LINK*

http://www.communityschools.org

0-09—INCLUSIVE PROCESS FOR POLICY DEVELOPMENT, COMMUNICATION[14,39]

Involve students, families, staff, administrators, and school board members in development of school health and safety policies and communicate these policies to them. Provide necessary training to implement policies. Monitor and evaluate policies' implementation and impact.

▶ RATIONALE

New policies receive a broader base of support when those affected by them have had the opportunity to contribute to their development. There is a decreased likelihood that a policy will be misunderstood, poorly communicated, or misapplied when its dissemination is planned, people are trained to implement it, and its implementation is monitored to ensure uniform application and enforcement.

▶ COMMENTARY

To help ensure broad support for school health- and safety-related policies, students, families, staff, administration, and the school board should contribute to their development and implementation. The school health and safety coordinator, working with the health and safety advisory council, may be helpful with coordinating community involvement. When families, school staff, and others affected by policies are left out of the policy development process, the rationale for a policy is more likely to be misunderstood, implementation challenges may multiply, and the policy is more likely to be ignored in practice.

All health- and safety-related policies should be available in writing. Communication can occur through a variety of modalities, including routine staff development opportunities, routine communication such as newsletters to staff and to families, pay slips, policy manuals given to all school employees on hire (and annually thereafter), Internet-based formats, e-mail messages, or specially convened staff meetings. Those on the staff with direct responsibility for implementing a given policy require more communication and monitoring than other staff or families. For certain policies, all staff members need training. School policy makers at the local level must determine who needs specialized training on specific policies.

▶ RELATED LINKS

http://www.nasbe.org
http://www.nsba.org

◀ Overarching Guidelines ▶

PROGRAM RELATED

0-10—PROGRAMS BASED ON NEEDS ASSESSMENT[40–42]

Schools and districts need to base plans for developing their coordinated health and safety programs on a thorough needs assessment of the health, mental health, and safety-related needs of students and staff as well as school and community assets and resources.

▶ *RATIONALE*

Proper planning of a coordinated school health and safety program is essential to meet identified needs of the population and to identify resources and services needed to implement the program. Only by assessing population characteristics, school policies, practices, and the school environment can schools be sure they are meeting the specific needs of their population and determine what additional policies, curricula, resources, and services are still required. Proper planning drives budget development, program implementation, and helps to assure inclusion of essential components.

▶ *COMMENTARY*

Although students of a given age share many characteristics, unique aspects of a community and its students must be documented and taken into account when planning. Resource materials from the Centers for Disease Control and Prevention,[40] as well as individuals with expertise in assessment and evaluation, can provide advice on this process—a process that is critically helpful to schools.

A group of people who know the community or are familiar with its students, including persons with expertise in conducting needs assessments as well as analysis and interpretation of data, should work together to gather and examine relevant information. This group may include teachers, administrators, other school health staff, community and public health professionals, medical professionals, clergy, family members, and students. Districts' school health and safety advisory councils (Guideline 0-05) might serve as such a group. The process of developing a needs assessment should include a plan to handle the information so that the process does not stigmatize a school or a student. A needs assessment might include student and community surveys, as well as information from focus groups of students and family members.

Surveying students for sensitive health and safety information (eg, suicide ideation, sexual activity, substance use, child abuse, and domestic violence) can make community acceptance difficult to attain. Ironically, these are the very same issues that may most interfere with students' ability to learn.

Surveillance can also involve environmental scans looking for community assets and resources as well as toxins, potential safety hazards, inconsistent health and safety messages, and barriers to physical activity and to other health and safety enhancing practices. School nurses, hospitals, mental health providers, substance abuse prevention and treatment programs, and/or local health departments can provide information about health and safety concerns they encounter regularly. The information should not identify health and safety problems of specific students but rather, trends and students' highest risks and risks relative to others their age.

▶ *RELATED LINKS*

http://www.cdc.gov
http://www.mchb.hrsa.gov
http://www.mchoralhealth.org

0-11—PROGRAMS WITH EVIDENCE FOR EFFECTIVENESS[43–51]

Select and implement curricula, programs, and services that have scientific evidence for effectively reducing health risks or injuries; for improving health (including oral and mental health), safety, or academic outcomes; or for improving related knowledge, practices, and/or attitudes. For content areas that are new or emerging or for which there are little data, choose curricula, programs, and services that utilize effective theories, practices, and/or principles.

▶ RATIONALE

Evidence of program effectiveness derived from research is an important criterion a school should use when selecting an intervention. Programs funded by the US Department of Education under Safe and Drug-Free Schools[43] must adhere to "Principles of Effectiveness," which states that programs are to be "based on scientifically based research that provides evidence that the program to be used will reduce violence and illegal drug use."

▶ COMMENTARY

Findings from evaluated school health programs are available, but just because a program has undergone evaluation does not guarantee that it is effective. Many effective strategies for health and safety education curricula are described in Guideline 2-05. Synthesis research helps to identify research-based characteristics of effectiveness for a number of components of school health and safety programs, but for many aspects of these programs, this research is not available. When no research exists to support one intervention over another, schools should consider characteristics of effective programs and services and then select or develop an intervention that is based on models with proven effectiveness (ie, best practices). When using untested interventions, the importance of including an evaluation component with the program is paramount.

Although many effective programs are narrow in scope, all chosen programs, curricula, and services should contribute to a district's or school's coordinated health and safety program.

▶ RELATED LINKS

http://www.ada.gov
http://www.asfsa.org
http://www.ashaweb.org
http://www.nasn.org
http://www.nasponline.org
http://www.samhsa.gov
http://www.ed.gov

0-12—ENGAGING COMMUNITY STAKEHOLDERS[28,52-57]

Engage students' families and homes, service agencies, youth-serving organizations, local businesses, faith-based institutions, and other community resources to enhance school health, mental health, and safety programs.

▶ *RATIONALE*

Schools are one element in a community that can help families keep children safe and healthy and promote their learning and citizenship skills. As schools do not and should not have sole responsibility for students' health, mental health, and safety, the support of families and community agencies is essential for school programs.

▶ *COMMENTARY*

Schools often have insufficient resources to provide a comprehensive and multifaceted continuum of interventions. By having direct contact with families and key informants in the community, schools are better able to identify barriers to student success and well-being and better equipped to develop solutions that overcome these barriers. Schools can enhance home-school links by sharing concerns with families and developing solutions that address students' unique needs.

In addition to the benefits for students' education and well-being, students' families, and school staff, there are reciprocal benefits for community agencies who partner with schools. Businesses, the justice system, community health and safety systems, and others may benefit from a healthier population. Community agencies and organizations that provide services to children and families often gain a more visible profile when they become partners with schools.

Examples of neighborhood stakeholders in student health and well-being are students themselves as well as their families and teachers. Other school staff; community business owners; police; faith-based institutions; universities and colleges; local health departments; health and mental health service providers; dentists; emergency medical services; educators of first-aid; departments of health, justice, education, and social services; and other agencies that serve families have stakes in the well-being of the student population and school staff. Communicate regularly with partners and potential partners in order to learn what each has to offer.

▶ *RELATED LINKS*

http://www.cdc.gov
http://www.schoolnurse.com/publicationshealtynews.html
http://www.sedl.org/connections/resources
http://www.csos.jhu.edu/p2000/default.htm
http://www.pta.org
http://www.ed.gov

0-13—EVALUATION OF SCHOOL HEALTH AND SAFETY PROGRAMS[58–64]

Conduct periodic and ongoing evaluation of coordinated school health and safety programs and their components. Include process evaluation and quality assurance, evaluation of programs' effectiveness (including performance measurements), and evaluation of programs' impact on the entire school population.

▶ RATIONALE

Program evaluation enables program improvement, appropriate allocation of resources, and objective support for continuation of effective programs. Routinely conducted evaluation of school health and safety policies, curricula, programs, and services can help decision makers determine whether planned interventions are consistent with what students actually receive and demonstrate the effectiveness of these interventions. Information from a well-designed data collection system can help school administrators make decisions about policies, about maintaining or modifying programs, and about allocating future resources.

▶ COMMENTARY

Most schools have only limited resources for evaluation. Partnerships with local community planning agencies, universities, foundations, and governments can sometimes augment school resources for planning and implementing an evaluation. Three levels of sophistication for evaluation are monitoring, assessment (more rigorous than monitoring with an additional focus on process measures), and applied research (experimental design and statistical data analysis). To conduct any level of evaluation, allocate adequate time, funds, and other resources. Evaluate and collect data on all school programs designed to promote wellness or reduce illness, injuries, suicide, and violence (ie, all health-, mental health-, and safety-related services and programs). Evaluation can include student outcomes and outcomes of programs on the school environment (eg, a sense of community, a sense of safety). When schools use programs with preexisting evidence of effectiveness, evaluation can assess implementation effectiveness as well as relevance in the specific setting and for the specific population to which they are being applied. School administrators often choose to reserve the most sophisticated level of evaluation (applied research) for programs that are either new or cost- or time-intensive, until the program is proven effective.

"Process evaluations" of programs, curricula, policies, and services assess the effectiveness of implementation. Evaluation data can help decision makers modify and improve scrutinized programs and ascertain whether programs were efficient in addition to being effective. Data can consist of administrative information already being collected (such as attendance, injuries, and health office visits) as well as data derived from new surveillance efforts. Examples of data to collect, analyze, and act on are:

- student incident report forms that include cause, location, and other characteristics of incidents of violence and of injuries.[58] All schools should collect data on injuries and violence;
- logs of student visits (nature and number) to school health professionals (eg, nurses);
- classroom behavior, referrals for disciplinary measures and specialized assistance, interpersonal functioning;
- attendance, timely completion of assignments, involvement in extracurricular activities, satisfaction with programs and services, progress toward long-term goals;

- individual families' basic needs and involvement in schooling;
- surveys of students, families, and staff for their awareness and satisfaction with programs and services; and
- frequency of "copy-cat" incidents after a suicide or suicide attempt.

▶ *RELATED LINKS*

http://www.cdc.gov
http://www.nasbhc.org
http://www.uchsc.edu/schoolhealth

◀ **Overarching Guidelines** ▶

PERSONNEL RELATED

0-14—QUALIFICATIONS OF SCHOOL HEALTH STAFF [65–67]

Hire or contract with health-, mental health-, and safety-related professionals who have completed the appropriate academic training for their field and are licensed, credentialed, or certified to provide the services and education for which they are responsible.

▶ *RATIONALE*

Appropriate academic training and formal credentialing and licensing can help ensure the quality of the health, mental health, social, nutrition, dental, and safety services and of the health education and physical education provided in schools.

▶ *COMMENTARY*

Licensing, credentialing, and certification procedures vary by profession. Where licensure, credentialing, and certification are available, staff should be licensed, credentialed, and certified. In many cases, licensure is required, but certification is voluntary. In some cases, evidence of specialized training is desirable, such as specialized training with adolescents or in school settings. If it pertains to professionals' roles and functions at school, require training and experience in specific developmental stages of childhood and adolescence.

Certification and credentialing are often, but not exclusively, achieved through a national body. Licensure always occurs through the state. Districts interested in the availability of licensing for a profession by the state or in the requirements of professional licensure should contact their state professional licensing boards. A number of health- and safety-related professions are listed in Appendix C. Each is accompanied by contact information for a national certification body that is associated with the profession or with a national professional organization that is in a position to recommend qualifications for school practice.

For those professionals already on staff and successfully performing health- and safety-related tasks for which they are not fully qualified, require that necessary training or credentials are obtained within 3 to 5 years. Maintenance of licenses and certifications requires continuing education credits in most professions. School administrators should try to provide time and financial support to assist employed professionals in obtaining continuing education. Facilitating school health and safety professionals' attainment of required continuing education credits may be an assigned responsibility of the school or district health and safety coordinator.

RELATED LINKS

See Internet resources in Appendix C.

O-15—HEALTH PARAPROFESSIONALS[68-71]

Personnel who are not members of a health profession but are trained to assist these professionals (ie, paraprofessionals) may provide many services that students need at school. Establish clearly written guidelines and policies outlining what responsibilities may be delegated to health and mental health paraprofessionals.

▶ RATIONALE

The delegation of some health-related services to unlicensed assistive personnel requires that assistants are trained, oriented, and supervised by the appropriate professional. Assigning such duties to untrained employees may provide a poor quality of care and expose schools to legal risk.

▶ COMMENTARY

Trained paraprofessionals can safely perform many routine functions, which relieves professional staff to provide more complex services. Minor first aid, vision screenings, hearing screenings and occupational therapy are examples of services that school professionals often delegate to unlicensed assistants or paraprofessionals. Examples of health-related paraprofessionals working in schools include health aides, nursing assistants, audiology assistants, occupational therapy assistants (OTAs), and physical therapy assistants (PTAs). In some states, certain paraprofessionals may be certified (eg, certified physical therapy aides).

Through consultation with professional staff, school administrators should specifically and clearly identify the duties of paraprofessionals who provide school health-, mental health-, and safety-related services. The fully qualified professional supervising the paraprofessional must determine whether the paraprofessional has met the required level of training to perform a given function. Paraprofessionals must have the knowledge and competency to perform the designated activities. In no case should paraprofessionals provide or be asked to provide services beyond their level of training or competency.

In schools, administrative assistants or secretaries are often responsible for providing services such as first aid. Administrative assistants who provide first aid services also require appropriate training and supervision. In no case should these staff members provide or be asked to provide services beyond their level of training.

Some states have legislation or regulations that define what services may be delegated to paraprofessionals and other nonprofessionals. For example, in some states the Nurse Practice Act outlines those nursing tasks that may and may not be delegated to others.

Several Internet resources listed in Appendix C are useful for researching the potential role of paraprofessionals in many health and health-related fields.

▶ RELATED LINKS

See Appendix C.

0-16—STAFF DEVELOPMENT FOR HEALTH/SAFETY PERSONNEL[47,72]

Support the participation of health- and safety-related staff members in professional development opportunities that are designed to help them remain current in their fields and maintain credentials and/or licenses.

▶ *RATIONALE*

Ongoing updates and reviews for staff with health- and safety-related roles are required to help ensure the quality of health-, mental health-, nutrition-, dental-, and safety-related services and health and physical education provided in school.

▶ *COMMENTARY*

To implement coordinated school health programs of high quality, professionals and other staff working in health- and safety-related school programs must be properly prepared and stay current in their fields. This includes those who teach health and safety (eg, a certified health educator, an elementary school teacher) and those who provide health- and safety-related services. Rapid advances in health sciences and in the field of teaching methodology necessitate continuing education for those who provide nursing, primary health care, counseling, other mental health services, injury and violence prevention, physical therapy, occupational therapy, speech therapy, school food services, and other services as well as for teachers who provide health education and physical education instruction. Many, but not all, staff members with these health- and safety-related roles in school require continuing education to maintain their certification or license.

Staff development programs that address educators' needs are often too generic and inadequate to help these staff members function optimally in their health- and safety-related roles. Even within one's professional field, ongoing training must be targeted to cover issues specific to the age groups and developmental levels of students encountered. (For example, a staff member working with high school populations requires updates pertinent to adolescent development and is less likely to benefit from training on early childhood development.) Knowledge about growth and development must include any new information on how student transitions (between grades or schools, for example) are affected by or affect a young person's health and educational status. Relevant staff development should include skills practice with feedback in a training setting as well as on-site mentoring.

In addition to updating personnel on matters related to their area of responsibility, it is beneficial for staff to be familiar with the underlying theory and conceptual framework of the district's health and safety program. Since educational systems evolve over time, health professionals working in school systems may also need to be updated on skills required for working within an educational system and on relevant educational policies.

Staff development programs for those with health- and safety-related roles are often available through regional health and educational centers, local and state education agencies, local and state health and safety agencies, colleges and universities, professional meetings and conferences, national or regional training centers, safety agencies (eg, American Heart Association (http://www.americanheart.org), American Red Cross (http://www.redcross.org); emergency medical services), and through others in the school or district who have themselves remained up-to-date professionally. Administrators should assist and encourage staff to participate in a variety of professional development activities (eg, study groups, action research, in-service programs, mentoring programs) and to join relevant local, state, and national professional organizations (see Appendix C for list of national professional associations).

▶ *RELATED LINKS*

http://www.aaaai.org
http://www.aahperd.rg/aahe
http://www.ashaweb.org
http://www.edc.org
http://www.nasbhc.org
http://www.nasbe.org
http://www.nsba.org

0-17–CRIMINAL BACKGROUND CLEARANCE[73,74]

Before allowing new employees or volunteers to have contact with students, ensure that they have no criminal background, particularly in child abuse or in child sexual molestation or assault.

▶ RATIONALE

Schools are liable if a school employee, whose criminal history was available but not checked by school authorities, harms a student. Schools have a responsibility to protect students.

▶ COMMENTARY

Have each prospective employee disclose whether he or she has ever been found by either a court of law or disciplinary board to have sexually assaulted or exploited a minor or to have physically abused a minor. A criminal record might not, by itself, indicate that an adult poses a threat to students or other staff. However, a criminal background check would expose any convictions for child molestation or violence that might pose a threat to students or other staff. Many states have regulations that define schools' responsibilities for criminal record screening.

In many school districts, staff members are selected for employment by the office of the superintendent. Subsequently, employment is based on approval by the school board. Information on criminal background for sexual assault or physical abuse of a minor needs to be made available to these persons who have a responsibility to make employment decisions.

The information on employees with records of prosecution must be protected, just as health information is protected. Criminal background disclosures and fingerprinting information is highly confidential and schools must have policies and procedures to protect against unwarranted dissemination.

▶ RELATED LINKS

http://www.nsba.org
http://www.safechild.org

CHAPTER REFERENCES

1. Community and Family Health Multicultural Work Group. *Building Cultural Competence: A Blueprint for Action.* Olympia, WA: Washington State Department of Health; 1995

2. Davis BJ, Voegtle KH. *Culturally Competent Health Care for Adolescents: A Guide for Primary Care Providers.* Chicago, IL: American Medical Association; 1994

3. *Emergency Medical Services for Children. Cultural Competence.* Washington, DC: EMSC National Resource Center; 1999. Available at: http://www.ems-c.org/Cultural/framecultural.htm

4. Epstein JL. School/family/community partnerships: caring for the children we share. *Phi Delta Kappan.* 1995; 76:701–712

5. Ginsburg KR, Winn RJ, Rudy BJ, Crawford J, Zhao H, Schwarz DF. How to reach sexual minority youth in the health care setting: the teens offer guidance. *J Adolesc Health.* 2002;31:407–416

6. Haynes NM, Comer JP. Integrating schools, families, and communities through successful school reform: the School Development Program. *Sch Psychol Rev.* 1996;25:501–506

7. King MA, Sims A, Osher D. *How is Cultural Competence Integrated in Education? Center for Effective Collaboration and Practice.* Available at: http://cecp.air.org/cultural/Q_integrated.htm

8. Uladson-Billings, G. *Crossing Over to Canaan: The Journey of New Teachers in Diverse Classrooms.* San Francisco, CA: Jossey-Bass; 2001

9. Messina SA. *A Youth Leader's Guide to Building Cultural Competence.* Washington, DC: Advocates for Youth; 1994. Available at: http://www.advocatesforyouth.org/publications/guide.pdf

10. National Education Association. *NEA Handbook, 1991–1992.* Washington, DC: National Education Association; 1991

11. Parents, Families and Friends of Lesbians and Gays. *From our House to the School House: A Brochure for Educators.* Washington, DC: Parents, Families and Friends of Lesbians and Gays; 2002. Available at: http://www.pflag.org/publications/schools.pdf

12. Payne RK. *A Framework for Understanding Poverty.* Baytown, TX: RFT Publishers; 1998

13. Sobocinski MR. Ethical principles in the counseling of gay and lesbian adolescents: issues of autonomy, competence, and confidentiality. *Prof Psychol.* 1990;21:240–247

14. Bogden JF. *Fit, Healthy, and Ready to Learn: A School Health Policy Guide.* Alexandria, VA: National Association of State Boards of Education; 2000

15. US Department of Health and Human Services, Public Health Service. *Food Code.* Washington, DC: US Food and Drug Administration; 2001. Available at: http://www.cfsan.fda.gov/~dms/fc01-toc.html

16. Family Educational Rights and Privacy Act. 20 USC 1232g, 34 CFR 99 (2002)

17. Bergren MD. HIPAA hoopla: privacy and security of identifiable health information. *J Sch Nurs.* 2001;17:336–340

18. Lewis KD, Bear BJ. *Manual of School Health.* 2nd ed, St. Louis MO: Saunders-Elsevier Science; 2002

19. National Association of School Nurses. *Issue Brief: School Health Nurse's Role in Education: Privacy Standards for Student Health Records.* Scarborough, ME: National Association of School Nurses; 2002. Available at: http://208.5.177.157/briefs/hippa.htm

20. National Task Force on Confidential Student Health Information. *Guidelines for Protecting Confidential Student Health Information.* Kent, OH: American School Health Association; 2000

21. American Cancer Society. *School Health Program Elements of Excellence: Helping Children to Grow Up Healthy and Able to Learn.* Atlanta, GA: American Cancer Society; 2000

22. Fetro JV. Implementing coordinated school health programs in local schools. In: Marx E, Wooley SF, eds. *Health Is Academic: A Guide to Coordinated School Health Programs.* New York, NY: Teachers College Press; 1998:15–42

23. Resnicow K, Allensworth D. Conducting a comprehensive school health program. *J Sch Health.* 1996;66:59–63

24. Smith DW, Steckler AB, McCormick LK, LeRoy KR. Lessons learned about disseminating health curricula to schools. *J Health Educ.* 1995;26:37–43

25. Valois RF, Hoyle TB. Formative evaluation results from the Mariner Project: a coordinated school health pilot program. *J Sch Health.* 2000;70:95–103

26. American Academy of Pediatrics. Section 6. Establishing a school health council. In: *School Health Leadership Training Kit.* Elk Grove Village, IL: American Academy of Pediatrics; 2001. Available at: http://www.schoolhealth.org/

27. American Cancer Society. *Improving School Health: A Guide to School Health Councils.* Atlanta, GA: American Cancer Society; 1999

28. Carlyon P, Carlyon W, McCarthy AR. Family and community involvement in school health. In: Marx E, Wooley SF, eds. *Health Is Academic: A Guide to Coordinated School Health Programs.* New York, NY: Teachers College Press; 1998:67–95

29. Epstein JL, Coates L, Clark-Salinas K, Sanders MG, Simon B. *Partnership 2000 Schools Manual: Improving School-Family Community Connections.* An Inventory of Present Practices of School-Family-Community Connections. Baltimore, MD: Johns Hopkins University; 1997

30. Iowa Department of Public Health, Division of Family and Community Health. *Promoting Healthy Youth, Schools, and Communities: A Guide to Community-School Health Advisory Councils.* Des Moines, IA: Iowa Department of Public Health; 2001. Available at: http://208.142.197.5/hkn/pdfs/PDF-Part 1.pdf

31. American Academy of Pediatrics, Committee on Children With Disabilities. Provision of educationally-related services for children and adolescents with chronic diseases and disabling conditions. *Pediatrics.* 2000;105:448–451

32. American Academy of Pediatrics, Committee on School Health. Guidelines for emergency medical care in school. *Pediatrics.* 2001;107:435–436

33. American Red Cross. *Community First Aid and Safety.* Washington, DC: American Red Cross; 2002

34. Nebraska Department of Health and Human Services. *Emergency Guidelines for School Personnel.* Lincoln, NE: Nebraska Department of Health and Human Services; 1997

35. Ohio Chapter American Academy of Pediatrics. *Emergency Guidelines for Schools.* Worthington, OH: Ohio Chapter American Academy of Pediatrics; 2000. Available at: http://www.ems-c.org/downloads/pdf/emscguide.pdf

36. Bernado LM, Anderson L. *Preparing a Response to Emergency Problems: A Self-study Module.* Scarborough, ME: National Association of School Nurses; 1998

37. Hodgkinson HL. *Beyond the Schools: How Schools and Communities Must Collaborate to Solve the Problems Facing America's Youth.* Arlington, VA: American Association of School Administrators; 1991

38. Melaville A. *Community Schools: Partnership for Excellence.* Washington, DC: Coalition for Community Schools. Available at: http://www.communityschools.org/partnerships.html

39. Bogden JF. *Someone At School Has AIDS: A Complete Guide to Developing Education Policies Regarding HIV Infection.* Alexandria, VA: National Association of State Boards of Education; 2000

40. Centers for Disease Control and Prevention. *School Health Index for Physical Activity and Healthy Eating: A Self-Assessment and Planning Guide. Middle School/High School Version.* Atlanta, GA: Centers for Disease Control and Prevention; 2000. Available at: http://www.cdc.gov/nccdphp/dash/SHI/

41. American Academy of Pediatrics. Section 7. Assessing community needs. In: *School Health Leadership Training Kit.* Elk Grove Village, IL: American Academy of Pediatrics; 2001. Available at: http://www.schoolhealth.org

42. Marx E, Northrop D. *Educating for Health: A Guide to Implementing a Comprehensive Approach to School Health Education.* Newton, MA: Education Development Centers Inc; 1995

43. US Department of Education. Safe and drug-free schools program: notice of final principles of effectiveness. *Federal Register.* 1998;63:29901–29906

44. Allensworth D. The research base for innovative practices in school health education at the secondary level. *J Sch Health.* 1994;64:180–187

45. American School Health Association. *School Health: Findings from Evaluated Programs.* 2nd ed. Washington, DC: US Department of Health and Human Services, Public Health Service; 1998

46. Drug Strategies. *Making the Grade: A Guide to School Drug Prevention Programs.* Washington, DC: Drug Strategies; 1999

47. Irvine Doran DM, Baker GR, Murray M, et al. Achieving clinical improvement: an interdisciplinary intervention. *Health Care Manage Rev.* 2002;27:42–56

48. Nastasi BK, Varjas K, Bernsetin R. *Exemplary Mental Health Programs: School Psychologists as Mental Health Service Providers.* Bethesda MD: National Association of School Psychologists; 1997

49. Office of National Drug Control Policy. *Understanding Substance Abuse Prevention: Toward the 21st Century: A Primer on Effective Programs.* Brounstein PJ, Zweig JM, eds. Washington, DC: US Department of Health and Human Services; 2001. DHHS Publication No. SMA 99–3301. Available at: http://www.whitehousedrugpolicy.gov/prevent/high_Frisk/index.htm

50. Redding CA, Rossi JS, Rossi SR, Velicer WF, Prochaska JO. Health behavior models. *Int Elec J Health Educ.* 2000;3:180–193

51. American School Health Association. *School Health: Findings from Evaluation Programs.* 2nd ed. Kent, OH: American School Health Association, Office of Disease Prevention and Health Promotion; 1998. Available at: http://www.ashaweb.org

52. Adelman HS. Intervening to enhance home involvement in schooling. *Int Sch Clin.* 1994;29:276–287

53. Comer JP, ed. *Rallying the Whole Village: The Comer Process for Reforming Education.* New York, NY: Teachers College Press; 1996

54. Epstein JL, Hollifield JH. Title I and school-family-community partnerships: using research to realize the potential. *J Educ Stud Risk.* 1996;1:263–278

55. National Association of Partners in Education. *Seven Stage Partnership Development Process: Creating, Managing and Sustaining School-Community Business Partnerships.* Alexandria, VA: National Association of Partners in Education; 2001

56. Sheridan SM. Best Practice in fostering school/community relationships. In: Thomas A, Grimes J, eds. *Best Practices in School Psychology—III.* Washington, DC: National Association of School Psychologists; 1995:203–212

57. Zetlin A, Ramos C, Valdez A. Integrating services in a school-based center: an example of a school-community collaboration. *J Community Psychol.* 1996;24:97–107

58. Centers for Disease Control and Prevention. School health guidelines to prevent unintentional injuries and violence. *MMWR Morb Mortal Wkly Rep.* 2001;50(RR-22):1–73

59. Centers for Disease Control and Prevention. *Coordinated School Health Program Infrastructure Development: Process Evaluation Manual.* Atlanta, GA: US Centers for Disease Control and Prevention; 1997

60. Fetro JV. *Step by Step to Health Promoting Schools: A Guide to Implementing Coordinated School Health Programs in Local Schools and Districts.* Santa Cruz, CA: ETR Associates; 1998

61. Institute of Medicine. *Schools and Health: Our Nation's Investment.* Washington, DC: National Academy Press; 1997

62. Newton J, Adams R, Marcontel M. *The New School Health Handbook: A Ready Reference for School Nurses and Educators.* 3rd ed. Paramus, NJ: Prentice Hall, 1999

63. *Survival of the Fittest: A Tool Kit for Creating Lasting Comprehensive School Health Programs.* Washington, DC: Public Education Network. Available at: http://www.publiceducation.org/sc-tools-survival.asp

64. Windsor R, Baranowski T, Clark N, Cutter G. *Evaluation of Health Promotion, Health Education, and Disease Prevention Programs.* 2nd ed. Mountain View, CA: Mayfield Publishing Company; 1994

65. National Association for Sport and Physical Education. *National Standards for Athletic Coaches.* Dubuque, IA: Kendall/Hunt Publishing; 1995

66. National Association of School Nurses. *Scope and Standards of Professional School Nursing Practice.* Scarborough, ME: National Association of School Nurses; 2001

67. National Association of School Psychologists. *Standards for the Credentialing of School Psychologists.* Bethesda, MD: National Association of School Psychologists; 2000

68. Fryer GE Jr, Igoe JB. Functions of school nurses and health assistants in US school health programs. *J Sch Health.* 1996;66:55–58

69. National Association of School Nurses. *The School Nurse's Role in Delegation of Care: Guidelines and Compendium.* Scarborough, ME: National Association of School Nurses; 1996

70. National Association of State School Nurse Consultants. Delegation of school health services to unlicensed assistive personnel: a position paper of the National Association of State School Nurse Consultants. *J Sch Health.* 1996;66:72–74

71. Schwab N. *Guidelines for School Nursing Documentation: Standards, Issues, and Models.* Scarborough, ME: National Association of School Nurses; 1998

72. Greene MT, Puetzer M. The value of mentoring: a strategic approach to retention and recruitment. *J Nurs Care Qual.* 2002;17:63–70

73. Fossey R, Gregory V. Should colleges conduct criminal background checks before hiring instructors? A Louisiana court says yes. *J Personnel Eval Educ.* 2000;14:193–197

74. Hardy L. Trust betrayed. *Am Sch Board J.* 2002;189:14–18

75. Drug Strategies. *Safe Schools, Safe Students: A Guide to Violence Prevention Strategies.* Washington, DC: Drug Strategies; 1998

76. Mukherjee S, Lightfoot J, Sloper P. Communicating about pupils in mainstream school with special health needs: the NHS perspective. *Child Care Health Dev.* 2002;28:21–27

77. National Education Association. *Report of the NEA Task Force on Sexual Orientation.* Washington, DC: National Education Association; 2002. Available at: http://www.nea.org/nr/02taskforce.html

78. US Department of Education, Office of Special Educational Research and Improvement, Office of Reform Assistance and Dissemination. *Safe, Disciplined, and Drug-Free Schools Programs.* Washington, DC; 2001

79. US Department of Health and Human Services. *What You Need To Know About Youth Violence Prevention.* Rockville, MD: Substance Abuse and Mental Health Services Administration; 2002

CHAPTER-RELATED LINKS

American Academy of Allergy, Asthma, and Immunology
http://www.aaaai.org/
Includes a school nurse tool kit for asthma and allergy
  management.

American Association for Health Education
http://www.aahperd.org/aahe

American Cancer Society
http://www.cancer.org/
In addition to health education curricula, the ACS has
  a training program for school health coordinators
  and resources for forming school health advisory
  councils.

American Dental Association
http://www.ada.org/
Includes information on National Dental Board
  examinations.

American Diabetes Association
http://www.diabetes.org
Includes information on nondiscriminatory practices
  for students with diabetes.

American Heart Association
http://www.americanheart.org

American Red Cross
http://www.redcross.org

American School Food Services Association
http://www.asfsa.org/

American School Health Association
http://www.ashaweb.org/
Resources for practicing school health professionals
  (Health in Action) and policy resolutions of many
  school health and safety issues.

Centers for Disease Control and Prevention (CDC)
http://www.cdc.gov/

Centers for Disease Control and Prevention (CDC)—
  Division of Adolescent and School Health
http://www.cdc.gov/nccdphp/dash/index.htm
Includes youth risk behavior surveillance and guidelines
  for school health programs.

Centers for Disease Control and Prevention (CDC)—
  Strategies for Addressing Asthma within a
  Coordinated School Health Program
http://www.cdc.gov/HealthyYouth/asthma/index.htm

Centers for Medicare and Medicaid Services
http://cms.hhs.gov/
Formerly Health Care Financing Administration (HCFA);
  Federal agency administers child insurance
  programs, HIPAA, (Health Insurance Portability and
  Accountability Act), CLIA (Clinical Laboratory
  Improvement Amendments), and other federally
  funded health programs and policies.

Centers for Medicare and Medicaid Services—Health
  Insurance Portability and Accountability Act (HIPAA)
http://www.cms.hhs.gov/hipaa/
Addresses the security and privacy of health data and
  describes national standards for electronic health
  care transactions and patient identifiers to be used
  by providers, health plans, and employers.

Coalition for Community Schools
http://www.communityschools.org/
Information on school partnerships with community
  agencies, parents, volunteers.

Collaborative for Academic, Social, and
  Emotional Learning
http://www.casel.org/

Colorado Anti-Bullying Project
http://www.no-bully.com/
Part of the Center for the Study and Prevention of
  Violence. Provides information for teachers, parents,
  and students to prevent bullying, including resources,
  links, and a bullying quiz.

Consumer Product Safety Commission
http://www.cpsc.gov/
Safe playground equipment and other products.

Council of Chief State School Officers
http://www.ccsso.org/

Education Development Center
http://www.edc.org/
A nonprofit organization with model projects that
  enhance learning and promote health.

Emergency Medical Services for Children (EMS-C)
http://www.ems-c.org/

Environmental Protection Agency
http://www.epa.gov/

Gay Lesbian Straight Education Network (GLSEN)
http://www.glsen.org/
Includes a comprehensive training program for educators
to increase knowledge, skills, and tools that build
sexual orientation awareness and inclusive school
environments from K–12.

Healthy Newsletters
http://www.schoolnurse.com/publicationshealtynews.html
A biannual publication of information on health and
family issues.

Maternal and Child Health Bureau; Health Resources and
Services Administration
http://www.mchb.hrsa.gov/

Maternal and Child Health Bureau; Health Resources and
Services Administration—Child Health USA
http://mchb.hrsa.gov/chusa02/index.htm
Annual report on health status and service needs of
American children.

National Association for Multicultural Education
http://www.nameorg.org/

National Assembly of School-Based Health Centers
http://www.nasbhc.org/
In regard to school-based health centers, this site
provides resources and support related to advocacy,
public policy, technical assistance, training,
evaluation, and quality.

National Association of School Nurses
http://www.nasn.org

National Association of School Psychologists
http://www.nasponline.org/

National Association of State Boards of Education
http://www.nasbe.org

National Asthma Education and Prevention Program
http://www.nhlbi.nih.gov/about/naepp/

National Center for Family and Community Connections
with Schools
http://www.sedl.org/connections/resources/

National Education Association
http://www.nea.org/

National Education Association—Code of Ethics
http://www.nea.org/aboutnea/code.html

National Highway Traffic Safety Administration (US
Department of Transportation)
http://www.nhtsa.dot.gov
Information on child safety restraint systems, training
for child passenger safety technicians, and laws
and regulations governing transporting children.
The "Child Passenger Safety" pages include information on transporting children with disabilities
and school bus safety.

National Maternal and Child Health Oral Health Resource
Center
http://www.mchoralhealth.org/
Information on current and emerging public oral health
issues.

National Network of Partnership Schools
http://www.csos.jhu.edu/p2000/default.htm

National PTA
http://www.pta.org

National School Boards Association
http://www.nsba.org/
Includes sample school policies (including health-
related), resources for school attorneys, school
governance, and advocacy.

Occupational Safety and Health Administration
http://www.osha.gov/

Office of School Health, University of Colorado
http://www.uchsc.edu/schoolhealth/
Includes a School Health Evaluation Services (SHES)
site that assists schools with school health quality
assurance issues.

Safe Child
http://www.safechild.org
Teaches prevention of sexual, emotional, and physical
abuse of children.

Substance Abuse and Mental Health Services
Administration (SAMHSA)
http://www.samhsa.gov/
Includes information on researched prevention programs
for substance abuse, violence, and other mental
health-related problems affecting youth.

US Department of Agriculture
http://www.usda.gov/
National school lunch program and school breakfast
program regulations.

US Department of Education
http://www.ed.gov/

US Department of Education—Family Educational Rights and Privacy Act (FERPA)
http://www.ed.gov/offices/OM/fpco/ferpa/
A US Department of Education Web site that describes a federal law that protects the privacy of student education records.

US Department of Education—Individuals with Disabilities Education Act (IDEA)
http://www.ed.gov/offices/OSERS/Policy/IDEA/

US Department of Education—Office of Civil Rights
http://www.ed.gov/about/offices/list/ocr/504faq.html
Provides information on Section 504

US Department of Education—Office of Safe and Drug-Free Schools
http://www.ed.gov/about/offices/list/osdfs/index.html
Includes publications on effective violence and substance abuse prevention programs.

US Department of Education—Partnership for Family Involvement in Education
http://www.ed.gov/pubs/whoweare/title.html

US Department of Health and Human Services, Office for Civil Rights
http://www.hhs.gov/ocr/

US Department of Justice, Americans with Disabilities Act
http://www.ada.gov/
Information and technical assistance on compliance with the Americans with Disabilities Act.

US Department of Labor, Family and Medical Leave Act
http://www.dol.gov/elaws/fmla.htm
Information about employee eligibility, employee/employer notification responsibilities, and employee rights and benefits.

◀ Family and Community Involvement ▶

1-01—FAMILY INVOLVEMENT IN HEALTH/SAFETY PROGRAMS, POLICIES[1–15]

Involve parents, families, students, and community members in the decision-making process for the selection of health and safety messages, curricula, learning activities, and policies. Inform them of characteristics that make these programs/policies effective.

▶ *RATIONALE*

Family and community input into health and safety messages sent home from school increases the likelihood that they will be helpful. When parents, families, and community members reinforce school health and safety programs and provide input into curricular decision making, these programs are more likely to be sustained. Strong family and community involvement on school health and safety councils (Guideline 0-05) can promote health and safety messages that are most needed in a community, emergency and safety plans that are consistent with families' resources, and program formats that are most acceptable to students, families, and community members.

▶ *COMMENTARY*

Inform parents of characteristics of effective health, safety, and physical education messages, activities, and curricula (Guidelines 0-11, 2-02). Informed parents can better advocate for and participate in effective implementation of health, safety, and physical education curricula. Provide families with training, seminars, and information on health, mental health, and safety topics that relate directly to lessons taught in classroom health and safety education. Teach family members how to reinforce these messages. Possible approaches include: providing helpful, easy-to-read health and safety information that offers a health perspective for families; assigning homework that requires family discussion; encouraging staff visits to students' homes; including families in the planning and implementation of health- and safety-related academic events; and welcoming family members into health classrooms as volunteers or casual observers. Family involvement through home-learning activities enhances instruction.

Families and students can be remarkably powerful advocates when they are also decision makers and involved in the selection of curricula. They can be helpful in setting reasonable goals, planning and implementing evaluations of the school health and safety program, and disseminating results of educational programs. Engagement in decision-making processes can occur through participation in venues such as curriculum advisory committees. A health and safety advisory council that includes a diversity of family and community members can help build broad community support for comprehensive health and safety education. Work with members who have opposing viewpoints to create a shared vision and program goals.

When schools provide materials for families to reinforce health and safety teaching with students within the home, family and student input can be invaluable in developing new or tailoring existing materials so that they provide a context that is best understood by students' families.

Collaboration between school and community groups is sometimes strengthened by formal agreements. Publications of the National PTA[1,2] describe effective strategies for involving families. The National Network of Partnership Schools (http://www.csos.jhu.edu/p2000/default.htm) defines 6 ways that families and community members can become involved in school and describes sample practices. Two of these, "Learning at Home" and "Decision Making," are useful for achieving goals of this guideline.

▶ **RELATED GUIDELINES**

0-05, 0-09, 0-11, 2-01, 2-02

▶ **RELATED LINKS**

http://www.nes.org
http://www.csos.jhu.edu/p2000/default.htm
http://www.pta.org

1-02–COMMUNICATION AMONG SCHOOL, HOME, AND HEALTH PROVIDERS[1,14,16–22]

Implement and support consistent, timely, and meaningful communication among school, home, and students' community-based health professionals in order to effectively address any health, mental health, or safety matter that affects a student.

▶ RATIONALE

Communication is the foundation for a solid partnership between schools and families. When parents and educators communicate effectively about a child, parents become more engaged with the school and their child's education, relationships between school and parent are more likely to be positive, problems are solved more easily, and students may progress more favorably. Communication among school health professionals, other school staff, parents, and students' health care providers can result in earlier access to health, oral health, and mental health services and a more comprehensive understanding (by all the aforementioned) of a student's health and safety needs and how best to manage these needs.

▶ COMMENTARY

It is primarily parents' responsibility to care for their children's health and mental health. But school staff are often the first to recognize health, mental health, and safety issues that confront children. Clear communication among schools, parents, and health care providers can facilitate diagnosis and problem management.

All communication should be respectful in its tone. Be certain that all written and oral communications with families are available in a language, literacy level, and level of understanding that will be understood. Venues of communication for health, mental health, and safety matters can include telephone calls, e-mail, home visits, "meet the teacher" evenings with time to address students' issues, and appointments at school that are scheduled during times that are convenient for families. Teachers, school staff, and school administrators should receive training on communicating with diverse populations and on effective communication techniques. Tips for school staff on gaining cultural competency are outlined in Appendix B.

Inform families about any injuries, health complaints, or concern about signs or symptoms that school staff observe. When staff feel that a problem requires further investigation, follow-up, or ongoing care, express this clearly to the family.

Collect health-related information directly from families as well as from health providers. This includes information on allergies, any health condition that may affect education or safety in school, any condition that may require treatment or emergency intervention during the school day, medications, all emergency contact information, and name and phone number of students' primary health care providers (eg, doctor, dentist). School health professionals should review this information to determine whether specific emergency plans need to be developed and whether a care plan needs to be implemented for a chronic condition.

Health information needs to be stored where confidentiality can be maintained but where the information can be utilized by those who need it, for example, in response to an emergency. Forms that permit exchange of information and that define the limits of information to be exchanged should be developed and utilized.

▶ *RELATED GUIDELINES*

0-03, 0-08, 0-09, 4-09, 4-13, 4-15, 4-19, 4-22, 5-04, 6-02, 7-03

▶ *RELATED LINKS*

http://schoolhealth.org
http://www.ashaweb.org
http://www.sedl.org/connections/resources

1-03–INFORMING FAMILIES ABOUT HEALTH/SAFETY PROGRAMS, POLICIES[1,2,15,16,18–20,22–24]

Regularly inform students, families, and other community stakeholders about school programs, services, and outcome data that are related to health, safety, oral health, and mental health.

▶ *RATIONALE*

Families and community members must know about successes and challenges related to schools' health and safety programs and policies if they are to utilize them, abide by them, contribute to them, and advocate for them. Often, community stakeholders are looking for a way to participate and support schools' health- and safety-related efforts and only need an invitation to participate.

▶ *COMMENTARY*

Informed students, families, and other community stakeholders can provide advocacy for programs and partnerships with community groups and services. By providing regular reports to the school board about school health and safety issues, students and educators can focus attention on the value of school health and safety programs and on the benefits of investing in these programs as part of schools' improvement plans. Communicate with potential stakeholders in the community (eg, agencies providing services to youth, recreation groups and agencies, health and safety organizations, universities, and faith groups). Involve a diversity of community members with a broad range of experiences with service provision, the development of health- and safety-related programs, or staff training.

Regularly inform students and families about:
- times when teachers, school health professionals, security staff, and administrators are available to meet with parents
- health, mental health, and social services available at school and elsewhere
- school policy delineating when a physician's note is required for return to school
- need for updated student health information that may impact school performance
- how to find a regular source of care within the community for families who do not have one, such as a medical home, a dental home, and a professional who can prescribe and dispense corrective lenses and help with other vision issues (offer families multiple options, including public, private, and charitable resources)
- plans for and results of screening programs, such as vision screening
- policies on weapon-carrying, bullying, fighting, tobacco, alcohol, and illicit drugs
- how health information is shared and remains confidential in school
- consent forms that allow exchange of information
- any foods or ingredients that are restricted from school grounds (if that is how a school is dealing with a student's food allergy)

Families can also benefit from receiving health and safety information of a more general nature. This could include injury and violence prevention, child and adolescent developmental milestones, protective factors for children, asset-building strategies that can assist parents with parenting and progression through school, and the importance of health promotion activities through recreation, leisure, and educational opportunities.

Communication tools that schools can use on a regular basis to convey health- and safety-related messages to community members and parents include: a parent handbook, newsletters, surveys, e-mail, Web sites, academic and social events, homework hotlines, parent libraries, and asset-building progress reports.

▶ *RELATED GUIDELINES*

0-03, 0-09, 6-02

▶ *RELATED LINKS*

http://www.nes.org
http://www.csos.jhu.edu/p2000/default.htm
http://www.pta.org
http://www.ed.gov/pubs/whoweare/title.html

1-04—PARENTING RESOURCES FOR FAMILIES[1,8,20,25]

Provide resources that help families on matters of: parenting, progression in school, knowledge of child developmental milestones, and communication with their child or adolescent about relationships, safety, tobacco, alcohol, illicit drugs, sexuality, violence, and diet.

▶ *RATIONALE*

Research has shown that children and adolescents are less likely to engage in risk behaviors (including sexual risk behaviors) if their families discuss these health- and safety-related issues with them and make their personal positions known. Families often do not feel equipped to engage in meaningful discussions with their children about sensitive topics, and many school staff members do have this expertise. Reduction in high-risk behaviors can help to enhance student performance.

▶ *COMMENTARY*

As emphasized by the National PTA (http://www.pta.org),[1] parents are their children's first and most influential teachers. Helpful actions that schools can take to promote positive parental influences include providing information and workshops on parenting, child-rearing skills, and child and adolescent development, as well as linking parents to resources in the community that will provide support. School staff members who recognize parenting traditions and practices within the community's faiths and cultural groups can more effectively communicate with families (Cultural Competence, Appendix B).

Resources should increase families' levels of comfort in addressing health and safety issues with their children. Workshops and programs can help improve the ability of families to provide accurate information and to listen to their children's concerns, questions, and thoughts in all areas of health and safety. Other examples include encouraging parents to avoid overcompetitive and aggressive behavior during sports, not allowing their child to play sports after being injured until medically cleared to return, and understanding the developmental limitations of children's behavior and how to assist with homework.

Strategies include offering sessions for parents where they can acquire skills for optimal communication with their children, providing written materials for families, meeting with families to discuss health and safety education programs, and encouraging families to discuss their expectations with their children. If a school has a staffed family resource center, materials and expertise can be housed there.

▶ *RELATED GUIDELINES*

2-08, 3-04, 3-06, 4-06, 4-16, 5-05, 7-03

▶ *RELATED LINKS*

http://www.connectforkids.org/
http://familysupportamerica.org/
http://www.schoolnurse.com/publicationshealtynews.html
http://www.nes.org/
http://www.pta.org/
http://kidshealth.org/

1-05—PROMOTING FAMILY RECREATION[1,8,20,26]

Provide families with information that encourages healthy and safe recreational and educational activities for the student and the family.

▶ *RATIONALE*

There are many opportunities for schools to promote community institutions that enhance children's mental and physical well-being. By transmitting such information to parents, schools benefit from improved student learning as well as healthy growth and development. Students who are healthy physically, emotionally, and socially are stronger learners.

▶ *COMMENTARY*

Schools should assist families to provide healthy and safe recreational, leisure, and educational opportunities for their children. Parents may be informed through Internet sites and newsletters. School personnel should be thoroughly apprised of resources. Having a staffed family resource center on school property is an efficient way to inform parents of community resources.

Link families to community resources such as the YMCA, YWCA, Boys and Girls Clubs, 4-H, Girls Incorporated, Girl Scouts, Boy Scouts, Campfire Boys and Girls, Big Brothers and Big Sisters, departments of parks and recreation, community centers, faith-based institutions, junior colleges, and universities. Linkages can also be to schools' own after-school programs. The "21st Century Community Learning Centers" (http://www.ed.gov/21stcclc) are examples of how schools can help to promote opportunities for students and their families to learn new skills and discover new abilities after the school day has ended.

Schools can initiate partnerships with community agencies. The nature of partnerships can range from exchanging informational flyers to having a community agency operate a before- and after-school program on the school campus. Partnerships can be initiated by schools' health and safety coordinators (Guideline 0-04); other health, administrative, or educational staff; or district-level health and safety advisory councils (Guideline 0-05).

▶ *RELATED GUIDELINES*

0-04, 0-05, 0-12, 3-04

▶ *RELATED LINKS*

http://www.ed.gov/21stcclc
http://www.cdc.gov/nccdphp/dash/index.htm
http://www.nes.org
http://www.pta.org
http://kidshealth.org

1-06–FUNDING FOR FAMILY/COMMUNITY INVOLVEMENT[27-30]

Secure financial and technical assistance to increase student, family, and community involvement in school health and safety programs and activities. Engage local, state, federal, and tribal governments, as well as philanthropic organizations, foundations, universities, and private sources for these resources.

▶ *RATIONALE*

The need for funding to attract and maintain parent and community involvement is often a hurdle to realizing success for this important aspect of a coordinated school health and safety program.

▶ *COMMENTARY*

Community and family involvement in schools often improves when there is external assistance, including financial assistance. Schools require financial resources to send health and safety information to families, for training parents and volunteers (eg, to assist in classrooms), for conducting needs assessments, for programs such as health fairs, and for supporting community partnerships. Schools or districts usually apply for these funds. Families and community liaisons to schools can help examine existing resources, consolidate funding, and seek potential new funding sources. Assistance may also be sought from local, state, and federal governments. A tribal government is comparable to the structure of other elected governments and should be considered as well. Partnerships with universities and colleges can provide assistance with research and evaluation of school health and safety programs. Look to philanthropic organizations, foundations, corporations, and other private sources for partnerships and financial assistance. Engage them by demonstrating how the effectiveness of school health, safety, and educational programs can be enhanced with family and community involvement.

Resources that are available to schools may be dependent on characteristics of the local community. Each community is unique in its composition of citizens, racial and ethnic groups, facilities, traditions, spiritual practices, economics, climate, geography, and governance.

RELATED GUIDELINES

0-12, 3-04, 4-33

RELATED LINKS

http://www.childadvocacy.org

CHAPTER REFERENCES

1. National PTA. *Building Successful Partnerships: A Guide for Developing Parent and Family Involvement Programs.* Bloomington, IN: National Educational Services; 2000

2. National PTA. *National Standards for Parent/Family Involvement Programs, Standard 1: Communicating.* Chicago, IL: National PTA; 1998. Available at: http://www.pta.org/parentinvolvement/standards/state.asp

3. Abrams L, Gibbs JT. Planning for change: school-community collaboration in a full-service elementary school. *Urban Educ.* 2000;35:79–103

4. Benson PL, Galbraith J, Espeland P. *What Teens Need to Succeed: Proven, Practical Ways to Shape Your Own Future.* Minneapolis, MN: Free Spirit Publishing; 1997

5. Birch DA. *Step by Step to Involving Parents in Health Education.* Santa Cruz, CA: ETR Associates; 1996

6. Carolyn P, Carolyn W, McCarthy AR. Family and community involvement in school health. In: Marx E, Wooley SF, eds. *Health is Academic: A Guide to Coordinated School Health Programs.* New York, NY: Teacher's College Press; 1998:67–95

7. Darby L, ed. *Learning Partners: A Guide to Educational Activities for Families.* Washington, DC: US Department of Education; 1997

8. Epstein JL, Coates L, Clark-Salinas K, Sanders MF, Simon B. *Partnership 2000 Schools Manual: Improving School-Family-Community Partnerships.* Baltimore, MD: Johns Hopkins University; 1997

9. Epstein JL. School-family-community partnerships: caring for the children we share. *Phi Delta Kappa.* 1995;79:701–712

10. Haynes NM, Comer JP, Hamilton-Lee M. School climate enhancement through parental involvement. *J Sch Psychol.* 1989;27:87–90

11. Haynes NM, Comer JP. Integrating schools, families, and communities through successful school reform: the School Development Program. *Sch Psychol Rev.* 1996;25:501–506

12. Kirby D. *Emerging Answers. Research Findings on Program to Reduce Teenage Pregnancy.* Washington, DC: National Campaign to Prevent Teen Pregnancy; 2001

13. *Making the Grade: A Guide to School Drug Prevention Programs.* Washington, DC: Drug Strategies; 1999

14. McCarthy AR. Teens, families, and schools. In: *Healthy Teens: Facing the Challenges of Young Lives.* 3rd ed. Birmingham, MI: Bridge Communications; 2000:19–34

15. Starkman N, Scales PC, Roberts C. *Great Places to Learn: How Asset-Building Schools Help Students Succeed.* Minneapolis, MN: Search Institute; 1999

16. Allen R. Forging school-home links: a new paradigm for parent involvement. *Educ Update.* 2000;42:1, 4, 8

17. Bogden JF. *How Schools Work and How to Work with Schools: A Primer for Professionals who Serve Children and Youth.* Alexandria, VA: National Association of State Boards of Education; 2003

18. Brand S. Making parent involvement a reality: help teachers develop partnerships with parents. *Young Child.* 1996;51:76–81

19. Chavkin NF. Making the case for school, family, and community partnerships: recommendations for research. *Sch Community J.* 1998;8:9–21

20. McCarthy AR. *Healthy Teens: Facing the Challenges of Young Lives.* 3rd ed. Birmingham, MI: Bridge Communications; 2000

21. National Task Force on Confidential Student Health Information. *Guidelines for Protecting Coordinated Student Health Information.* Kent, OH; American School Health Association; 2000

22. Resnicow K, Allensworth D. Conducting a comprehensive school health program. *J Sch Health.* 1996;66:59–63

23. Dauber SL, Epstein JL. *Parent Attitudes and Practices of Parent Involvement in Inner-city Elementary and Middle Schools.* Report No. 33. Baltimore, MD: Center for Research on Elementary and Middle Schools; 1989

24. US Department of Education. Goal No. 8: parental participation. In: *Sec 102 National Education Goals 2000.* Available at: http://www.ed.gov/legislation/GOALS2000/TheAct/sec102.html

25. Merrell KW. School-based prevention and treatment: preventing kids with depression, anxiety from slipping through the cracks. Brown University. *Child Adolesc Behavior Lett.* 2001;17(11)

26. US Department of Education, Office of the Under Secretary. *When Schools Stay Open Late: The National Evaluation of the 21st-Century Learning Centers Program, First Year Findings.* Washington, DC: US Department of Education; 2003

27. Calfee C, Wittwer F, Meredith M. *Building a Full-Service School: A Step-by-Step Guide.* San Francisco, CA: Jossey-Bass Publishers; 1998

28. Gans JE, Mc Manus MA, Newacheck PW. *Adolescent Health Care: Use, Costs, and Problems of Access*. Chicago, IL: American Medical Association; 1991

29. National PTA. *National Survey of Parents of Public School Students: Executive Summary*. Chicago, IL: National PTA; 1999. Available at: http://www.PTA.org/programs/parentsur/summary.htm

30. US Department of Education, National Center for Education Statistics. *Parent Involvement in Children's Education: Efforts by Public Elementary Schools*. Washington, DC: US Department of Education; 1998. Statistical Analysis Report NCES 98–032

CHAPTER-RELATED LINKS

21st Century Community Learning Centers
http://www.ed.gov/21stcclc

American Academy of Pediatrics — School Health
http://www.schoolhealth.org

American School Health Association
http://www.ashaweb.org

Centers for Disease Control and Prevention: Division of Adolescent and School Health
http://www.cdc.gov/nccdphp/dash/index.htm
Includes Guidelines for Schools and link to "After School Care Programs."

Connect for Kids
http://www.connectforkids.org
Resources for teachers and parents with advice from mental health professionals.

Council of Chief State School Officers
http://www.ccsso.org

Education Development Center
http://www.edc.org
A nonprofit organization with model projects that enhance learning and promote health.

Emergency Medical Services for Children (EMS-C)
http://www.ems-c.org

Environmental Protection Agency
http://www.epa.gov

Family Resource Coalition of America
http://familysupportamerica.org
Includes a nationwide database of family support programs.

Gay Lesbian Straight Education Network (GLSEN)
http://www.glsen.org
Includes a comprehensive training program for educators to increase knowledge, skills, and tools that build sexual orientation awareness and inclusive school environments from K–12.

Healthy Newsletters
http://www.schoolnurse.com/publicationshealtynews.html
A biannual publication of information on health and family issues.

Maternal and Child Health Bureau; Health Resources and Services Administration
http://www.mchb.hrsa.gov

Maternal and Child Health Bureau; Health Resources and Services Administration—Child Health USA
http://mchb.hrsa.gov/chusa02/index.htm
Annual report on health status and service needs of American children.

National Assembly of School-Based Health Centers
http://www.nasbhc.org
In regard to school-based health centers, this site provides resources and support related to advocacy, public policy, technical assistance, training, evaluation, and quality.

National Association for Multicultural Education
http://www.nameorg.org

National Association of Child Advocates / Voices for America's Children
http://www.childadvocacy.org
Dedicated to improving safety, security, health, and education for all children.

National Association of School Nurses
http://www.nasn.org

National Association of School Psychologists
http://www.nasponline.org

National Association of State Boards of Education
http://www.nasbe.org

National Asthma Education and Prevention Program
http://www.nhlbi.nih.gov/about/naepp

National Center for Family and Community Connections
    with Schools
http://www.sedl.org/connections/resources

National Education Association
http://www.nea.org

National Education Association—Code of Ethics
http://www.nea.org/aboutnea/code.html

National Educational Service
http://www.nes.org
For educators and other youth professionals to help
    foster environments where all youth succeed.

National Network of Partnership Schools
http://www.csos.jhu.edu/p2000/default.htm

National Highway Traffic Safety Administration
    (US Department of Transportation)
http://www.nhtsa.dot.gov
Information on child safety restraint systems, training
    for child passenger safety technicians, and laws and
    regulations governing transporting children. The
    "Child Passenger Safety" pages include information
    on transporting children with disabilities and school
    bus safety.

National Maternal and Child Health Oral Health
    Resource Center
http://www.mchoralhealth.org
Information on current and emerging public oral
    health issues.

National Network of Partnership Schools
http://www.csos.jhu.edu/p2000/default.htm

National PTA
http://www.pta.org

National School Boards Association
http://www.nsba.org
Includes sample school policies (including health-
    related), resources for school attorneys, school
    governance, and advocacy.

Nemours Foundation
http://kidshealth.org
A site for parents and children that addresses behavior,
    nutrition, fitness, first-aid, and safety.

Occupational Safety and Health Administration
http://www.osha.gov

Office of School Health, University of Colorado
http://www.uchsc.edu/schoolhealth
Includes a School Health Evaluation Services (SHES)
    site that assists schools with school health quality
    assurance issues.

Safe Child
http://www.safechild.org
Teaches prevention of sexual, emotional, and physical
    abuse of children.

Substance Abuse and Mental Health Services
    Administration (SAMHSA)
http://www.samhsa.gov
Includes information on researched prevention programs
    for substance abuse, violence, and other mental
    health-related problems affecting youth.

US Department of Agriculture
http://www.usda.gov
National school lunch program and school breakfast
    program regulations.

US Department of Education
http://www.ed.gov

US Department of Education—Family Educational
    Rights and Privacy Act (FERPA)
http://www.ed.gov/offices/OM/fpco/ferpa
A US Department of Education Web site that describes
    a federal law that protects the privacy of student
    education records.

US Department of Education—Individuals with
    Disabilities Education Act (IDEA) Web site
http://www.ed.gov/offices/OSERS/Policy/IDEA

US Department of Education—Office of Civil Rights
http://www.ed.gov/about/offices/list/ocr/504faq.html
Provides information on Section 504.

US Department of Education—Office of Safe and
    Drug-Free Schools
http://www.ed.gov/about/offices/list/osdfs/index.html
Includes publications on effective violence and substance
    abuse prevention programs.

US Department of Education—Partnership for Family
    Involvement in Education
http://www.ed.gov/pubs/whoweare/title.html

US Department of Health and Human Services,
    Office of Civil Rights
http://www.hhs.gov/ocr
Information and technical assistance on compliance with
    the Americans with Disabilities Act.

US Department of Justice, Americans with Disabilities Act
http://www.ada.gov

US Department of Labor, Family and Medical Leave Act
http://www.dol.gov/elaws/fmla.htm
Information about employee eligibility, employee/
    employer notification responsibilities, and
    employee rights and benefits.

◀ **Health and Safety Education** ▶

PROGRAM PLANNING AND STAFFING

2-01–INSTITUTIONAL SUPPORT, AMPLE TIME FOR HEALTH/SAFETY EDUCATION[1-12]

Adopt policies and provide resources that institutionalize health and safety education so that the education is high quality and provides sufficient time and materials for students to master essential knowledge and skills.

▶ RATIONALE

Effective implementation of health and safety education requires administrative support and sufficient time and resources. Policies help to ensure that support continues and becomes institutionalized. Studies show that adequate instructional time and opportunities to learn are crucial if students are to develop mastery of essential knowledge, skills, and competencies for health and safety.

▶ COMMENTARY

Policies that support high-quality health and safety education include making these topics part of the educational system's core academic content (Guideline 2-04) and requiring that these topics are taught by qualified teachers who stay current in the subject (Guideline 2-03). Other forms of administrative support include providing release time for teachers to attend professional development sessions (Guideline 0-16) and ensuring that health and safety instructional needs are included in the budget. Resources required for high-quality health and safety education include ample classroom space, access to a computer and audiovisual equipment, relevant and current library materials, and regularly updated instructional materials, curricular guides, and hands-on materials (such as anatomic models and mannequins for teaching cardiopulmonary resuscitation skills). Health and safety courses should receive the same level of support as other core academic subjects for time, space, teaching staff, support staff, and instructional materials.

Having sufficient time for health and safety education allows students time to model, practice, receive feedback, and develop competency in relevant skills. When time is insufficient, teachers often omit skills practice, which is an essential part of health and safety lessons. To address the concern of insufficient time in the school day, some schools have sought funding to lengthen the school day or year. The United States has the equivalent of 175 to 180 6-hour school days per year compared with a mean of 194 days in 38 other countries. Those additional hours have allowed some schools to allot adequate time for health and safety education.

▶ RELATED GUIDELINES

0-09, 0-16, 1-01

2-02—PROCESS FOR SELECTING HEALTH/SAFETY CURRICULA[8,13-16]

Establish a review and adoption process to select, adapt, or develop health and safety education curricula. Include multidisciplinary and community input, a needs assessment, a review of curricula, and an agreed-on process for approval.

▶ RATIONALE

A curriculum review and adoption process that involves multiple stakeholders is most likely to result in the approval of health and safety curricula that meet students' needs and that reflect and respect the variety of cultures, races, ethnic groups, and faiths among students. Employing such a process generates widespread buy-in and ownership of the curricula.

▶ COMMENTARY

A broad-based curriculum committee should include representatives of stakeholder groups, such as parents, students, other community members, school health and safety educators, and health services providers. Members of the school health and safety advisory council (Guideline 0-05) might serve this function.

The process of curriculum selection often includes conducting a needs assessment (Guideline 0-10) as well as a review of policies and existing resources. The Rocky Mountain Center for Health Promotion and Education[13] (http://www.rmc.org) provides a curriculum selection criteria worksheet divided into 3 sections: district-needs driven criteria, instructional criteria, and scientific research and evaluation criteria. To determine district priorities for curricula, the curriculum committee should consider data on risks for students and using data that are local and recent. This committee should also consider local resiliency factors, community assets, and community perceptions about health risks.

To determine instructional criteria, review national, state, and district standards for health and safety education, performance measures, and recent professional literature. Identify and review curricula and programs that have undergone evaluation using appropriate control or comparison groups and that have evidence for effectively addressing targeted behaviors.

Once the committee agrees on selection criteria (eg, on the basis of evidence of effectiveness, scientific accuracy, inclusion of approved messages), it is ready to review potential curricula and then make the decision to adopt, revise, or adapt existing curricula. It also needs to define who has the authority to make the final decision regarding selection of curricula as well as the frequency of future review and reconsideration. At some point in the process, the committee needs to consider how it will evaluate the program's effectiveness in terms of successful implementation and student outcomes.

▶ RELATED GUIDELINES

0-05, 0-10, 0-11, 0-13, 1-01

▷ *RELATED LINKS*

http://www.redcross.org

http://www.ccsso.org

http://www.healthypeople.gov

http://www.rmc.org

http://www.cdc.gov/nccdphp/dash/yrbs

2-03—CERTIFIED HEALTH TEACHERS [17-19]

Hire health education teachers for secondary schools who have appropriate qualifications for teaching health and safety classes. At the elementary level and for anyone who is assigned to teach health and safety but is not certified, require at least 6 hours of academic course work or 30 hours of in-service training on health and safety content and pedagogy. Training must include content of the health and safety topics the person is being assigned to teach and methods of teaching relevant social skills.

▶ RATIONALE

The teaching of health and safety is complex and dynamic. Those who teach health and safety education should have previous education about health and safety content as well as teaching methodologies that research has shown to be effective.

▶ COMMENTARY

Appropriate delivery and accurate information are essential components of effective health and safety education. Those who teach health and safety must have the necessary education, qualifications, and skills to perform their tasks, including the ability to deliver skills-based instruction, be effective agents of behavior change, and communicate and work effectively with administrators, other teachers, students, families, and community representatives.

Minimum qualifications of a certified health educator are a bachelor's degree from an accredited college or university and a valid state credential authorizing him or her as a teacher of health education. Credentialing indicates there is a commitment to the discipline and to ongoing professional development. The National Council on Accreditation of Teacher Education (NCATE [http://www.ncate.org]) approves colleges and universities to prepare teachers who are content specialists in health education. State credentialing ensures that teachers have met that state's requirements and completed course work on knowledge and skills that are necessary to teach health and safety subjects. Those teachers certified as health education specialists (CHESs) have met standards of competence established by the National Commission for Health Education Credentialing (http://www.nchec.org), and have successfully passed the CHES examination.

Accomplished teachers might also choose to go through a rigorous review process and become board certified. Standards for certification in the field of health education have been established by the National Board for Professional Teaching.[17]

▶ RELATED GUIDELINES
0-14

▶ RELATED LINKS
http://www.aahperd.org/aahe
http://www.nchec.org
http://www.ncate.org

◀ Health and Safety Education ▶

CURRICULUM AND INSTRUCTION

2-04—HEALTH/SAFETY EDUCATION AS A CORE SUBJECT [6,20,21]

Provide health/safety education as a core academic subject in grades kindergarten through 12.

▶ *RATIONALE*

Healthy and safe students are better able to learn than those who feel unsafe or have unaddressed health issues. Education can enhance a person's health and safety. When curricula include health and safety courses and when standards include health and safety content, teachers make time to teach these topics. Otherwise, many teachers consider health and safety as "add-ons" that they can eliminate if time is short.

▶ *COMMENTARY*

Health/safety education is best taught as a separate course of study at every grade, with reinforcement across the curriculum and in the school environment. When schools rely on integration into other academic areas as the sole means of providing health and safety education, they provide less instructional time for health and safety and cover fewer topics than when health is a separate course. In integrated teaching, skill-development is rarely addressed. Without skills development, education in health and safety has limited effectiveness. Effective health/safety education involves repeated exposure to key topics as appropriate for students' developmental stages.

Reinforcing health and safety concepts in other subjects helps make those academic areas more relevant to students' everyday life and enhances students' learning of health and safety concepts and skills. Many elementary school teachers realize that education in health and safety issues is central to what they already do on a daily basis. Math, science, social studies, art, and English/language arts teachers can teach about specific health and safety issues from a variety of perspectives. An illustrative example of reinforcing health and safety while teaching other subjects is "Risk Watch" (http://www.nfpa.org). This curriculum (prekindergarten through eighth grade) meets learning objectives in mandated subject areas other than health and safety, yet provides comprehensive injury prevention education.

RELATED GUIDELINES

3-02

RELATED LINKS

http://www.aahperd.org/aahe
http://www.ashaweb.org
http://www.nfpa.org

2-05–HEALTH/SAFETY EDUCATION: PLANNED, SEQUENTIAL, MEETS STANDARDS[3,6,7,22–24]

Provide planned, sequential, comprehensive health and safety education (K–12) that is culturally, linguistically, developmentally, and age appropriate and is consistent with state and national health education standards. Content should include community, personal, environmental, mental and emotional health; prevention of substance abuse, diseases, injury, and violence; family life; human sexuality; media literacy; nutrition; and first aid and basic emergency lifesaving skills.

▶ **RATIONALE**

Health and safety education curricula for students that are sequential and include essential knowledge and skills related to specified topics are more effective in changing health and safety behaviors than are occasional educational programs on single health and safety topics. Content that affects major intermediate- and long-term health and safety risks has the biggest impact. Teachers need to employ a variety of instructional methods when teaching concepts and skills in order to meet various learning styles.

▶ **COMMENTARY**

A sequential curriculum addresses topics in developmentally appropriate ways and builds on concepts and skills learned in previous grades. This results in fewer omissions and less redundancy than having each teacher select content based on personal interest or perceived importance. A curriculum can either cover different aspects of each content area annually or cover several issues in depth each year, eventually covering all by the end of grade 12.

Standards serve as a gauge for excellence; they describe the challenging goals schools should aspire to for expanding and improving education. National Health Education Standards[6] identify standards for health and safety education overall, with specific indicators at grades 4, 8, and 11. A limited number of behaviors contribute markedly to contemporary major causes of death and health problems (Centers for Disease Control and Prevention [http://www.cdc.gov/nccdphp/dash/yrbs]). They are tobacco use, unhealthy diets, inadequate physical activity, abuse of alcohol and other drugs, sexual behaviors that can result in unintended pregnancies and sexually transmitted diseases including human immunodeficiency virus (HIV), and behaviors that can result in violence or unintentional injuries (eg, motor vehicle, pedestrian, weapon, playground). Information about environmental and personal health can reduce the frequency or severity of diseases such as colds and dental decay. Information about mental and emotional health can enhance students' quality of life and lessen the negative influence of poor mental and emotional health on risk behaviors.

Using standards, districts should develop goals, objectives, content sequence, and specific classroom lessons that use interactive, experiential activities and actively engage students. Appendix D lists examples of creative strategies teachers have used in health classes. Information should be basic, accurate, developmentally appropriate (Guideline 2-06); address social and media influences on behavior; strengthen individual values and group norms that support health- and safety-enhancing behaviors (Guideline 2-08); provide opportunities to become competent in social skills (Guideline 2-07); and provide incentives and remove disincentives for healthy and safe behaviors. Learning is most effective when activities and materials are consistent with students' physical, cultural, social, mental, and emotional states and when they address diverse languages and cultures as well as cognitive, physical, and sensory disabilities.

▶ *RELATED GUIDELINES*

0-11, 0-16, 7-03

▶ *RELATED LINKS*

http://www.aahperd.org/aahe
http://www.americanheart.org
http://ems-c.org
http://www.cdc.gov/nccdphp/dash/yrbs

2-06–FUNCTIONAL KNOWLEDGE OF HEALTH AND SAFETY ISSUES[3,16,25–35]

Include in health and safety curricula functional knowledge that is critical to the topic, is scientifically accurate, and is associated with the acquisition of related skills.

▶ *RATIONALE*

One characteristic of health and safety curricula that generates positive behavior change is that "functional knowledge" (ie, basic facts students need to make behaviorally relevant decisions) is taught. Determining functional knowledge in each selected content area (versus whatever interests the teacher or curious students or appears on a test) allows the most effective use of available instructional time. Even though knowledge is necessary, it is not sufficient for changing or maintaining healthy and safe behaviors. Other characteristics of effective curricula are skills development and social influences (Guidelines 2-07, 2-08).

▶ *COMMENTARY*

In many situations, functional knowledge crosses a number of content areas. For example, teaching about the relationship between drug use and sexual activity uses instructional content from substance abuse prevention, human growth, development and sexuality, disease prevention, and emotional/mental health. Education related to providing first aid and cardiopulmonary resuscitation (CPR) draws from content areas of community safety and personal health. Sports nutrition programs that teach the effects of using performance-enhancing or weight-controlling pharmacologic and nutritional supplements draw from content areas such as substance abuse and information related to nutrition, hydration, physical activity, disease prevention, and mental health. A focus on tobacco use draws from content areas of consumer and environmental health, physical activity, oral health, addiction, personal appearance, development of heart and lung disease, and development of a variety of cancers.

Examples of content areas and of functional knowledge associated with the content areas are:
- Tobacco, alcohol, and other drug use prevention: long-term and short-term negative physiologic and social consequences of use, and social influences on use.
- Growth, development, sexuality, and family life: biopsychosocial sexual development (eg, reproductive cycle); abstinence as the only 100% effective way to avoid unwanted pregnancy, human immunodeficiency virus (HIV), and other sexually transmitted diseases; contraception; and parenting.
- Personal and oral health: hand washing, proper tooth brushing, flossing, and diet.
- Injury prevention and safety: recognizing emergencies; rendering first aid such as cardio-pulmonary resuscitation and other emergency lifesaving skills; proper use of protective gear (eg, seat belts, helmets, wrist pads, guards for mouth and face); smoke and carbon monoxide alarms; rules for motor vehicle, pedestrian, and cycle safety; safe storage, handling, and avoid-ance of weapons; work-related safety principles (eg, agriculture, food services); using proper lifting technique by teaching about the handling of heavy backpacks.
- Violence prevention: healthy relationships, conflict resolution, empathy, impulse control, expressions and control of anger.
- Nutrition and physical activity: healthful food choices, recommended serving sizes, exercise.

▶ *RELATED GUIDELINES*

3-09, 4-30, 5-03, 6-05, 6-11, 6-12

▶ *RELATED LINKS*

http://www.americanheart.org
http://www.redcross.org
http://ems-c.org
http://www.fs4jk.org
http://www.safekids.org

2-07–LEARNING SOCIAL SKILLS[3,5,6,10,12,16,22,25–28,30,31,36]

Provide opportunities in a variety of context-specific ways for students to model and practice social skills that are important for implementing healthy and safe decisions. These include interpersonal communication, goal setting, anger management, and advocacy skills.

▶ RATIONALE

One characteristic of curricula found effective for influencing behaviors is the provision of opportunities for students to model and practice social skills. The National Health Education Standards[6] include interpersonal communication, goal-setting, decision-making, and advocacy skills, among several overall standards, that students should achieve through health and safety education. A few skills such as negotiation, refusal, goal-setting, stress management, and effective communication can help students engage in health-enhancing behaviors and avoid unsafe behaviors. Students need to practice the same or similar skills in a variety of contexts so that they gain proficiency and the ability to apply them in new situations. The same social skills can lead to a reduction in violence, drug abuse, unsafe sexual activity, and other risk behaviors. Effective curricula include not only skills development, but also functional knowledge (Guideline 2-06) and analysis of social in Guideline 2-08).

▶ COMMENTARY

Practice with social skills helps students develop these skills and gain the self-confidence needed to use the skills in appropriate situations. Social learning theory identifies self-efficacy, or the belief that one can use a skill and that using it will make a difference, as a key element in adopting new behaviors. Repeated use of the same skill in different contexts increases the chance that students who learn a skill for one situation, such as refusing an offer to try a drug, will transfer the skill to another situation, such as refusing to engage in theft or sexual activity.

Examples of context-specific skills include:
- refusal skills for tobacco, alcohol, and other drugs;
- goal-setting, negotiation, and refusal skills for interpersonal relationships;
- problem-solving, anger management, and coping skills for stressful situations such as bullying and interpersonal conflict;
- goal setting for maintaining and achieving an appropriate weight through healthy food intake and exercise;
- negotiation skills with families on changing roles and responsibilities within the family as a result of maturation;
- negotiation and conflict resolution skills in situations with a potential for violence;
- problem-solving skills regarding risk-taking behaviors on the basis of likelihood for injury; and
- developing healthy, interpersonal relationship skills.

RELATED GUIDELINES

3-09, 5-03, 6-20, 7-07

RELATED LINKS

http://brightfutures.aap.org/web
http://www.chef.org

2-08—ANALYZING MEDIA AND OTHER SOCIETAL INFLUENCES[16,30,31,36–40]

Provide opportunities for students to analyze how family, peers, culture, media, technology, and other factors influence the development of their own attitudes, beliefs, values, and behaviors.

▶ RATIONALE

Two characteristics of curricula found effective in influencing behaviors are attention to social and media influences on behaviors and accuracy of students' perceptions of what their peers are doing. Skill development (Guideline 2-07) and functional knowledge (Guideline 2-06) are 2 additional characteristics of effective curricula.

▶ COMMENTARY

Effective health and safety education addresses attitudes, beliefs, and values as well as content and skills. The first and often strongest influence on the development of a person's attitudes, beliefs and values is a child's family. As children grow, messages from others—peers, the media, faith-based leaders—often reinforce or challenge family and values messages. Understanding these influences helps students sort out their feelings and values.

Examining popular media (including the Internet) for verbal and nonverbal messages, which are often contradictory, is one example of an opportunity for students to conduct analyses of such influences. Students can learn to locate accurate information, to distinguish fact from opinion and deliberately misleading information, and learn to recognize attempts at manipulating people (eg, subliminal messages). Areas conducive to such analyses include, but are not limited to, social and emotional health, sexuality, and the choice of health care products and services.

As children grow, acceptance by peers becomes more important and peers' opinions can influence attitudes, beliefs, and values as well as health and safety behaviors. Peer influences are both overt and implied. For example, youth tend to overestimate their peers' participation in risky behaviors such as sexual activity, alcohol consumption, and drug use. Such overestimates can lead to internalized pressure to "be like everyone else." Correcting misperceptions can help to reduce a wide variety of risk-taking behaviors such as continuing to play a sport after a head injury, using tobacco or alcohol, being sexually active, or failing to wear a helmet or use a safety belt. Sources of accurate information that can serve to reinforce that other young people are abstaining from risky behaviors include the Youth Risk Behavior Surveillance System (http://www.cdc.gov/nccdphp/dash/yrbs), a national substance abuse survey called Monitoring the Future (http://monitoringthefuture.org), and the Substance Abuse and Mental Health Service Administration (SAMHSA [http://www.samhsa.gov]) household survey of drug use. Students may obtain local data by conducting anonymous surveys of their peers. Data that are culturally relevant and collected from a local student population are most likely to correct misconceptions that "everyone is doing it."

Channel youths' attention and energies toward positive activities. Encourage "service learning" for youth and promote student involvement in youth councils. These experiences provide youth with opportunities to make meaningful contributions to their communities. These are examples of "positive youth development."

▶ *RELATED GUIDELINES*

1-01, 1-04, 5-10, 6-11

▶ *RELATED LINKS*

http://www.communityschools.org
http://www.mediaed.org
http://www.ncate.org
http://www.samhsa.gov
http://www.cdc.gov/nccdphp/dash/yrbs

2-09–GRADE ASSIGNMENT FOR HEALTH/SAFETY EDUCATION[14,41–43]

Use a variety of strategies to assess students' achievement in health and safety education. Report students' progress in the same manner used to report progress in other core subjects.

▶ RATIONALE

Alignment of curriculum, instruction, and assessment is sound educational practice. When students are assessed on a topic or skill, students, teachers, administrators, and parents perceive the subject area as important for their child.

▶ COMMENTARY

Although health and safety education help students acquire knowledge about a variety of health and safety content areas, the primary intended outcome is to help students develop and apply health and safety promoting skills and behaviors.

Students can demonstrate achievement through a range of assessment strategies from traditional paper and pencil tests and quizzes to authentic assessment activities where they participate in processes, produce products, perform, and make presentations. Additional types of assessment strategies are reports, demonstrations, projects, cooperative activities, journals, and portfolios. The Council of Chief State School Officers (http://www.ccsso.org) is a resource for identifying health education assessment measures.

Teachers should consider the varying levels of students' abilities and learning styles when planning assessments of health and safety knowledge and skills. All students need adequate time and opportunity to complete assessments. Use of multiple assessment strategies allows all students to demonstrate mastery and competency of essential health and safety knowledge and skills in ways that are meaningful to teacher and student.

Reporting student achievement in health and safety education in a manner that is consistent with other subjects and incorporating these grades into overall grade point averages serves to reinforce the importance of these subjects.

Some states assess students' acquisition of health- and safety-related knowledge and skills as part of standardized testing. Scores help to monitor progress on student achievement as well as gauge program effectiveness. Assess teaching strategies and program effectiveness (Guideline 0-13) by comparing instructional objectives to the extent to which students are mastering essential knowledge and skills.

▶ RELATED GUIDELINES

0-13, 3-02

▶ RELATED LINKS

http://www.ccsso.org

CHAPTER REFERENCES

1. American Academy of Family Physicians. *AAFP Policies on Health Issues: Health Education.* Leawood, KS: American Academy of Family Physicians; 1999

2. Bogden JF. *Fit, Healthy, and Ready to Learn: A School Health Policy Guide. Part 1: Physical Activity, Healthy Eating, and Tobacco Use Prevention.* Alexandria, VA: National Association of State Boards of Education; 2000

3. Centers for Disease Control and Prevention. School health guidelines to prevent unintentional injuries and violence. *MMWR Recomm Rep.* 2001;50(RR-22):1–73

4. Connell DB, Turner RR, Mason EF. Summary of findings of the school health education evaluation: health promotion effectiveness, implementation, and cost. *J Sch Health.* 1985;55:316–321

5. Jellinek M, ed. *Bright Futures in Practice: Mental Health.* 2nd ed. Arlington VA: National Center for Education in Maternal and Child Health, 2002

6. Joint Committee on *National Health Education Standards. National Health Education Standards: Achieving Health Literacy.* New York, NY: American Cancer Society; 1995

7. Lohrmann DK, Wooley SF. Comprehensive school health education. In: Marx E, Wooley SF, eds. *Health is Academic: A Guide to Coordinated School Health Programs.* New York, NY: Teachers College Press; 1998:43–66

8. Marx E, Northrop D. *Educating for Health: A Guide to Implementing a Comprehensive Approach to School Health Education.* Newton, MA: Education Development Centers Inc; 1995

9. National PTA. *Position Statement on Comprehensive School Health Education.* Chicago, IL: National PTA; 1987

10. Patrick K, ed. *Bright Futures in Practice: Physical Activity.* Arlington, VA: National Center for Education in Maternal and Child Health; 2001

11. Smith DW, Steckler AB, McCormick LK, McLeroy KR. Lessons learned about disseminating health curricula to schools. *J Health Educ.* 1995;26:37–43

12. Story M, ed. *Bright Futures in Practice: Nutrition.* 2nd ed. Arlington VA: National Center for Education in Maternal and Child Health; 2002

13. RMC Health Promotion and Education. What works: curriculum selection process. *Colorado School Health News.* 1998;14(1):1

14. Council of Chief State School Officers. *Health Education Assessment Project of the State Collaborative on Assessment and Student Standards* (CD-ROM). Available at: http://www.ccsso.org/scass

15. National PTA. *Building Successful Partnerships: A Guide for Developing Parent and Family Involvement Programs.* Bloomington, IN: National Educational Service; 2000

16. Neutens JJ, Drolet JC, DaShaw M, Jubb W, eds. *Sexuality Education Within Comprehensive School Health Education.* 2nd ed. Kent, OH: American School Health Association; 2003

17. National Board for Professional Teaching Standards. *Health Education Standards for Teachers of Students Ages 11–18.* Arlington VA: National Board for Professional Teaching Standards, 2002. Available at: http://www.nbpts.org/pdf/healthstandards.pdf

18. Allensworth DD. Health education: state of the art. *J Sch Health.* 1993;63:14–20

19. Teacher not certified to teach health loses job. *Sch Health Prof.* 1999;5:4

20. Kann L, Brener ND, Allensworth DD. Health education: results from the School Health Policies and Programs Study 2000. *J Sch Health.* 2001;71:266–278

21. The Gallup Organization. *Values and Opinions of Comprehensive School Health Education in US Public Schools: Adolescents, Parents, and School District Administrators.* Atlanta, GA: American Cancer Society; 1994

22. Fetro JV. *Personal and Social Skills.* Santa Cruz, CA: ETR Associates; 2000

23. Gilbert GG, Sawyer RG. *Health Education: Creating Strategies for School and Community Health.* Sudbury, MA: Jones & Bartlett; 2000

24. Report of the 2000 Joint Committee on Health Education and Promotion Terminology. *Am J Health Educ.* 2001; 32:89–104

25. Centers for Disease Control and Prevention. Guidelines for effective school health education to prevent the spread of AIDS. *MMWR Morb Mortal Wkly Rep.* 1988;37(S-2):1–14

26. Centers for Disease Control and Prevention. Guidelines for school and community programs to promote lifelong physical activity among young people. *MMWR Recomm Rep.* 1997;46(RR-6):1–36

27. Centers for Disease Control and Prevention. Guidelines for school health programs to prevent tobacco use and addiction. *MMWR Recomm Rep.* 1994;43(No. RR-2):1–18

28. Centers for Disease Control and Prevention. Guidelines for school health programs to promote lifelong healthy eating. *MMWR Morb Mortal Wkly Rep.* 1996;45(RR-9):1–41

29. Children's Safety Network. *Protecting Working Teens: A Public Health Resource Guide.* Newton, MA: Children's Safety Network; 1995

30. Cortese P, Middleton K, eds. *The Comprehensive School Health Challenge: Promoting Health Through Education.* Vol I. Santa Cruz, CA: ETR Associates; 1994

31. Kirby D, Short L, Collins J, et al. School-based programs to reduce sexual risk behaviors: a review of effectiveness. *Public Health Rep.* 1994;109:339–360

32. Massachusetts Department of Public Health. *Teens at Work: Injury Surveillance and Intervention Project, Occupational Health Surveillance Program.* Boston, MA: Massachusetts Department of Public Health; 2000. Available at: http://www.state.ma.us/dph/bhsre/ohsp/ohsp.htm

33. National Children's Center for Rural and Agricultural Health and Safety. *Creating Safe Play Areas on Farms.* Marshfield, WI: Marshfield Clinic; 2003. Available at: http://research.marshfieldclinic.org/children/safeplay.pdf

34. National Research Council and Institute of Medicine, Committee on the Health and Safety Implications of Child Labor. *Protecting Youth at Work: Health, Safety, and Development of Working Children and Adolescents in the United States.* Washington, DC: National Academy Press; 1998

35. Posner M. *Preventing School Injuries: A Comprehensive Guide for School Administrators, Teachers, and Staff.* New Brunswick, NJ: Rutgers University Press; 2000

36. Dusenbury L, Falco M. Eleven components of effective drug abuse prevention curricula. *J Sch Health.* 1995;65:420–425

37. American Academy of Pediatrics, Committee on Public Education. Media education. *Pediatrics.* 1999;104:341–343

38. Dryfoos J, Maguire S. *Inside Full-Service Community Schools.* Thousand Oaks, CA: Corwin Press; 2002

39. Rosenthal DA, Smith AM, de Visser R. Personal and social factors influencing age at first sexual intercourse. *Arch Sex Behav.* 1999;28:319–333

40. Vanoss Marin B, Coyle KK, Gomez CA, Carvajal SC, Kirby DB. Older boyfriends and girlfriends increase risk of sexual initiation in young adolescents. *J Adolesc Health.* 2000;27:409–418

41. Lohrmann DK. Overview of curriculum design and implementation. In: Mahoney BS, Olsen LK, eds. *Health Education Teacher Resource Handbook: A Practical Guide for K–12 Health Education.* Millwood, NY: Kraus International Publications; 1993:35–58

42. Wiggins G, McTighe J. *Understanding by Design.* Alexandria, VA: Association for Supervision and Curriculum Development; 1998

43. Wiggins GP. *Educative Assessment: Designing Assessments to Inform and Improve Student Performance.* San Francisco, CA: Jossey-Bass; 1998

44. American Red Cross. *Community First Aid and Safety.* Washington, DC: American Red Cross; 2002

45. Centers for Disease Control and Prevention. Guidelines for school programs to prevent skin cancer. *MMWR Recomm Rep.* 2002;51(RR-4):1–20

46. Drug Strategies. *Making the Grade: A Guide to School Drug Prevention Programs.* Washington, DC: Drug Strategies; 1999:95

47. Summerfield LM. *Drug and Alcohol Prevention Education.* Washington, DC: ERIC Digest Educational Resources Information Center Clearinghouse on Teaching and Teacher Education; 1991. Publication No. ED330675

CHAPTER-RELATED LINKS

American Association for Health Education
http://www.aahperd.org/aahe

American School Health Association
http://www.ashaweb.org/

American Heart Association
http://www.americanheart.org

American Red Cross
http://www.redcross.org/
Educational programs include first aid and cardiopulmonary resuscitation.

Bridge Communications, Inc. Healthy Newsletters
http://www.bridge-comm.com/

Bright Futures
http://brightfutures.aap.org
Resources to promote healthy behaviors; reduce morbidity and mortality; develop partnerships between health professionals, families, and communities; and improve child health outcomes.

Child Trends Data Bank

http://www.redcross.org/

Latest data on leading causes of morbidity and mortality
at various ages (national, state, local, international).

Coalition for Community Schools

http://www.communityschools.org/

Coalition to bring together partners to offer a range
of supports and opportunities to children, youth,
families, and communities—before, during, and
after school, 7 days a week.

Comprehensive Health Education Foundation

http://www.chef.org/

Resources for supporting school-aged youth, among
other populations, to have healthier lives through
health education.

Council of Chief State School Officers

http://www.ccsso.org/

This organization's State Collaborative on Assessment
and Student Standards includes the Health Education
Assessment Project (HEAP), which identifies
and develops assessment measures in the area
of health education.

Emergency Medical Services for Children

http://ems-c.org/

Resources available through their clearinghouse,
including: Basic Emergency Lifesaving Skills
(BELS): A Framework for Teaching Emergency
Lifesaving Skills to Children and Adolescents.

Farm Safety 4 Just Kids

http://www.fs4jk.org

Fact sheets for educators to promote safe farm
environments for children and youth.

Healthy People 2010

http://www.healthypeople.gov/

National health objectives designed to identify the
most significant preventable threats to health
and to establish national goals to reduce
these threats.

Media Education Foundation

http://www.mediaed.org/

A nonprofit educational organization devoted to media
research and production of resources that aids
educators to foster analytical media literacy.

Monitoring the Future

http://monitoringthefuture.org/

An ongoing study of behaviors, attitudes, and values
of American secondary school students, college
students, and young adults.

National Commission for Health Education Credentialing

http://www.nchec.org/

National Council on Accreditation of Teacher Education

http://www.ncate.org/

National Fire Protection Association

http://www.nfpa.org/

Has a model injury prevention program designed for
the classroom called Risk Watch.

National Safe Kids Campaign

http://www.safekids.org/

Includes a "teachers' desk" with resources for
teaching children safety

North American Guidelines for Children's
Agricultural Tasks

http://www.nagcat.org/

For an example of defining "developmentally appropriate,"
which has defined developmental readiness for
children to be able to engage in a variety of specific
agricultural chores.

Rocky Mountain Center for Health Promotion
and Education

http://www.rmc.org/

Substance Abuse and Mental Health Service
Administration (SAMHSA)

http://www.samhsa.gov/

SAMHSA is An Agency of the US Department of
Health and Human Services and its site publishes
a national household survey on drug abuse.

Youth Risk Behavior Surveillance System

http://www.cdc.gov/nccdphp/dash/yrbs/

A surveillance system of the Centers for Disease
Control and Prevention designed to assess
health risk behaviors.

◀ **Physical Education and Activities** ▶

CURRICULUM, STANDARDS, RESOURCES, AND OPPORTUNITIES

3-01—DAILY PHYSICAL EDUCATION[1-10]

Provide all students in kindergarten through grade 12 with daily physical education, with no substitutions allowed for participation in other courses or activities.

▶ RATIONALE

Daily physical education and activity allows students to acquire skills and attitudes necessary for lifelong participation in physical activity. Physical activity is a proven treatment strategy for obesity and may also be effective to prevent future obesity. High student physical activity levels are associated with higher grades, less substance abuse, and healthier psychological profiles.

▶ COMMENTARY

Physical education is essential to a student's total education. Planned, successfully-conducted physical education programs can provide many benefits for children and adolescents. These include improved levels of physical fitness, self-discipline, enhanced self-confidence, development of many skills, and reinforcement of knowledge learned in other subject areas. Physical activity has been correlated with physical and emotional health, such as better relationships, less depression, fewer risk-taking behaviors, and higher grades. Inactive adults show increased rates of obesity, diabetes, hypertension, coronary heart disease, and certain cancers, all of which can lead to premature illness and death. Physical education should be offered every day to provide sufficient teaching time and ample opportunities for students to learn skills and be physically active.

Exemptions from physical education should not be permitted for participation in activities such as athletic teams, community recreation programs, Reserve Officers Training Corps (ROTC), or marching band. Instruction in physical education is an integral part of each student's education (including students with special needs), has value beyond the physical activity itself, and students should not be exempt from it. A student may be excused from physical education when a physician states in writing that specific physical activities will jeopardize the student's health.

▶ RELATED GUIDELINES

2-04

▶ RELATED LINKS

http://www.actionforhealthykids.org
http://www.cdc.gov
http://www.aahperd.org/naspe

3-02—PHYSICAL EDUCATION STANDARDS AND QUALITY[2,3,5,6,11–18]

Provide physical education instruction based on a sequential curriculum that is consistent with state physical education standards and the National Standards for Physical Education.[6] Hire physical education teachers with appropriate qualifications.

▶ RATIONALE

Planned, sequential physical education will help students acquire skills, knowledge, and experiences that will help them adopt and maintain physically active lifestyles and enjoy numerous benefits of being physically active.

▶ COMMENTARY

High-quality physical education programs develop students' knowledge, movement and motor skills, safety skills, self-management skills, and health-related physical fitness. Classes should build on previous learning. All students should be kept active for most of the class time and have a variety of enjoyable physical activities, both competitive and noncompetitive. A high-quality program also emphasizes opportunities for students to assume leadership, cooperate with others, accept responsibility for one's behavior, build confidence, and have fun.

Physical education teachers must have appropriate qualifications for teaching physical education and maintaining safety. The National Board for Professional Teaching Standards' *Physical Education Standards for Teachers of Students Ages 3–18*[11] lays the foundation for physical education certificates. *National Standards for Physical Education*[6] provides a framework for developing a sound physical education curriculum, as described above. These standards outline how to create a physical education program that is well balanced with a combination of motor skills, concepts, fitness activities, and games. This resource will assist schools with designing a program that enhances development of students' psychomotor and cognitive skills, development and maintenance of physical fitness, and promotion of lifelong physical activity. Sample benchmarks for each grade level are offered. For example, at sixth grade this set of standards advises that students should be able to perform hand dribbles and foot dribbles while preventing an opponent from stealing the ball.[6] This resource also includes physical education goals for students outside of school (eg, "exhibits a physically active lifestyle.") and suggests ways to assess students for all of its recommended standards. Many states have used the *National Standards for Physical Education* to develop their own state standards.

Reporting student achievement in physical education in a manner that is consistent with other subjects and incorporating this grade into overall student achievement scores reinforces the importance of physical education. Schools should not deny students physical activities or force physical activities as disciplinary measures (Guideline 7-08).

▶ RELATED GUIDELINES

0-14, 2-02, 2-05, 2-06, 2-09, 7-08

▶ RELATED LINKS

http://www.actionforhealthykids.org
http://www.cdc.gov
http://www.aahperd.org/naspe

3-03—PHYSICAL ACTIVITY AND SPECIAL NEEDS[12,16,19–24]

Establish and enforce policies and practices that enable students with disabilities and other special health care needs to participate fully and safely in physical education and other school physical activity programs.

▶ RATIONALE

Students with disabilities need to experience the same quality of physical education and be offered equivalent opportunities for physical activity that are offered to other students, but with modifications to meet their needs. These students require physical activities that are designed to increase physical endurance, strength, and skills.

▶ COMMENTARY

Each student with a special health care need or disability requires an assessment of how the disability or special health care need will impact participation in any given activity. This includes assessments of cognitive abilities and social skills. Physical activity and physical education programs must be tailored to meet each student's specific disability and goals and allow them to experience success.

Depending on need, physical activity for students with disabilities may be delivered in a regular physical education class or in an adapted physical education class. Sometimes specialized instruction is required for students with disabilities in order to deal effectively with special learning styles and modes of communication. In addition, protective equipment, safety gear, and surfaces may require modifications to accommodate students. Teachers with national certification for adapted physical education are best equipped to design these programs. Standards from the National Consortium for Physical Education and Recreation[19] guide physical educators on accommodating the needs of students with disabilities. Resources are also available to guide community and school health professionals on specific cautions for athletic participation of students with cardiac disorders, neurological problems, cystic fibrosis, Down Syndrome, and other conditions.[20–22]

▶ RELATED GUIDELINES

0-01, 0-14, 4-15, 4-20, 6-01, 7-01

▶ RELATED LINKS

http://brightfutures.aap.org
http://www.cdc.gov
http://www.dsusa.org
http://www.aahperd.org/naspe
http://www.nscd.org

3-04—ACTIVITY OPPORTUNITIES BEYOND PHYSICAL EDUCATION[2,12,25-29]

Provide a variety of opportunities for physical activity in addition to physical education that meet all students' needs and interests. Opportunities include daily recess, active play during after-school programs, access to school facilities outside of school hours, interscholastic sports, intramural programs, and physical activity clubs.

▶ RATIONALE

Schools are in a unique position to provide many opportunities for students to participate safely in physical activity, and to motivate them to stay physically active. These positive experiences can contribute to students' physical and emotional development and to enjoyment of their school experience.

▶ COMMENTARY

To the extent possible, offer a diverse selection of competitive and noncompetitive, structured and unstructured activities. Cocurricular physical activity programs should focus on facilitating participation of all students who are interested, regardless of their athletic ability or disability. Intramural programs can be beneficial for students who dislike competitive sports or who lack the skills or confidence to play competitive sports.

Recess provides opportunities for unstructured but supervised play, helps students focus in class, and provides social benefits. Healthy children and adults fare better without extended periods of inactivity. Studies show that students who do not participate in recess become fidgety and less able to concentrate. Students become less attentive the longer they sit without a recess break. However, recess should not be a substitute for physical education classes.

After-school programs have the opportunity to provide health-enhancing physical activity and time to practice skills taught in physical education classes. Increased access to school facilities could help facilitate increases in physical activity for populations that lack access to appropriate facilities and where this is a barrier to an active lifestyle. Community-based youth sports and recreation programs can work together with schools to ensure school facilities are used to a maximum advantage.

Encourage parents to avoid overcompetitive and aggressive behavior while observing their children participate in sports, to keep children from playing sports after injury, and to understand the cognitive and physical limitations of children's ability during sports based on their developmental stage.

▶ RELATED GUIDELINES

0-12, 1-04, 1-05, 2-07, 6-07

▶ RELATED LINKS

http://www.actionforhealthykids.org
http://www.ipausa.org
http://www.cdc.gov
http://www.aahperd.org

3-05—AMPLE RESOURCES FOR ENTIRE CLASS IN PHYSICAL EDUCATION[2,3,5,13–15,17,18,25,30,31]

Provide teacher-student ratios for physical education and activity programs that are comparable with other subjects. Activities that require close supervision to ensure student safety should be staffed accordingly. Provide a sufficient amount of equipment and supplies to keep students active during most of the class.

▶ *RATIONALE*

Maximum student safety, involvement, and achievement in physical education can best be obtained when students are provided with appropriate supervision and adequate materials.

▶ *COMMENTARY*

Large class sizes are a barrier to quality physical education, which must cover a great deal of content. Teacher-student ratios should be comparable to those in other subjects. If children with disabilities require additional attention when active, then the ratio of teachers to students needs to be increased, as appropriate to the circumstances.

Students waste valuable time when they must stand in line waiting for equipment or waiting for their turn. This is often an outcome of inadequate supplies of equipment or suboptimal staffing.

▶ *RELATED GUIDELINES*

6-01, 6-05, 6-08

▶ *RELATED LINKS*

http://www.childrenssafetynetwork.org
http://www.aquaticisf.org
http://www.nata.org

◀ Physical Education and Activities ▶

SAFETY

3-06—OUTDOOR SAFETY FOR PHYSICAL ACTIVITY [2,25,30,32-37]

Establish and enforce policies for participation in outdoor activities to protect students and staff from health risks and hazards. This includes exposure to heat, cold, inclement weather, ultraviolet radiation, air pollution, traffic, unsafe surfaces, poor lighting, and poorly maintained equipment.

▶ *RATIONALE*

The health and safety of students and staff need to be considered first and foremost when making decisions about conducting outdoor physical activities.

▶ *COMMENTARY*

Policies should include specific information about appropriate clothing, hydration practices, screening for signs of dehydration, rest periods, indications to cancel activities, frostbite, protection from sun exposure, and a plan for reaching medical assistance when necessary. Specific recommendations for each of these weather conditions are outlined in Appendix E. On days when air quality is poor or the weather is inclement, the intensity of physical activity must be reduced or classes must be held indoors. There is evidence that high ozone levels, particularly for students with asthma and other respiratory conditions, induce or worsen symptoms. Ozone levels, other measures of air quality, and guidelines specific to physical activity and air pollution are available from the US Environmental Protection Agency (http://www.epa.gov/airnow), the American Lung Association (http://www.lungusa.org), and resources in Appendix E.

Fewer injuries occur when there is a shock-absorbent playing surface. Surfaces should be observed carefully when there are students with compromised gait, wheelchairs, canes, or crutches in order to be certain that ground surfaces allow free and easy movement. Playing areas should also be free from debris and water. Separation of motor vehicles and other traffic from play areas is essential for maintaining a safe environment and reducing injuries.

For schools where swimming pools are part of physical education or activity programs, safety procedures include maintenance of pool water chemistry, enforcing rules of student conduct, constant staff observation of all students, and staff trained in the prevention of drowning, in near drowning resuscitation, and in prevention and initial management of diving injuries. The Foundation for Aquatic Injury Prevention (http://www.aquaticisf.org) offers useful recommendations, such as having a telephone available at pools, and sample rules of conduct for students (eg, no running or pushing).

▶ *RELATED GUIDELINES*

5-06, 6-01, 6-04, 6-07, 6-08, 6-19

▶ *RELATED LINKS*

http://www.lungusa.org
http://www.redcross.org
http://www.childrenssafetynetwork.org
http://www.epa.gov/airnow
http://www.aquaticisf.org
http://www.nata.org
http://www.lightningsafety.com/nlsi_info.html

3-07—PREPARTICIPATION PHYSICAL EXAMINATION FOR SPORTS[20,32,38–40]

Require a preparticipation sports physical examination conducted by the student's primary care provider within a year of participation for students participating in interscholastic sports.

▶ *RATIONALE*

Preparticipation physical examination for student athletes can identify conditions that may predispose to injury or be life-threatening or disabling. Such examinations may meet state regulatory or district insurance requirements.

▶ *COMMENTARY*

A preparticipation physical examination allows for the counseling of student athletes on health-related issues, including mental health, and the assessment of students' fitness levels. It is extremely useful to have a standard form for purposes of documentation and continuity. Require students who have been excluded from participation for reasons of illness or injury to receive an additional preparticipation physical evaluation or sports clearance examination after recovery.

When the preparticipation physical examination is conducted by students' own physicians, this allows for continuity of care by someone who is familiar with the student and family. This also allows time for discussion of adolescent risk taking issues. For students without access to their own health care providers, it is sometimes necessary to arrange for examination of students at school-based health centers or through other school-based screening programs. Locker-room methods of lining students up to be examined affords little privacy or atmosphere for a good exchange between patient and doctor and is not the best environment to detect subtle abnormalities on the physical examination. The "station method," whereby a physician, a nurse, an athletic trainer, and perhaps others are each assigned one task as students move from one station to another, is better than the locker room method as there is an excellent yield of identified abnormalities. But this still falls short of developing a rapport with a student athlete for more comprehensive historical information. When there is a well-trained health care provider and students have access to this level of care, the office or clinic-based method is best because it allows a student and practitioner to converse on a one-to-one level.

Students who receive annual physical assessments by their primary health care provider may already have all the information that is necessary for the preparticipation physical examination. Some schools require that the presports medical assessments occur within weeks of the start of the athletic season. This has never been proven to be important from the medical perspective and it poses an unnecessary inconvenience for both students and examining doctors who cannot then schedule office visits at other times over the course of a year.

▶ *RELATED GUIDELINES*

4-13, 4-16, 4-26, 4-27

▶ *RELATED LINKS*

http://www.aap.org

3-08—PHYSICAL ACTIVITY EXEMPTION/RESUMPTION[20,21,38,39]

Require written and specific health verification from the school nurse, a primary care provider, or other licensed health care provider to allow a student to be exempt from physical education and activity programs on the basis of health reasons. Require the same verification to resume physical activity.

▶ RATIONALE

There are valid health and safety-related reasons for restricting some students from all or some physical activities. Schools need to know when it is safe for students to return to regular physical activity. Some health care providers are not aware that activity programs can be tailored and they may excuse students from participation in all physical education activities, even when fewer limitations would be permissible. Communication with school personnel may correct this misunderstanding.

▶ COMMENTARY

Students commonly have health excuses to be exempt from participating in physical activity. Menstrual cramps, asthma, minor or significant injuries, and being on a medication are common excuses. When a student presents a health excuse prior to the physical activity and the excuse is not supported by medical verification, the school nurse and/or physical education teacher need to use their best judgment to decide whether to allow the exemption—erring on the side of caution. A referral to the student's health care provider may need to be made at this time. Repetitive health complaints leading to reduced participation in physical activity should initiate a referral to students' health care provider.

Many students and their families mistakenly feel that a diagnosis such as asthma or temporary conditions such as menstrual cramps are best managed by avoiding physical activity. Communication between school staff, parents, students, and the student's health care provider can correct common misperceptions. Some health care providers in the community are misinformed about the flexibility of schools' physical activity programs and may appear to be recommending more restrictions than they intend to. For example, children experiencing side effects of a medication may still perform many activities. Modified or adapted physical education programs can be provided in many cases to students with valid reasons for partial exemption. Discussion among the family, the prescribing physician (or nurse practitioner, physician assistant), the physical education teacher, and the school nurse (and/or school physician) will help to establish the limits of participation and the duration of limitations for the student.

▶ RELATED GUIDELINES

1-02, 4-13

▶ RELATED LINKS

http://www.aap.org
http://www.lungusa.org
http://brightfutures.aap.org

3-09—PHYSICAL EDUCATION AND SAFETY CURRICULUM[3,30,32,41–45]

Educate students and staff about the dangers of substance abuse, misconduct during physical activity, excessive weight control (rapid weight gain or loss), and the importance of using safety gear as well as other aspects of safe participation in physical activities. Safety education must be a major component of the physical education program.

▶ RATIONALE

Substance abuse and misconduct adversely affect safety during physical activity. Alcohol, other psychoactive drugs, and excessive weight control are examples of student practices that can have long-term adverse consequences on the body.

▶ COMMENTARY

Use of alcohol and other drugs increases chances of injury through impaired judgment and delayed reaction time. Many performance-enhancing products, such as creatine and substances related to anabolic steroids, are readily available and often legally purchased. Most of these substances have never been tested for safety for use in the long-term or for use by children and adolescents. Many of these substances may pose numerous or significant health hazards.

Bullying, harassment, unsportsmanlike behavior, and violent behavior are hazardous to student and staff safety and discourage many students from wanting to participate in physical activities. Educate students about behavior in play areas. Inform them of rules and the consequences for breaking them. Coaches, physical education teachers, and those supervising other physical activities must be trained to recognize and educate students on signs and symptoms of injuries, including muscle, bone, head, and abdominal injuries, and actions to be taken when they occur. Teach students the rationale for removing a student from a physical activity after an injury and for seeking medical assessment and assistance.

Young athletes must be discouraged from trying to gain weight for sports such as football and body building and from trying to lose weight for sports such as wrestling or dance/ballet. Excessive weight control may impair athletic performance and safety in the short-term (eg, dehydration). Water-loading to increase short-term weight before measurement also poses danger to health. Surveys of youth find that youth practice weight control through self-induced vomiting, binge eating, and use of diuretics, diet pills, and laxatives. These practices and disordered eating may lead to suboptimal calcium deposition into bones, menstrual disorders, anorexia nervosa, and bulimia. The consequences of the latter 2 can be fatal.

Dietary supplements, such as protein powders and amino acids, are commonly perceived by athletes as healthier than ordinary foods. To correct erroneous associations between nutritional supplements and athletic accomplishment, teachers and coaches should emphasize that a nutritious diet of healthy foods also promotes muscle growth and optimal performance. Encourage students to keep records of their own practice, training, and improvement in performance so that accomplishments in athletic endeavors are easily seen to be more closely associated with effort and practice.

▶ *RELATED GUIDELINES*

2-06, 2-07, 4-07, 5-03, 6-01, 6-08, 7-05, 7-07

▶ *RELATED LINKS*

http://www.aap.org
http://www.childrenssafetynetwork.org
http://www.nata.org

3-10—USE OF PROTECTIVE EQUIPMENT IN SPORTS[26,30,32,46]

Require the use of appropriate safety and protective equipment in physical education, inter-scholastic and intramural sports, and all other physical activity programs.

▶ RATIONALE

Minimizing physical activity-related injuries and illnesses for students is a joint responsibility of teachers, supervisors of recess and physical activity programs, coaches, athletic trainers, students and families.

▶ COMMENTARY

Safety and protective equipment include such items as helmets, goggles, mouth and shin guards, and wrist, elbow, knee, and shoulder pads. Safety gear should be sport-specific and required. Examples are: footwear appropriate for the specific activity; helmets for bicycling; shin guards for soccer; reflective clothing for walking and running; helmets, face masks, mouth guards, and protective pads for football and ice hockey; and chest protectors for fencing. Protective gear and equipment should be frequently inspected and replaced if worn, damaged, or outdated. Safety gear worn by a student should fit properly. Protective gear should be worn during practice sessions as well as during competition.

▶ PELATED GUIDELINES

6-01, 6-05, 6-06, 6-08, 6-19

▶ RELATED LINKS

http://www.childrenssafetynetwork.org
http://www.nata.org
http://www.safeusa.org/school/safescho.htm

CHAPTER REFERENCES

1. Aarts H, Paulussen T, Schaalma H. Physical exercise habit: on the conceptualization and formation of habitual health behaviours. *Health Educ Res.* 1997;12:363–374

2. Bogden JF. *Fit, Healthy, and Ready to Learn: A School Health Policy Guide. Part I: Physical Activity, Healthy Eating, and Tobacco-Use Prevention.* Alexandria, VA: National Association of State Boards of Education; 2000

3. Centers for Disease Control and Prevention. Guidelines for school health programs to promote lifelong healthy eating. *MMWR Morb Mortal Wkly Rep.* 1996;45(RR-9):1–41

4. Field T, Diego M, Sanders CE. Exercise is positively related to adolescents' relationships and academics. *Adolescence.* 2001;36:105–110

5. Napper-Owen G. *Opportunity to Learn: Standards for Elementary Physical Education.* Reston, VA: National Association for Sport and Physical Education; 2000

6. National Association for Sport and Physical Education. *Moving into the Future: National Standards of Physical Education.* 2nd ed. Reston, VA: National Association for Sport and Physical Education; 2004

7. Paluska SA, Schwenk TL. Physical activity and mental health: current concepts. *Sports Med.* 2000;29:167–180

8. Seefeldt VD. Physical education. In: Marx E, Wooley SF, eds. *Health is Academic: A Guide to Coordinated School Health Programs.* New York, NY: Teachers College Press; 1998:43–66

9. Steinbeck KS. The importance of physical activity in the prevention of overweight and obesity in childhood: a review and an opinion. *Obes Rev.* 2001;2:117–130

10. Trost SG, Pate RR, Dowda M, Ward DS, Felton G, Saunders R. Psychosocial correlates of physical activity in white and African-American girls. *J Adolesc Health.* 2002;31:226–233

11. National Board for Professional Teaching Standards. *Physical Education Standards for Teachers of Students Ages 3–18.* Arlington VA: National Board for Professional Teaching Standards; 1999. Available at: http://www.nbpts.org/pdf/ecya_pe.pdf

12. Centers for Disease Control and Prevention. *Promoting Better Health for Young People Through Physical Activity and Sports: A Report to the President From the Secretary of Health and Human Services and the Secretary of Education.* Atlanta, GA: Centers for Disease Control and Prevention; 2000

13. National Association for Sport and Physical Education. *Appropriate Practices for Elementary School Physical Education.* Reston, VA: National Association for Sport and Physical Education; 2000

14. National Association for Sport and Physical Education. *Appropriate Practices for Middle School Physical Education.* Reston, VA: National Association for Sport and Physical Education; 2001

15. National Association for Sport and Physical Education. *Appropriate Practices for High School Physical Education.* Reston, VA: National Association for Sport and Physical Education; 1998

16. National Association for Sport and Physical Education. *Including Students With Disabilities in Physical Education.* Reston, VA: National Association for Sport and Physical Education; 1995

17. National Association for Sport and Physical Education. *Physical Education Program Improvement and Self-Study Guide: High School.* Reston, VA: National Association for Sport and Physical Education; 1998

18. National Association for Sport and Physical Education. *Physical Education Program Improvement and Self-Study Guide: Middle School.* Reston, VA: National Association for Sport and Physical Education; 1998

19. National Consortium for Physical Education and Recreation for Individuals with Disabilities. *Adapted Physical Education National Standards.* Champaign, IL: Human Kinetics; 1995

20. American Academy of Pediatrics, Committee on Sports Medicine and Fitness. Medical conditions affecting sports participation. *Pediatrics.* 2001;107:1205–1209

21. Patrick K, ed. *Bright Futures in Practice: Physical Activity.* Arlington, VA: National Center for Education in Maternal and Child Health; 2001

22. Sullivan JA, Anderson SJ, eds. *Care of the Young Athlete.* Rosemont, IL: American Academy of Orthopaedic Surgeons/American Academy of Pediatrics; 2000

23. Block ME. *A Teacher's Guide to Including Students With Disabilities in Regular Physical Education.* Baltimore, MD: Brookes; 1994

24. National Heart, Lung, and Blood Institute. *Asthma and Physical Activity in the School: Making a Difference.* Bethesda, MD: National Institutes of Health; 1995. Publication No. 95–3651

25. Centers for Disease Control and Prevention. Guidelines for school and community programs to promote lifelong physical activity among young people. *MMWR Recomm Rep.* 1997;46(RR-6):1–36

26. Council on Physical Education for Children. *Recess in Elementary Schools. A Position Report from the National Association for Sport and Physical Education.* Reston, VA: National Association for Sport and Physical Education; 2001

27. National Association for Sport and Physical Education. *National Standards for Athletic Coaches.* Dubuque, IA: Kendall/Hunt Publishing; 1995

28. National Association for Sport and Physical Education. *Position Paper. Guidelines for After School Physical Activity and Intramural Sports Programs.* Reston, VA: National Association for Sport and Physical Education; 2002

29. Roman J, ed. *The NSACA Standards for Quality School-Age Care.* Boston, MA: National School-Age Care Alliance; 1998

30. Centers for Disease Control and Prevention. School health guidelines to prevent unintentional injuries and violence. *MMWR Recomm Rep.* 2001;50(RR-22):1–73

31. Dougherty NJ, ed. *Principles of Safety in Physical Education and Sport.* 3rd ed. Reston, VA: American Alliance for Health, Physical Education, Recreation and Dance; 2002

32. Adirim TA, Cheng TL. Overview of injuries in the young athlete. *Sports Med.* 2003;33:75–81

33. American Academy of Pediatrics, Committee on Sports Medicine and Fitness. Climatic heat stress and the exercising child and adolescent. *Pediatrics.* 2000;106:158–159

34. American Red Cross. *Lifeguard Management.* Washington, DC: American Red Cross; 2003

35. Blanksby BA, Wearne FK, Elliott BC, Blitvich JD. Aetiology and occurrence of diving injuries. A review of diving safety. *Sports Med.* 1997;23:228–246

36. Centers for Disease Control and Prevention. Guidelines for school programs to prevent skin cancer. *MMWR Recomm Rep.* 2002;51(No.RR-4):1–20

37. DeVivo MJ, Sekar P. Prevention of spinal cord injuries that occur in swimming pools. *Spinal Cord.* 1997;35:509–515

38. American Academy of Family Physicians, Preparticipation Physical Evaluation Task Force. *Preparticipation Physical Evaluation.* 2nd ed. Minneapolis, MN: The Physician and Sports Medicine; 1997

39. Barrett JR, Kuhlman GS, Stanitski CL, Small E. The pre-participation physical evaluation. In: Sullivan JA, Anderson SJ, eds. *Care of the Young Athlete.* Rosemont, IL: American Academy of Orthopaedic Surgeons/American Academy of Pediatrics; 2000:43–56

40. Fahrenbach MC, Thompson PD. The pre-participation sports examination. Cardiovascular considerations for screening. *Cardiol Clin.* 1992;10:319–328

41. Congeni J, Miller S. Supplements and drugs used to enhance athletic performance. *Pediatr Clin North Am.* 2002;49:435–461

42. Griesemer BA. Performance enhancing substances. In: Sullivan JA, Anderson SJ, eds. *Care of the Young Athlete.* Rosemont, IL: American Academy of Orthopaedic Surgeons/American Academy of Pediatrics; 2000:95–104

43. Ross JG, Eihaus KE, Hohenemser LK, Green B. School health policy prohibiting tobacco use, alcohol and other drug use, and violence. *J Sch Health.* 1995;65:333–338

44. Stainback RD. *Alcohol and Sport.* Champaign, IL: Human Kinetics; 1997

45. Steen SN, Bernhardt DT. Nutrition and weight control. In: Sullivan JA, Anderson SJ, eds. *Care of the Young Athlete.* Rosemont, IL: American Academy of Orthopaedic Surgeons/American Academy of Pediatrics; 2000:81–94

46. American Academy of Pediatric Dentistry. Prevention of sports-related injuries. *Pediatr Dent.* 1999;21:32

47. Murdock CG. Excuse from physical education. *J Sch Health.* 1967;37:387–390

48. National Association for Sport and Physical Education, Middle and Secondary School Physical Education Council. *Position Paper. Substitution for Instructional Physical Education Programs.* Reston, VA: National Association for Sport and Physical Education; 1999

49. Patel DR, Greydanus DE. The pediatric athlete with disabilities. *Pediatr Clin North Am.* 2002;49:803–827

CHAPTER-RELATED LINKS

Action for Healthy Kids
http://www.actionforhealthykids.org
Resource for health-promotion in schools with an
emphasis on promotion of sound nutrition and
increased physical activity.

American Academy of Pediatrics
http://www.aap.org/

American Association for the Child's Right to Play
http://www.ipausa.org
Includes: The Case for Elementary School Recess.

American Lung Association; 1-800-LUNGUSA
http://www.lungusa.org
Ozone and the Air Quality Index: A Program
Resource Guide.

American Red Cross
http://www.redcross.org/

Bright Futures
http://brightfutures.aap.org
Resources to promote healthy behaviors; reduce
morbidity and mortality; develop partnerships
between health professionals, families, and
communities; and improve child health outcomes.

Centers for Disease Control and Prevention (CDC)
http://www.cdc.gov/

Centers for Disease Control and Prevention (CDC)—
Division of Adolescent and School Health
http://www.cdc.gov/nccdphp/dash/index.htm
Includes youth risk behavior surveillance, guidelines
for school health programs, physical activity, and
after-school care programs.

Centers for Disease Control and Prevention (CDC)—
"School Health Index for Physical Activity and
Healthy Eating: A Self Assessment & Planning Guide"
http://www.cdc.gov/nccdphp/dash/SHI/index.htm

Children's Safety Network
http://www.childrenssafetynetwork.org
Resources on child safety in school and on employed
youth.

Disabled Sports USA
http://www.dsusa.org/

Environmental Protection Agency
http://www.epa.gov/airnow/
For information on daily air quality across the
United States.

Environmental Protection Agency—"Keeping Kids Safe
from Sun and Smog"
http://www.epa.gov/sunwise/doc/summertime.pdf
Includes a color-coded air quality index that relates
to ozone levels and a UV index that relates to
harmful effects of sun.

Foundation for Aquatic Injury Prevention
http://www.aquaticisf.org/

National Association for Sport and Physical Education
http://www.aahperd.org/naspe
The "store" includes published national guidelines.

National Athletic Trainers Association
http://www.nata.org/
Publications include "Minimizing the Risk of Injury in
High School Athletics."

National Lightning Safety Institute
http://www.lightningsafety.com/nlsi_info.html

National Sports Center for the Disabled
http://www.nscd.org/

Safe USA
http://www.safeusa.org/school/safescho.htm
Resources for safety on playgrounds and in sports
and for violence prevention.

◀ Health and Mental Health Services ▶

STAFFING AND ORGANIZATION

4-01—STUDENT ASSISTANCE TEAMS AT EACH SITE[1-2]

Provide a multidisciplinary student assistance team individualized to assist each student experiencing problems (educational, behavioral, developmental, or any health- or safety-related problem). At a minimum, include a school nurse, mental health professional, the student's teachers, and school administrator on the team.

▶ *RATIONALE*

Multidisciplinary student assistance teams are essential if educational staff are to understand all potential health and social causes that may be contributing to a student's academic and behavior problems and if they are to achieve resolutions that can lead to improved student performance.

▶ *COMMENTARY*

Student assistance teams are known by many different names. "Student study teams" and "site consultation teams" are other examples. Parents are typically invited to be a part of the team when their child's concerns are being addressed. The student is also invited when appropriate.

A multidisciplinary approach is necessary to address problems with a student's learning, ability to attend to academics, attendance, social problems, emotional problems, misbehavior, unaddressed medical needs, and other health-related problems. As many educational, peer relationship, and student behavior problems are associated with health and safety issues, health and mental health personnel need to be an integral part of schools' multidisciplinary team approach.

▶ *RELATED GUIDELINES*

7-02, 7-03, 7-04, 7-05, 8-06

4-02—SUPERVISION OF CLINICAL ACTIVITIES[3-7]

Require that fully qualified, credentialed, and licensed health professionals supervise clinical health professionals and health care services. The leading clinical supervisor of the district should be part of the district's central administrative team and have formal training in management and administration.

▶ RATIONALE

Informed, competent oversight of health professionals delivering clinical services requires supervision by professionals with appropriate clinical training. This level of supervision is necessary for optimal student development, health, safety, and education.

▶ COMMENTARY

Examples of school health services that require such supervision include nursing, occupational therapy, physical therapy, oral health, and mental health. Selection of supervisors should be on merit, competency and expertise, not merely seniority. This applies to supervision of health, rehabilitation, dental, and mental health service providers working in schools, both licensed and unlicensed, as well as to both school-employed and contracted personnel. The ratio of school health professionals to supervisors must be adequate to allow competent supervision and assessment of delivered services. The clinical supervisor need not be located on site.

It may be appropriate for principals and other school administrators to select, supervise, and evaluate personnel who perform clinical functions. But supervision and evaluation of these professionals' clinical activities require someone qualified to properly assess clinical skills and services delivered.

▶ RELATED GUIDELINES

0-14, 0-15, 0-16, 6-06, 6-17

▶ RELATED LINKS

http://www.aota.org
http://www.apta.org
http://www.schoolcounselor.org
http://www.asha.org
http://www.nasn.org
http://www.nasponline.org
http://www.sswaa.org

4-03—STUDENT ACCESS TO A CERTIFIED SCHOOL NURSE[5,8-10]

In order to meet students' physical and emotional needs, provide daily access to an on-site school nurse. School nurses should be registered nurses who have specialization in school nursing.

▶ RATIONALE

For many students, achievement, attendance, and graduation are dependent on access to health- and safety-related services at school. Certified school nurses are best equipped to communicate with physicians, dentists, and other health professionals, understand student health and safety needs, and educate individual students and their families on health and safety matters.

▶ COMMENTARY

A ratio of 1 nurse to every 750 students is a goal written in *Healthy People 2010*[8] (Appendix A; http://www.healthypeople.gov) from the US Department of Health and Human Services. The National Association of School Nurses (NASN; http://www.nasn.org) recommends one school nurse to no more than 225 students when students with special health needs are mainstreamed with other students. Assisting families with access to health care, case management (Guideline 4-09), presence at individualized education program (IEP) meetings, education of other students and staff, medical procedures, and home visits are examples of tasks that take extraordinary amounts of time. The NASN recommends one school nurse to no more than 125 students for severely chronically ill or developmentally disabled student populations. Medically fragile students require a ratio based on individual needs. Schools with many students having special health needs will require more nursing time, clerical help, or other staff support. Suboptimal ratios of other health professionals (school counselors, for example) and assignment of non-nursing tasks to nurses can increase the number of nurses required to meet student needs.

Certification for school nurses is state-specific. National certification is an option that is available through the National Board for Certification of School Nurses or the American Association of Nurse Certification. Training for a school nurse goes beyond material covered in baccalaureate preparation. School nurse training prepares nurses for educational functions that are needed to address health, safety, and psychosocial issues specific to children in the school setting. Critical knowledge gained includes the relationship between health and academic performance, normal child and adolescent growth and development, established standards of clinical practice, legal issues related to children with special health care needs in school, ethical issues, and skills to work within an educational setting and to communicate with parents, family, and primary care providers as a representative of the school.

▶ RELATED GUIDELINES

0-06, 0-14, 0-15, 0-16

▶ RELATED LINKS

http://www.healthypeople.gov
http://www.nasn.org

4-04–THE SCHOOL PHYSICIAN[11-15]

Hire, or contract with, a school physician who has training and/or experience in child, adolescent and/or school health, to work with school nurses and others on the health and safety team. The physician's function should be specified in a written agreement and may include support of school staff with health and safety roles, interaction with community health professionals, guidance of district policy, and/or specific clinical responsibilities.

▶ RATIONALE

A physician with interest and experience in school health and safety on the school's health and safety team can assist districts and schools to interact more efficiently with students' physicians and others on complex health and safety problems and help design ongoing communication systems between the school health office and primary care providers. Physicians need to acquire experience that is pertinent to schools in order to perform these tasks well and maintain quality of service delivery, particularly for schools that provide comprehensive clinical and support services.

▶ COMMENTARY

Physicians can play many roles within a school district or school. Depending on the school district, the school physician may play a role in any or all of the components of a coordinated school health and safety program. In addition, the school physician may act as a liaison to community providers and participate on a school health and safety advisory council (Guideline 0-05). School physicians should be board certified in pediatrics or family medicine or have subspecialty training in adolescent medicine. In a rural area where there is no physician with specialty certification in a medical field that includes child-specific training, a county public health physician is able to provide some school physician functions.

Depending on resources and need, physicians can be assigned to a school district for as little as several hours per year to as much as full-time. To locate a physician that is willing and qualified to work for or consult to a school or district, contact one or more professional physician associations such as the American Academy of Family Physicians (http://www.aafp.org) and the American Academy of Pediatrics (http://www.aap.org) or multidisciplinary associations such as the Society for Adolescent Medicine (http://www.adolescenthealth.org) and the American School Health Association (http://www.ashaweb.org). These national associations have many local affiliates that may be very helpful. Some professional associations also provide school physicians with continuing education on school health and safety issues.

▶ RELATED GUIDELINES

0-05, 0-06, 0-14

▶ RELATED LINKS

http://www.aafp.org
http://www.adolescenthealth.org
http://www.aap.org
http://www.ashaweb.org

4-05—DELEGATION OF ROUTINE CLINICAL SERVICES[16]

Nurses, other school health professionals (eg, occupational, physical, and speech and language therapists), paraprofessionals, and unlicensed assistive personnel should provide only those assessments and procedures (including medical observations, dental services, and administration of medications) that are appropriate to their level of training, competency, and licensure.

▶ *RATIONALE*

To protect student safety as well as school district and school staff liability, health-related services should never be provided by someone not fully qualified or licensed.

▶ *COMMENTARY*

Many routine medical procedures (eg, blood sugar testing, gastric tube feeding) are commonly performed by parents and others who are not trained as health professionals outside of school and may be safely performed in school by individuals who have been specifically trained and supervised to do so. Persons delegated to providing clinical services at school should demonstrate competencies and be reviewed for continued proficiency on a regular basis.

Delegation of health-related care may depend on states' professional practice acts (eg, Nurse Practice Act) or with the state professional boards. A licensed occupational therapist, physical therapist, or speech and language therapist may delegate certain duties to aides and other unlicensed personnel under conditions defined by most states' professional licensing boards and/or practice acts relevant to these professions. In certain states, school districts are exempt from many stipulations contained in their Nurse Practice Acts. In special circumstances, such as delivery of some emergency procedures (Guideline 4-07) or in very rural communities where nurses are unavailable, school staff without health expertise may be allowed to perform some procedures that would otherwise be done only by a nurse. Even in these cases, training and supervision of designated personnel for clinical procedures must be provided by a registered nurse or physician.

▶ *RELATED GUIDELINES*

0-14, 0-15, 6-06

▶ *RELATED LINKS*

http://www.aota.org
http://www.apta.org
http://www.asha.org
http://www.nasn.org
http://www.ed.gov

◀ Health and Mental Health Services ▶

SCHOOL'S CAPACITY TO PROVIDE HEALTH, MENTAL HEALTH SERVICES

4-06–MENTAL HEALTH PROBLEMS: CAPACITY TO IDENTIFY, REFER, MANAGE[17-28]

Have the capacity to identify students with or at risk of mental health problems, to refer them for assessment and interventions appropriate to their needs, and to monitor and manage their behavioral, mental health, and emotional needs at school.

▶ *RATIONALE*

Early identification of students with, or at risk of, transient or ongoing mental disorders, followed by early intervention can mitigate the severity and duration of these problems and reduce personal, social, educational, and financial costs to the student and family and the educational and health systems. Up to three quarters of US children receiving professional care for a mental health problem obtained services through a school-based program.

▶ *COMMENTARY*

Schools must be able to assess students for immediate risks they might face, have the capacity to stabilize immediate behavioral, mental health, and emotional situations, and protect all those involved in crisis situations. Identify school- and community-based services for students facing immediate risks as well as for those requiring intervention in the long-term. Students with behavioral, emotional, and other mental health needs that interfere with functioning may require a referral to special education or a modified school program designed to accommodate their needs.

Most schools sustain specialized programs and adequate expertise and staffing to meet students' needs by maintaining a staff of school-based counselors, psychologists, social workers, nurses, nurse-practitioners, and/or other professionals trained to deal directly with emotional, behavioral, and mental health issues and to assist educators and administrators with students. Many schools establish a crisis response team, a suicide prevention team, and individual and/or group counseling services to assist these students.

Being sensitive to beliefs and practices relevant to mental health and child development includes keeping families involved and informed of the assessment process, of referrals, and of all services provided to their children. Schools sometimes need to refer students and families to primary health care providers, to mental health professionals with experience in managing children and adolescents (including but not limited to those who can assess for the need to prescribe psychotropic medications), to substance abuse and alcohol treatment centers, and to social support agencies. Whenever referrals to community-based agencies or professionals are warranted, ensure that families and students are effectively connected to these resources and follow up to determine that services provided were appropriate and effective. Coordinate and integrate community-based interventions with school health, mental health, and educational services.

Some schools provide extensive mental health services by hiring school-based mental health professionals or arranging for community-based mental health professionals to provide services at school. Campus-based arrangements can improve families' access to professional services and make coordination of mental health services with students' educational programs more comprehensive, reliable, and continual.

Reassess students' needs at intervals to clarify changes in their nature and scope. Evaluate school assessment procedures and interventions for their validity, reliability, and effectiveness.

RELATED GUIDELINES

0-08, 0-12, 7-03, 7-04, 8-03, 8-05

RELATED LINKS

http://brightfutures.aap.org/web
http://smhp.psych.ucla.edu
http://csmha.umaryland.edu

4-07—STAFF TRAINED FOR EMERGENCIES[29-34]

Ensure that at least one adult with current training in basic first aid and lifesaving techniques is available to students and staff on site and at all off-site school-sponsored activities. Skills include cervical spine protection, Heimlich maneuver, cardiopulmonary resuscitation (CPR), use of an automated external defibrillator (AED), and specialized emergency procedures for those who need them.

▶ RATIONALE

Schools are responsible for handling medical emergencies for all students, including students with special needs who may be prone to certain emergencies and/or require specific emergency equipment. A written plan and trained personnel are essential to the successful handling of medical and dental emergencies.

▶ COMMENTARY

The required number of staff trained to handle medical emergencies should be gauged by the number necessary to meet the anticipated needs of all students attending school. Having only one staff member trained for emergency response will be inadequate in mid-sized or large schools and on many field trips because students are spread around a large geographic campus and programs take subpopulations of students off campus. Calculations of staffing for emergency situations should include estimated days when trained staff will be absent.

Provide training to handle first aid for minor trauma and for serious problems such as bleeding, choking, musculoskeletal injuries, dental emergencies, and allergic reactions. Knowledge of emergency assistance numbers and their appropriate use is necessary (eg, poison control at 800/222-1222, emergency assistance at 911). The Ohio Chapter of the American Academy of Pediatrics[29] (http://www.schoolhealth.org) and Emergency Medical Services for Children (EMS-C) (http://www.ems-c.org) jointly developed emergency guidelines for schools. Many state departments of health or education have written guidelines on common emergency procedures. During the school day, a trained person should be designated to provide emergency assistance. Optimally, the school nurse fills this role. In many schools, staff who are not health professionals provide designated emergency assistance.

In some cases, a student's need demands that a nurse be available at the school site at all times. In rare cases, a nurse dedicated to one student is required for close observation and nursing procedures (eg, to detect and treat a blocked airway for a child with a tracheostomy). When it is determined that a nurse is not required to provide a specialized emergency procedure (eg, glucagon injections for students with diabetes and low blood sugar), then the school administrator should specify the person(s) designated to the task. Also, school policy should indicate for such procedures how and when a trained nurse will provide education and indirect supervision (Guideline 4-05). All emergency procedures require training (eg, use of predrawn epinephrine syringes and allergy kits for many students with insect or food allergies), and designated staff must know how to recognize symptoms and have written steps to follow. A prescribing physician must sign emergency plans (Guideline 4-20). Organizations such as the American Diabetes Association (http://www.diabetes.org) and the Asthma and Allergy Foundation of America (http://www.aafa.org) have developed sample emergency protocols specifically for use by schools.

RELATED GUIDELINES

0-07, 6-06, 6-15, 6-17, 6-22, 7-04, 7-05

RELATED LINKS

http://www.aaaai.org

http://www.schoolhealth.org

http://www.ada.org

http://www.diabetes.org

http://www.americanheart.org

http://www.redcross.org

http://www.aafa.org

http://www.ems-c.org

http://www.nasn.org

http://www.foodsafeschools.org

4-08—CHILD ABUSE REPORTING SYSTEM[35–46]

Establish and maintain a system to recognize and report suspected child abuse and neglect. Define schools' response to allegations of school employees' abuse or harassment of students.

▶ RATIONALE

School personnel must fully understand all aspects of defining, identifying, and reporting suspected child abuse, neglect, and family violence in order to follow mandatory reporting statutes. Children with special needs, such as those who are physically or mentally disabled, are often more susceptible to neglect and abuse and may not have the capacity to express occurrence of abuse or neglect to an adult.

▶ COMMENTARY

The terms "abuse" and "neglect" describe: deprivation of necessities so that a child's welfare is harmed or threatened or there is physical injury or maltreatment, including sexual and emotional maltreatment. Districts and schools need to establish written school protocols, reporting forms, and memoranda of understanding with local child protective services, health care facilities, and child advocacy centers. Some states do not require mandatory reporting of domestic violence despite significant overlap of child maltreatment and domestic violence. If domestic violence is not reportable by law, attempt to handle domestic violence cases through an agreement with local child protective services and partnerships with domestic violence programs and follow-up treatment programs for children and families.

All school personnel should receive training on recognizing suspected abuse and neglect, reporting suspicions, and recognizing cultural issues that pertain to suspected abuse. Cultural factors, including the conditions that bring immigrants to this country and acculturation gaps within families, have strong influences on the prevalence and nature of abuse. Certain populations of youth, such as those who are physically and mentally disabled, are at increased risk of various forms of abuse and neglect. Chapter references provide information on features of abuse in these populations.

District protocols should be developed by a panel that includes school administrative, health, and educational personnel, law enforcement, social services, and family representatives. The community's diversity should be represented so that differences in opinion about physical discipline, conventional health care, and faith/personal beliefs are considered. The protocol must include clear steps to be taken when a school employee is accused of abusing or harassing a student and it should include criteria of when to bring in and consult with local law enforcement officials. Most states have published reporting requirements (http://www.acf.dhhs.gov/programs/cb/publications/rpt_abu.htm) and some states, such as Colorado, have printed guides for school personnel.[35] Schools or districts might have one person complete all reports of suspected abuse or neglect. Accumulating reports in one site can be helpful for health and safety program evaluation. If a school has its own strong school-based child protection team and it is permitted by law, this team can conduct preliminary investigations on the validity of suspected abuse and decide on the necessity of reporting the case to child protective services. A school-based team requires the participation of a classroom teacher, a school administrator, school health personnel, and expert consultants from the medical, mental health, rehabilitation, and child protection communities.

▶ *RELATED GUIDELINES*

0-02, 0-05, 0-07, 0-13, 0-17, 7-04, 7-05, 7-08

▶ *RELATED LINKS*

http://www.acf.dhhs.gov/programs/cb/publications/rpt_abu.htm
http://www.safechild.org

4-09—HEALTH-RELATED CASE MANAGEMENT[10,47–52]

Provide case management for families of students who have complex health or safety needs, who have difficulty accessing required services, or whose needs preclude optimal participation or achievement at school.

▶ RATIONALE

Case management can enhance students' ability to learn by facilitating timely access to resources (eg, health, mental health, social, financial) and enhancing communication and coordination among school staff and community-based health professionals, families, social services providers, and others providing resources to the family and student.

▶ COMMENTARY

Case management is a collaborative process by which students' special health-related needs are assessed, planned, implemented, coordinated, monitored, and evaluated. It is also referred to as "care coordination" and "care management." It is a collaborative process whereby a case manager, the person primarily assisting the family, helps families to explore options and services that they and their children require. Referrals for case management may come from the student assistance team (Guideline 4-01). When a student has a community-based case manager, the school's role would be to communicate with that case manager.

Case management should not be limited to students with disabilities or special health needs. Those who are homeless, hungry, overwhelmed by family problems, and/or otherwise distracted from learning also require case management. School-based case managers can help families by advocating for family and student services, informing and educating families about such services, coordinating access to student and family services, taking on the role of liaison to community providers and organizations, and/or interpreting health-related information to school staff and family. School case management often differs from one community to another, as the location of the community (eg, urban versus rural) and characteristics of the population (eg, recent immigrants, families in military service careers) influence the nature of services students and families require.

Case management encompasses many of the key functions of the school nurse. Counselors, social workers, and other health professionals in the school setting also often perform case management functions. The category of the school professional assigned to take on a case management role will often depend on the nature of a student's and family's needs and on school staffing.

▶ RELATED GUIDELINES

1-02, 1-04, 7-02, 7-03

▶ RELATED LINKS

http://www.cmsa.org
http://smhp.psych.ucla.edu
http://csmha.umaryland.edu
http://www.ed.gov/offices/OSERS/Policy/IDEA
http://mchb.hrsa.gov
http://www.nasn.org
http://www.ed.gov

4-10—HEALTH RECORDS MANAGEMENT SYSTEM[53-57]

Utilize a comprehensive records management system, either electronic or paper-based, for student health and safety information.

▶ RATIONALE

A records management system that is efficient, reflects professional practice standards, and conforms to legal principles and state and federal laws and regulations is extremely useful to those who need the information, can save valuable staff time, and can assist schools with the evaluation of their health and safety programs.

▶ COMMENTARY

A comprehensive health records management system is a district's method of recording and filing students' health and immunization histories, problem lists, progress notes, special needs, health-related encounters with students and families, individualized health services plans, medication lists, records of medication administration, nonmedication management, third-party health information, demographic information (including emergency contact numbers), and information on health insurance and health care providers.

Health and mental health professionals, such as social workers, special education directors, nurses, psychologists, counselors, and occupational therapists as well as paraprofessionals require access to components of this information in order to provide effective and safe services. Software packages for managing student health information are available commercially and are helpful for school staff members who need to share information, protect information (using devices such as passwords), and compile health data. Using an electronic information management system requires that all relevant school staff have access to computers.

Sharing health information within and outside of the school district must follow regulations that deal with privacy and confidentiality (Guideline 0-03, Guideline 4-25).

▶ RELATED GUIDELINES

0-03, 0-13, 1-02, 6-18

▶ RELATED LINKS

http://www.ed.gov/offices/OSERS/Policy/IDEA
http://www.cms.hhs.gov/hipaa
http://www.nasn.org

4-11—CRISIS RESPONSE TEAM AND PLANS[9,29,31,58–67]

Establish a crisis response protocol to manage a crisis and its aftermath, including recovery.

▶ RATIONALE

Schools need to be prepared to address crises that have physical, emotional, social, and spiritual effects on all members of the school community. Only by preparing in advance for potential crises are schools able to come to the immediate aid of affected and vulnerable students, staff, and community members.

▶ COMMENTARY

Possible crises include violent events, suicide, attempted suicide, serious injuries, arrest of staff for criminal conduct, natural disasters, fire, bomb threats, terrorism, hostage-taking, kidnapping, and any threatening event occurring during school activities and/or involving members of the school community.

Preparation for schools to respond to crises include partnerships with other community agencies, as appropriate (eg, health and mental health service agencies, public health, public utilities, faith-based institutions, social service agencies, emergency medical services, fire department, police and other law enforcement agencies). Involve these agencies as well as families in developing clear written protocols for potential disasters. School personnel should be knowledgeable about these protocols and the protocols should be accessible to them. Protocols should include details of implementing an evacuation and a "lockdown" and the safest areas to evacuate building occupants for various types of disasters. Clearly identify personnel responsible for decision making and for coordinating the response to a crisis. Adequate training of school personnel and practice and testing of the responses are essential. A school crisis team should be formed to develop appropriate responses to crises and their aftermath; this team's interventions should address incidents that threaten the sense of security at a school or that are disruptive to teaching and learning.

As an example, after a suicide, school personnel and community resources must address the need for grieving and coping with feelings of loss that many in the general school population will experience. Schools also can anticipate the need to identify students at risk of "copy-cat" behavior and the need for partnerships that can assist certain students who require further evaluation and counseling services.

The US Departments of Justice and Education[58] have jointly developed guidelines for schools that help make schools safe and responsive. The Department of Education's *A Guide for Schools and Communities*,[59] as well as other recommended resources (see Internet Resources), guide development of prevention and response plans for crises. An Internet-accessible toolkit that guides schools on preventive measures, interventions, and staff training has been developed by the National Education Association (NEA).[60] Detailed instructions are provided for telephone trees (for staff notification), preparation of staff lists identifying staff trained in cardiopulmonary resuscitation and first aid, identification of makeshift reunion areas, prepared badges or orange jackets that enable students to identify key personnel, checklists for schools' preparedness, planning for orderly release of students, and dealing with the media. This NEA resource also addresses potentially disturbing physical reminders that might remain at school when students return after a crisis, curricula for first day back to school, and memorials. Evacuation plans and emergency supplies are covered in Guidelines 6-22 and 6-23.

RELATED GUIDELINES

0-07, 6-22, 6-23, 7-02, 7-04, 7-05

RELATED LINKS

http://www.aaets.org
http://www.aap.org
http://www.cdc.gov
http://www.ems-c.org
http://www.FEMA.gov
http://www.nasponline.org
http://www.ed.gov

4-12—ORAL HEALTH SERVICES[68-75]

Base the range of school-based oral health care services on the student population's needs. Services may include oral health screening, fluoride rinse programs, fluoride varnishes, dental sealants, access to dentists and/or dental hygienists, and emergency dental care.

▶ *RATIONALE*

Dental disease is the largest unmet health need among school-aged children. More than 51 million school hours are lost each year to dental-related illness. Access to oral health care through schools can minimize suffering in school and decrease absenteeism from untreated dental disease.

▶ *COMMENTARY*

In communities without fluoridated water supplies, schools are more likely to find a great need among their student populations for preventive and restorative oral health services. Children living in poverty suffer twice as much dental decay as their more affluent peers and the decay is less likely to be treated. School nurses and parents are often the first to recognize that students' oral health needs are unmet. Objective measures of the population's needs may be sought from state and local dental directors in departments of public health and from the National Maternal and Child Oral Health Resource Center (http://www.mchoralhealth.org). Once the need is understood, these public health experts, local dentists, dental hygienists, and other oral health professionals and agencies should be recruited by schools to help develop realistic goals, find funding sources, identify priority populations within the student body, choose the most cost-effective interventions and define measurable outcomes.

To be effective, interventions should be tailored to children's stages of dental development. *Bright Futures in Oral Health*[68] provides information on dental development, dental caries, periodontal disease, malocclusion, the effects of tobacco-use on oral health, oral injuries, and expected outcomes of various prevention and service programs.

To improve student oral health, schools may provide preventive interventions (eg, fluoride rinse programs, fluoride varnish application, dental sealants, oral health screening) and other services that are targeted to students differently, depending on whether they are in elementary, middle, or high school age groups. Staffing these services may be provided by school health staff, visiting dental professionals (eg, dentists, dental hygienists), or school-based health center professionals.

All students must receive school-based oral health education that is designed to prevent dental disease and injury. Services at school should complement what is accessible in the community. Grade-wide oral health screening programs (eg, all third-graders) and dental interventions at select schools have been found to successfully reduce the incidence of dental cavities, decrease pain, and minimize costs of treatment and missed classroom time. Some schools screen students without providing treatment but set up referral arrangements with local dental clinics. Models of school-based and school-linked programs also exist. Mobile dental clinics that visit schools have been shown to be one successful model. Another is having a dental clinic set up within a school-based health center.

▶ *RELATED GUIDELINES*

0-08, 1-03, 2-06, 3-10, 5-06

▶ *RELATED LINKS*

http://www.aapd.org
http://www.ada.org
http://brightfutures.aap.org/web
http://www.mchoralhealth.org

◀ Health and Mental Health Services ▶

STUDENT ASSESSMENTS AND SCREENS

4-13–MAINTAINING CURRENT STUDENT HEALTH INFORMATION[25,56,76,77]

Collect and assess student health information that pertains to students' functioning and safety in school prior to school entry, every 1 to 2 years thereafter, and whenever a significant change in health status has occurred. Share information with staff members whose access to the health information is necessary for maintaining student health and safety. Obtain parents' informed, written consent to share information.

▶ *RATIONALE*

An up-to-date health assessment is necessary to identify students' unique health and safety needs and to anticipate and meet the need for special or emergency services. Untreated health, mental health, and oral health problems are common and many impact students' attendance, attention to school work, or safe participation in school activities.

▶ *COMMENTARY*

Schools should maintain results of students' most recent health evaluation. As recommended by the American Academy of Pediatrics,[76] an assessment for school should include: health, family and social history that relates to functioning and safety in school, growth and development, allergies, medications, special needs, disabilities, vision and hearing screens, past problems, immunization status, and physical findings. Request results of dental and other oral health assessments, mental health information, recent injuries, and any other information necessary to optimally and safely accommodate a student in school and to optimize a student's safety in the event of an emergency. Relevant and appropriate information should be shared with school health services personnel, physical educators, coaches, recess monitors, food service personnel, or others, provided that the use of the information by the recipient is relevant to a student's safe functioning.

Injuries, new health problems, or new symptoms necessitate that schools collect updated health information, regardless of the date of the last assessment. Some schools require that preseason sport physical examinations be performed during a specific month of the year, but there is no evidence that this has any benefit over assessments done anytime during the year prior to initiating the sports activity. Recognize that regular dental health assessments may occur more frequently (ie, every 6 months) than general physical examinations (ie, every 1 to 2 years).

Regular health assessments for students may place a tremendous burden on families without health insurance or access to a provider. School personnel should be trained and assigned to assist families with identifying primary health care resources. The district can develop cooperative agreements with community health agencies to ensure student access to health assessments.

Some schools conduct comprehensive health assessments on students through school-based providers. Schools that provide complete histories and physical examinations on-site must not exclude the genital examination (ie, inspection and any gentle manipulation that allows for inspection of external genital organs), as this is part of a full assessment. This should be explained to parents and students when obtaining their permission for the physical examination. It is not acceptable to perform any health-related screen of students at school unless the school also has the capacity to arrange further assessment, follow-up visits, and management when these are required.

▶ *RELATED GUIDELINES*

0-03, 1-02, 3-07, 6-18

▶ *RELATED LINKS*

http://brightfutures.aap.org/web
http://www.ed.gov/offices/OM/fpco/ferpa

4-14–ASSESSMENT OF IMMUNIZATION STATUS[78-83]

Assess and document immunization status when a student enters school, transfers to
another school, or advances to a next level of schooling (eg, elementary to middle or middle
to high school).

▶ *RATIONALE*

It is in the best interest of individual students, the entire student body, and the population as a
whole to have all students up-to-date with recommended immunizations. Record keeping can
prevent unnecessary exclusion from school on the basis of state law and can ensure that appropriate and selective exclusion from school is recommended for students when there is an outbreak of a vaccine-preventable disease.

▶ *COMMENTARY*

Each state has immunization requirements for enrollment in school. All require immunization
against tetanus, diphtheria, pertussis, polio, rubella, and measles. Many also require immunization
against mumps, varicella, and hepatitis B. School health personnel should strongly encourage
important immunizations that are not required by state law, including influenza vaccine for those
at highest health risk from this viral infection. Allow an exception if a student has a specific medical condition that would make an immunization dangerous. Most states exempt students from
immunizations if they are from families with strong faith-based convictions that oppose immunization. State laws require that all other children who are not in compliance within a certain period
of time after enrollment be denied access to school.

Each school should have a mechanism to obtain documentation of immunizations from families,
to store immunization records, to notify families of children not in compliance, and to recommend
how students can obtain immunizations. Schools should consider participating in regional immunization databases to provide and receive the most up-to-date records. Students who have no
access to required immunizations may need the assistance of school staff to help them arrange
for immunizations.

▶ *RELATED GUIDELINES*

8-02

▶ *RELATED LINKS*

http://www.asaweb.org
http://www.nasn.org

4-15–IDENTIFICATION OF HEALTH/SAFETY NEEDS PRIOR TO SCHOOL ENTRY[52,84–86]

Develop a system to identify, prior to school entry, those students who require assistance with a special health or safety need (eg, new students, those returning from an extended absence, those experiencing a recent health or mental health problem, and those with one or more chronic illnesses). Reassess these students' needs at least annually and modify individualized health and safety care plans accordingly.

▶ *RATIONALE*

Early, regular, and skilled assessments of students' needs and of schools' resources to meet those needs will allow schools to provide an appropriate and safe educational program for all students with minimal or no disruption to students' education.

▶ *COMMENTARY*

A logical time to collect this information is when children register for school. Assessments for possible accommodations or interventions include the following examples of special need: medical, dental, orthopedic, nutritional, developmental, speech or language, auditory, visual, transportation-related, mental health, and emotional. School nurses, school psychologists, specially trained aides, or other school health professionals may perform initial screening in these areas. After initial screening, further exploration and clarification of these needs must be performed by professional staff who are trained and skilled for the areas of identified needs (for example, a nurse, physical therapist, nutritionist, or mental health professional). Schools require a system in place to communicate directly with community agencies, community-based professionals (eg, students' physicians, dentist, mental health therapist, other therapists), and students' families in order to complete these assessments. Assess school resources in relation to student needs. Outline all school interventions and accommodations to be made (Guideline 4-20).

Schools are financially and otherwise responsible for space, equipment, and personnel that are required to meet students' needs if these needs interfere with learning, school attendance, or access to school programs (Individuals with Disabilities Education Act and, for schools receiving federal funding, Section 504 of the Rehabilitation Act). If identified problems do not interfere with learning, school attendance, or participation, but school personnel find that these needs are inadequately addressed outside of school, schools may assist students and their families to access resources in the community.

RELATED GUIDELINES

0-01, 0-03, 1-02, 5-05, 6-06, 6-18

RELATED LINKS

http://www.cms.hhs.gov/hipaa
http://www.ed.gov/offices/OSERS/Policy/IDEA
http://www.ed.gov

4-16–STUDENTS WITH FREQUENT OR EXTENDED ABSENCES[76]

Require a comprehensive health evaluation for students with frequent or extended absences from school.

▷ RATIONALE

Formal health assessments of students with frequent or extended absences often uncover previously undiagnosed chronic conditions, recurrent health concerns that can be prevented or managed, and family issues that interfere with attendance (for example, difficulty accessing health care or a family's incomplete understanding of a health condition).

▷ COMMENTARY

There are many valid health-related causes for keeping students at home, but when these problems have been recurrent and are anticipated to continue, schools have an obligation to make accommodations that will allow safe school attendance for these students (eg, a school could provide short periods of rest and administer prescribed pain relievers for a student with recurrent headaches). Parents, acting in good faith, may keep their child at home for health-related reasons that in fact do not really warrant being home-bound (eg, mild symptoms of the common cold).

Request a note or other form of direct communication from the health care provider responsible for managing the problem thought to be causing the student's absence from school. Notify parents that school staff members are concerned about their child's frequent or extended absence from school. A form letter to parents can be used to explain district policy and to request medical verification of illness or injury. Offer to assist parents with finding a health evaluation if the student has no access to health care. Provide parents and the student's health care providers with details of potential health-related symptoms, signs, or patterns that are noticed by school staff.

State or local regulations may help determine time periods that students can be absent without physician verification. Where this is not regulated, school staff should consult with local health care providers to establish a magnitude of absenteeism that should raise concern and subsequent investigation (eg, "more than 3 consecutive days" or "more than 10 days a quarter, consecutive or not").

▷ RELATED GUIDELINES

0-03, 1-02, 1-03, 1-04, 7-02

▷ RELATED LINKS

http://www.cmsa.org
http://www.nasn.org

4-17—BEHAVIORS WITH UNDERLYING HEALTH CAUSES[39]

Assess students who are frequent users of health services, who are suspended or expelled, or who demonstrate other concerning behaviors. Use a school-based multidisciplinary assessment team to assess for potential learning, emotional, and physical health problems that often underlie such behaviors.

▶ RATIONALE

Exploring all aspects of students' physical, emotional, environmental, and psychosocial states will often uncover issues contributing to repeated school health office visits or concerning behaviors. Only by dealing with underlying health causes can school-related problems be successfully addressed so that students can focus on learning.

▶ COMMENTARY

Students who are frequent visitors to school health offices are often seeking to avoid a difficult situation or signaling that they need help. These frequent visitors should not be labeled or deterred from visiting, regardless of their grade level. Rather, the health team should explore possible reasons for these visits.

Most students who carry a weapon, threaten violence, engage in violent behavior, are aggressive towards others, or use illicit substances have a learning, attention, emotional, mental, or physical health problem or family circumstances underlying their behavior. Students who are unusually quiet, have difficulty making friends, or have few positive social interactions may also have such underlying problems.

Through discussion about students' behaviors and other known information, a school-based multi-disciplinary student assessment team (Guideline 4-01), which includes not only school health professionals but also teachers, school administrators, and students' parents, can help to determine likely underlying causes of the behaviors. This team should also establish the next best steps to take. This may be a school-based intervention, a community- or home-based intervention, and/or referral for further school-based or community-based professional assessment.

▶ RELATED GUIDELINES

0-08, 1-02, 7-02, 7-03

▶ RELATED LINKS

http://smhp.psych.ucla.edu
http://csmha.umaryland.edu

4-18–SCHOOL HEALTH SCREENING PROGRAMS[76,77,87–96]

Require health screenings on the basis of state and local mandates, public health principles, and the needs of the student population.

▶ *RATIONALE*

School health screenings are often the best way to detect problems that interfere with students' education, such as poor vision or hearing.

▶ *COMMENTARY*

Most schools are mandated to screen for hearing and vision. Some are required to screen for scoliosis, and many choose to screen for oral health problems. For all school screening programs, develop specific procedures for notifying and informing families and students about normal and abnormal results. Screenings should be carried out by trained individuals who follow clearly written protocols. Ensure that appropriate referrals are made to students' health care providers when needed.

The value of schools' screening programs should be regularly assessed. Determine the extent to which families follow through with school referrals. Ascertain the outcome of community-based assessments that occur as a result of school referrals of students with positive screens. If results of such assessments show that a screening program is inadequate, work with public health officials and community health practitioners to update screening techniques, redesign screening procedures, and/or reexamine current mandates. Involve families in the process of adopting screening programs and designing the screening process.

It is often suggested that schools screen for numerous health-related problems in addition to mandated screens. In recent years this list includes mental health problems, substance abuse, hypertension, obesity, type 2 diabetes, high cholesterol, asthma, tuberculosis, and head lice. Before implementing a school screening program, look for evidence that mass screening and school-based screening are effective and do not cause inadvertent harm. Evidence to support or oppose screening for many of the aforementioned health problems is still being developed. Work with public health authorities to evaluate the following before adopting a new screening program: difficulties incurred by not detecting the problem in school-aged children through a screening process; the effectiveness of therapy available; the relative efficiency of the screening procedure; the specificity, sensitivity, and positive predictive value of the screening tool; the relative efficiency of utilizing schools as the screening site; the availability of remediation and follow-up for all students with positive screening results; and the cost of the screening program.

▶ *RELATED GUIDELINES*

0-03, 0-10, 0-13, 1-01, 1-03, 3-07

▶ *RELATED LINKS*

http://smhp.psych.ucla.edu
http://csmha.umaryland.edu

◀ **Health and Mental Health Services** ▶

PROTOCOLS, PROCEDURES, AND QUALITY

4-19—ADMINISTERING MEDICATIONS IN SCHOOL[5-7,9,12,31,52,56,57,97,98]

Adopt medication administering policies that address prescription and nonprescription medications and outline responsibilities of student, family, prescribing clinician, and school staff.

▶ *RATIONALE*

Clear policies on medication administration are necessary to avoid misunderstandings, oversights, and medication errors so that students remain safe.

▶ *COMMENTARY*

Where states do not regulate school medication practices, school health professionals, consulting physicians, and the district's health and safety advisory council should contribute to these policies. Administering a long-term medication regimen in school requires a written statement from the student's parent and the prescribing clinician. Parents must be notified that it is their responsibility to provide labeled containers, supply medical devices (eg, insulin pumps, spacers for inhaled asthma medications), and keep medications current. Include the name of the medication, the dose, approximate time it is to be taken, and the diagnosis or reason the medication is needed. Educate school staff members about methods of administration (eg, by mouth or inhaled) and about factors that should alert them to not give the medication. Specify how medication will be delivered when the student is at out-of-school activities. Use protocols to document all emergency and routine therapies given (Guideline 4-07, Guideline 4-25). Report all errors in medication administration to at least one common supervisor so that patterns of error may be detected. Corrections taken for medication errors must be carefully considered so that they do not discourage staff from self-reporting errors.

If permitted, allow students to carry medications and self-medicate at school if parent, prescribing clinician, and school staff agree that the student is responsible to remember doses and to not over-use or share with others. Some schools obtain written parental notification acknowledging that the school bears no responsibility for ensuring the medication is taken. Distinguish between appropriate situations for self-medication (eg, rescue medications for asthma; insulin for diabetes) from situations where medications should be administered by school staff (eg, stimulants for attention-deficit disorders; episodic administration of antibiotics).

Herbal and over-the-counter medications taken on a regular basis should require a physician's note that, in essence, "prescribes" these nonprescription substances. In some states a written parental request for school staff to administer an over-the-counter medication for a brief period (eg, an antihistamine for hay fever for a period of 1 or 2 days) is insufficient unless the request is accompanied by a prescription. Where allowed by law, these requests need not be honored if a school nurse feels uncomfortable with the dose, the duration of treatment, or the appropriateness of the medication to the health problem. Schools should always retain the right to require a prescription or physician's note.

Some schools keep over-the-counter medications on stock for school nurses to administer on an "as needed" basis (eg, ibuprofen for menstrual cramps). If schools opt for such a program, require written parental permission that allows nurses to have the discretion to administer these medications. Notify parents in writing whenever medications are given. Have a physician-approved protocol for each medication that is kept in stock and place a limit on the frequency a medication may be given without a physician's note or prescription.

RELATED GUIDELINES

0-05, 1-02, 6-06, 6-22

RELATED LINKS

http://www.schoolhealth.org
http://www.aap.org
http://www.diabetes.org
http://www.aafa.org
http://www.ed.gov/offices/OSERS/Policy/IDEA
http://www.state.ma.us/dph/fch/schoolhealth/index.htm
http://www.ed.gov

4-20–INDIVIDUALIZED HEALTH SERVICES PLANS[48,52,55,56,85,99–102]

Provide written, individualized health services plans for students with special health care needs. Plans must be developed with a multidisciplinary core team and comply with federal laws.

▶ *RATIONALE*

A comprehensive written health care or health services plan facilitates communication among families, school health team members, and the student's own health professionals in the community and helps ensure that students receive necessary services.

▶ *COMMENTARY*

Written plans for student health care in school may be part of or an addendum to an individualized education program (IEP), a separate individualized health services plan (IHSP), a section 504 plan, an individual family service plan (IFSP), individualized health and support plan, or another plan. These plans should address emergency care needs, safety concerns, frequency of provided services, health education needs, allergies, special food service or nutritional needs, medications, special transportation and equipment needs, parameters to be monitored (medical and behavioral), school personnel to implement plan, duration of special need, expected results of providing school-based services, and how the health problem may affect learning, peer interactions, and participation in school activities. Include all pertinent medical, dental, family contact, insurance, and emergency information. Address all student activities and environments (eg, after-school programs, field trips, extended school year), plans for transition (eg, transition to other schools, to adult medical and dental care), and plans for students to gain independence. Notify families of their legal rights as plans are developed. With parental permission, share copies of individualized health services plans with students' own health care providers and coordinate school care with care that is community-based. Professional coordination involves interaction among all those who work with the student at school and elsewhere (eg, social worker, psychologist, occupational therapist, speech therapist, physical therapist, dentist, nutritionist, physical education teacher, bus driver, food service personnel).

The multidisciplinary core team should include the parent, teacher, school nurse, and additional team members (depending on the nature of the student's need) and have physician or other health care provider input. Assign one school member the role of case coordinator. A school-based health professional should screen all requests for special school health-related services. In compliance with laws of privacy and confidentiality, elicit information from parents and professionals who manage students' special health needs so that members of the staff fully understand these needs. Information collection may include data derived by school staff from home visits and school assessments from previous years. Utilize all information to consider various placement and service-delivery options for the student. Students, parents, physicians, and other health care providers usually have the best understanding of a child's special health-related needs. School nurses and other school personnel usually are most aware of various school options available to meet those needs and have the most experience in individualizing plans for students so that they are both safe and minimally restrictive. If there are discrepancies of opinion on what constitutes a level of care that is both least restrictive and safe for a student, establish an open dialogue among school health staff, students' parents, and health care providers managing these needs in order to finalize the plan.

▶ *RELATED GUIDELINES*

0-03, 3-03, 5-05, 6-06, 6-13, 6-18, 8-07

▶ *RELATED LINKS*

http://www.aaaai.org
http://www.ed.gov/offices/OM/fpco/ferpa
http://www.cms.hhs.gov/hipaa
http://www.ed.gov/offices/OSERS/Policy/IDEA
http://www.nasn.org
http://www.nhlbi.nih.gov/about/naepp
http://www.padrefoundation.org

4-21—PROTOCOLS FOR SPECIAL MEDICAL PROCEDURES[84,101,103–105]

Adopt and maintain a set of up-to-date protocols for specialized medical procedures to include as part of students' individualized health services plans. Allow modifications on a student-by-student basis when there is school nurse endorsement and written consent of the parent and of the prescribing health care provider.

▶ RATIONALE

Approved protocols for medical procedures optimize safety by reducing the chances of missing important steps when delivering medical services.

▶ COMMENTARY

Examples of procedures and use of equipment that might require protocols include: blood sugar testing, glucagon injections for low blood sugars, delivery of aerosolized medications using a nebulizer or metered-dose inhaler, monitoring a student's asthma severity using a peak flow meter, epinephrine injections for severe allergic reactions, gastrostomy tube feeding, urinary tract catheterization, postural drainage, and tracheostomy suctioning.

Many state departments of health or education have procedure manuals for schools that provide protocols for this purpose. Some of these manuals also specify the level of staff training or credential required or recommended to perform each procedure. Because students vary in type of equipment used and have other unique characteristics in their medical care and diagnoses, school health staff, families, and prescribing physicians often need to work together to modify the original template of approved protocol instructions.

Schools should periodically review approved protocols to ensure that they are up-to-date and meet current standards of medical care.

▶ RELATED GUIDELINES

0-06, 0-07, 0-08, 0-14, 0-15, 6-06, 6-18

▶ RELATED LINKS

http://www.aaaai.org
http://www.diabetes.org
http://www.aafa.org
http://www.state.ma.us/dph/fch/schoolhealt/index.htm
http://www.nasn.org
http://www.nhlbi.nih.gov/about/naepp
http://www.padrefoundation.org

4-22–EXCLUSION FROM SCHOOL FOR ILLNESS OR INJURY[80,106,107]

Assess students and staff with communicable diseases, sudden illnesses, and serious injuries to determine the need to exclude them from school. Exclusion from school should apply to students and staff whose presence poses a significant risk to themselves or others.

▶ *RATIONALE*

Explicit guidelines on exclusion of staff and students help to ensure that those who can safely attend school are not kept home or excluded from certain school activities by overly vigilant parents or school staff. Explicit guidelines also make it easier for schools to protect students and staff when exclusion policies need to be enforced.

▶ *COMMENTARY*

Students and staff with a disease, illness, or injury may attend school if their attendance does not pose a significant risk to themselves or others. Exclusion from attending school is warranted when that person is either too ill to participate in school activities, the condition creates an unsafe or unhealthy environment for others at school, or when the illness or injury requires a level of care or observation that cannot be managed at school.

Examples of reasons that justify exclusion, at least until cleared by a health care provider, are: chicken pox, bloody diarrhea, fever, lethargy, sudden breathing difficulties, and any undiagnosed rash that is accompanied by fever.

Students and staff who are well enough to carry on with school functions should not be sent home for colds, bronchitis, or the rash of fifth disease, because inclusion in these circumstances has not been found to increase the chances others will become ill. Exclusion from selected activities is also sometimes appropriate (eg, a student recovering from pneumonia may be exempt from certain vigorous physical activities).

Many other contagious illnesses justify exclusion only under certain circumstances. For example, sores from herpes simplex (the cause of cold sores of the lip) and herpes zoster (the cause of shingles) are not transmitted if they can be covered with clothing or bandages. Strep throat is infectious, but not after 24 hours of antibiotic treatment. Head lice are not a danger, only a nuisance. An extended absence for a student whose head lice condition is not treated properly is not warranted. There is no evidence that having only nits (the term for eggs that head lice produce) on one's hair is a risk of the spread of head lice to others.

Written protocols can never be so well outlined and up-to-date that they will answer all questions regarding exclusion for every possible situation. There are too many diseases and an almost infinite number of special circumstances, such as emerging diseases like severe acute respiratory syndrome (SARS). School protocols can affirm, however, that staff will verify whether any state or local law requires exclusion and that decisions will be based on science—not on fear. Utilize authoritative sources (eg, American Academy of Pediatrics' *Red Book*,[80] local public health offices, the Web site of the Centers for Disease Control and Prevention [http://www.cdc.gov]) to assist in making determinations on exclusion.

▶ *RELATED GUIDELINES*

0-02, 1-02, 6-14

▶ *RELATED LINKS*

http://www.schoolhealth.org
http://www.cdc.gov

4-23–STUDENTS WITH SYMPTOMS OF POOR HEALTH[55,56,108,109]

Assess and refer students for a comprehensive evaluation who appear to have physical or mental health-related disorders such as sudden weight loss, eating disorders, obesity, fatigue, poor attention span, behavior change, frequent urination, toothache, and any recurring symptom (eg, cough, abdominal pain, headaches).

▶ *RATIONALE*

Early identification, assessment, and management of health problems and problems that affect a student's safety are necessary to limit more serious consequences and to prevent ill health from affecting the child's emotional well-being and ability to learn.

▶ *COMMENTARY*

School staff members, including teachers, administrators, nurses, and others on the school health team, are in good positions to identify many health conditions in their students. Often, families do not recognize the onset of symptoms or signs or do not know where to seek help. School staff should appreciate how physical and mental health problems affect students. ("Mental health problems" include drug- and alcohol-related problems, social problems, problems with attention, and emotional problems. Guideline 4-06 provides details on schools' capacity to identify students with symptoms of poor mental health and to refer and manage suspected mental health problems.)

To ensure that assessments and referrals are appropriate, consistent, and confidential, schools should maintain written policies and plans for the assessment and referral process. Train and provide continuing education for all staff on:
- detecting signs that a student's behavior, performance, attitude, or achievement may be the result of an unmet health- or safety-related need;
- strategies that can reduce the impact of the problem (eg, how to capitalize on students' strengths and assets, foster protective factors, and change environmental circumstances to minimize risk factors);
- policies, regulations, and laws that protect confidentiality (Guideline 0-03, Guideline 4-25);
- approaches to addressing students' health problems in ways that don't penalize students or label them as unhealthy or problem students;
- bringing the problem to the attention of those responsible at school for further assessment and/or referral.

Policies should clearly identify staff members who have the responsibility to further assess the students and/or refer them from the school to a community professional or agency. These responsibilities should not threaten the health, safety, or comfort level of staff involved in the process or of other students. Schools' student assistance teams can play a significant role for this function (Guideline 4-01). Members of these teams require additional training on issues of assessment, referral, and confidential record keeping.

Identify school and community resources and services available to meet the needs of students. Have ways to ensure that parents, as well as community agencies and community professionals receiving school referrals, get pertinent school-derived information. Assign one school contact person to be primarily responsible for further inquiries and for following up on school-generated referrals.

▶ *RELATED GUIDELINES*

0-03, 0-08, 0-13, 7-03

▶ *RELATED LINKS*

http://www.aafp.org
http://www.schoolhealth.org
http://smhp.psych.ucla.edu
http://csmha.umaryland.edu
http://www.ed.gov/offices/OM/fpco/ferpa
http://www.cms.hhs.gov/hipaa
http://www.adolescenthealth.org

4-24–REPORTS TO THE PUBLIC HEALTH DEPARTMENT[80,110-112]

Manage and report communicable disease exposure as well as exposure to chemical, biological, or radiation hazards by complying with public health, environmental, and law enforcement codes and guidelines in local and state jurisdictions.

▶ *RATIONALE*

Reporting certain communicable diseases is mandated in many circumstances to contain spread of these diseases in school and in the community. Reporting outbreaks of food poisoning can trigger investigations to locate the cause. Reporting possible exposure to noncommunicable hazards is important to individual and public safety.

▶ *COMMENTARY*

There are laws that specify which communicable diseases must be reported to public health authorities and that outline reporting procedures. Most often, physicians, laboratories, and hospitals report diseases as they are confirmed. However, because school staff cannot always rely on external reporting having occurred, they may also make these reports when they become aware of the diagnosis. Examples of reportable diseases are several infectious gastrointestinal diseases and infectious causes of meningitis. Because the list is specific to each state and because lists change, school health professionals should be aware of diseases required to be reported in each state and obtain updates to this list at least annually. The school nurse and school physician should also be apprised of any communicable disease being reported.

Once staff and students are already known to have been exposed to an infectious agent, school health staff should determine the extent of exposure and take appropriate actions for those at risk. Sending out letters or calling parents is sometimes warranted, but other times it does little more than generate unnecessary concern. Schools must work with their school nurses and school physicians as well as use resource manuals.

Public health departments have expertise and updated information on matters related to chemical, biological, and radiation hazards. School staff must describe what they have observed (as far as symptoms or exposure) to the best of their abilities and report this information immediately to public health authorities.

▶ *RELATED GUIDELINES*

0-07, 6-14, 6-22, 6-23

▶ *RELATED LINKS*

http://www.aap.org
http://www.cdc.gov
http://www.ems-c.org
http://www.FEMA.gov
http://www.foodsafeschools.org

4-25—CONFIDENTIAL HEALTH RECORDS[55,56,113–115]

Keep health records of students and staff confidential and in a secured environment.

▶ RATIONALE

The use and release of health information belonging to staff members, students, and their families are often necessary to the development of health, safety, and inclusion plans for those with special needs. By having policies in place and making sure they are understood, schools will safeguard their students' and staff members' confidentiality as well as protect the district from liability.

▶ COMMENTARY

School district personnel offices often collect confidential health and safety information from many staff members. Students' health information often resides in many offices (eg, nurses' offices, counselors' offices). Schools must have written policies that define when and how often signed consent to exchange information is required, the limits of information to be exchanged, and terms of notification when this information is exchanged. Locked cabinets and exchange of information (verbal exchanges, written exchanges such as fax, e-mail, and other electronic forms) must all be considered when defining limitations to access. Aside from sensitivity to issues of confidentiality and protection of privacy, policies must also be congruent with local, state, and federal laws (eg, Family Educational Rights and Privacy Act [FERPA; http://www.ed.gov/offices/OM/fpco/ferpa]). FERPA regulates sharing information at school and sending school information to others. The Health Insurance Portability and Accountability Act (HIPAA; http://www.cms.hhs.gov/hipaa) regulates health providers sharing information with each other and with schools. Special considerations for school compliance with HIPAA often apply to schools, for example, when confidential information is housed in school-based health centers (Guideline 4-31).

Students should know that records of health services at school and elsewhere are confidential and should understand the extent of that confidentiality. The purpose of collecting and storing this information is to protect the health and safety of students and staff members, necessitating that some information is shared with certain members of the school staff. There are many circumstances whereby parents and students wish to disclose components of the health record to classmates. When this occurs, staff must also consider that these same students and families may still want to keep many other aspects of the health record private.

Someone knowledgeable about state and federal laws in each school should be designated to make decisions about the extent and the manner to which confidential information is shared. The school principal or the person creating the health record is usually the person responsible for this. For health information, this responsibility is often delegated to the school nurse. For mental health information, responsibility to protect student confidentiality is often assigned to the school nurse, school counselor, or school psychologist. All who have access to health-related information about a student or staff member must be counseled about policies and practices for maintaining confidentiality.

▶ *RELATED GUIDELINES*

0-03

▶ *RELATED LINKS*

http://www.ashaweb.org
http://www.ed.gov/offices/om/fpco/ferpa
http://www.cms.hhs.gov/hipaa
http://www.nasponline.org

4-26–QUALITY OF HEALTH SERVICES, QUALITY ASSURANCE[3,116–118]

Write, review, monitor, and regularly update school health services and safety policies, procedures, and protocols so that they include current evidence-based information that optimizes care and safety.

▶ RATIONALE

Policies and procedures for school health services and safety protocols require regular review and revision as science, technology, and standards change. Monitoring for adherence and intended outcome helps protect student health and safety, keep schools accountable for services provided, and limit district liability.

▶ COMMENTARY

Quality assurance is a process of monitoring and improving the quality of services (health-related for purposes of this guideline) through enforcement of health and safety standards, technical assistance, and dissemination of new technology and methodologies. The school nurse, the school health and safety coordinator, the district physician, the school health and safety team, and the school health and safety advisory council should agree on who has the responsibility to update each health- and safety-related procedure, protocol, piece of school equipment, and set of supplies.

School health professionals must keep up-to-date with state and local laws, new scientific information, and policies from key health- and safety-oriented national professional organizations, such as the American Public Health Association (http://www.apha.org), the National Association of School Nurses (http://www.nasn.org), and the American School Health Association (http://www.ashaweb.org). Policies and procedures that need regular updates include, but are not limited to: first aid, medication administration, cardiopulmonary resuscitation, medical procedures for students with chronic diseases, and all screenings (eg, vision, hearing, oral health, and scoliosis screening). The school health and safety coordinator and the school health and safety advisory council should review and monitor the quality assurance process.

To support the quality of health services, schools must build capacity with personnel, internal and external systems of communication, and other resources, plus reward those who achieve and strive for quality. Systems must encourage staff to report errors they encounter or cause when performing any health procedure, including medication administration. Consequences of errors must not be so punitive that they will deter reporting. Errors in performing all health-related procedures should be reviewed regularly in order to detect patterns, reeducate staff, and revise procedures.

School Health Evaluation Services (SHES) of University of Colorado's Office of School Health (http://www.uchsc.edu/schoolhealth) provides technical assistance, training, and onsite services to educational administrators, health professionals, and community groups so that they may manage data related to all aspects of school health service delivery.

▶ *RELATED GUIDELINES*

0-04, 0-05, 0-06, 0-13, 0-14, 0-16

▶ *RELATED LINKS*

http://www.ada.org
http://www.diabetes.org
http://www.americanheart.org
http://www.aota.org
http://www.apta.org
http://www.apha.org
http://www.redcross.org
http://www.schoolcounselor.org
http://www.ashaweb.org
http://www.asha.org
http://www.cdc.gov
http://www.state.ma.us/dph/fch/schoolhealth/index.htm
http://www.nasn.org
http://www.nasponline.org
http://www.uchsc.edu/schoolhealth
http://www.sswaa.org
http://www.umass.edu/umsshi

◀ Health and Mental Health Services ▶

SCHOOL-BASED HEALTH CENTERS

4-27–SCHOOL-BASED HEALTH CENTER: NEEDS ASSESSMENT [8,69,119–122]

Base the selection of physical, oral, and mental health services in a school-based health center (SBHC) on needs of the student population and the community.

▶ RATIONALE

School-based health centers have the best chances of succeeding when they meet the needs of schools, students, families, and community. Assessing these needs at regular intervals will help to ensure the success of a school-based health center.

▶ COMMENTARY

School-based health centers vary in the level of health services provided. An SBHC's role in primary prevention should complement services that are available and accessible to students and families elsewhere. In many communities, schools are the only place where many students can receive certain types of health care. Inclusion of the community in the planning and development of the center is one key to its success. Services provided must be appropriate for the developmental stages of the student population. Physical assessment, anticipatory guidance, some level of treatment services, referrals, follow-up, and case management are provided in most SBHCs. Other services should be selected on the basis of the needs assessment.

School-based oral health programs, including preventive or restorative dental care, are the only source of such care for some populations. Oral health needs of the community and its toll on student functioning should be assessed. Students with emotional problems often present first with physical complaints – an important factor to recognize during the needs assessment process so that mental health needs are not underestimated. Mental health screening, identification, treatment, and referral should always be considered. Assistance for students involved with substance abuse may also be provided in an SBHC. Some SBHCs provide testing for sexually transmitted diseases (including human immunodeficiency virus [HIV]), pregnancy testing, prenatal care, gynecologic examinations, and contraception. Determination of the scope of services offered should include consideration the following: community support, recognized need to provide services in school, and availability of appropriate follow-up and referral services.

▶ RELATED GUIDELINES

0-08, 0-09, 0-10, 1-01

▶ RELATED LINKS

http://www.cmsa.org
http://www.mchb.hrsa.gov/chusa02/index.htm
http://mchb.hrsa.gov
http://www.nasbhc.org

4-28—SCHOOL-BASED HEALTH CENTER: COMMUNITY HEALTH SERVICES[119,120,123–125]

Coordinate and integrate services delivered at a school-based health center (SBHC) with those delivered by the community's health care providers.

▶ RATIONALE

Student referrals to and from SBHCs are likely to occur expediently and effectively when SBHCs, community-based health care providers, and community agencies coordinate and integrate their efforts.

▶ COMMENTARY

School-based health center services should be integrated with the overall community public health, mental health, primary care, specialized medical, and dental systems of care. School-based health centers vary widely. Some are independent organizations, while others are satellites of larger health organizations. Attempt to integrate the activities of the SBHC with those of other community-based health care provider systems. This may be done by educating community-based health care providers about the services delivered at school, sharing information about specific students who are patients in more than one site (taking care to protect confidentiality), and encouraging community agencies to share information about specific students with the SBHC. Such coordination and integration of services may make it more likely that SBHCs will become and remain an important part of the continuum of care within a community.

▶ RELATED GUIDELINES

0-12, 1-02, 1-06

▶ RELATED LINKS

http://www.healthinschools.org
http://www.nasbhc.org

4-29–SCHOOL-BASED HEALTH CENTER: TRANSITIONING TO COMMUNITY-BASED CARE[119,120,124,125]

Encourage school-based health centers (SBHCs) to teach students to be good consumers of community-based health care, recognizing that school sites will not always be available for health care.

▶ **RATIONALE**

Students at schools with health centers are more likely to continue to receive mental and dental care after they graduate if they and their families are taught to use community-based health and oral health care.

▶ **COMMENTARY**

Some students and families do not seek access to health care services outside of their SBHC (or the emergency care system in hospitals) because they are unfamiliar with principles of primary care, do not have insurance or transportation, or do not feel comfortable with traditional health care delivery systems. For many, SBHCs are the only place they have felt comfortable accessing preventive health care services. Many community-based health services sites, including community health centers, physician practices, and dental offices, can work with SBHCs to become transition sites for students' health care. Examples of assistance that SBHCs might offer students so that they are likely to continue receiving comprehensive health care once they have graduated are: helping students and their families complete health insurance applications (eg, State Children's Health Insurance Plan or Medicaid), helping families choose a medical or dental home that most suits them, discussing logistics of making and keeping appointments, helping them find the best transportation options to reach a community-based medical or dental site, and teaching adolescents about their rights for confidential care. All these tactics can help students feel more comfortable with seeking comprehensive care in a traditional clinical setting. These activities should be part of the SBHC's stated objectives with provisions for financial compensation and incentives from external medical systems. School-based health centers should document their success in helping students access community-based health care services.

▶ **RELATED GUIDELINES**

0-12, 1-02

▶ **RELATED LINKS**

http://www.aapd.org
http://www.healthinschools.org
http://mchb.hrsa.gov
http://www.nasbhc.org

4-30—SCHOOL-BASED HEALTH CENTER: OTHER SCHOOL PROGRAMS[120,123-127]

Coordinate services and education provided in all regular school health programs (eg, school health office, classroom education) with services and education provided in school-based health centers (SBHCs).

▶ *RATIONALE*

The effects of health services management for students in school and of health and safety education in school are most likely to be effective when services and education are reinforced in numerous school settings. This can best occur when SBHCs and other school programs collaborate.

▶ *COMMENTARY*

Coordination of health education and health services among classroom teachers, school health and safety personnel (eg, school nurses, counselors), and the SBHC will help optimize complementary programs, improve continuity of care, reduce fragmentation, prevent duplication, and maintain affordable services. All school programs are better able to identify and address health needs acting as barriers to school achievement when personnel in each system are aware of the others' services and strengths, and they work together to assist students and their families.

School-based health center staff and school nurses, for example, offer individual and group counseling on health and safety matters based on students' unique needs. In contrast, educators of health and safety curricula target groups of students with a primary aim of changing high-risk behaviors. School-based health centers' staff may be invited to provide classroom instruction. While clinical and educational staff members can play very different roles, awareness of and integration with one another's resources and curricula can serve to enhance the health and safety messages students receive. Invite SBHC staff onto the school health and safety advisory councils so that they may enhance the curriculum selection process. Keep SBHC staff aware of health and safety curricula so that they can build on what students have learned and practiced in class.

▶ *RELATED GUIDELINES*

2-02, 8-06

▶ *RELATED LINKS*

http://www.ashaweb.org
http://www.healthinschools.org
http://www.communityschools.org
http://mchb.hrs.gov
http://www.nasn.org

4-31–SCHOOL-BASED HEALTH CENTER: CONFIDENTIALITY [55,56,115]

Develop policies and procedures that protect confidential student health information, yet allow for exchange of information between the school-based health center (SBHC) and school staff, as well as between the SBHC and community health professionals, whenever information exchange is determined to be in a student's best interest.

▶ RATIONALE

School-based health centers must maintain health records in a confidential manner in accordance with law, yet allow a degree of communication that is consistent with students' best interest and wishes.

▶ COMMENTARY

School-based health centers that are satellites of community-based health agencies or are supervised by physicians from community-based health agencies have medical records that belong to the partner health care organization instead of, or in addition to, the school's records.

Health care organizations must maintain confidentiality of patient records under a federal law known as the Health Insurance Portability and Accountability Act (HIPAA). Parents and students should be offered waivers to sign that allow information exchange with the school nurse, counselor, or other staff. Waivers to exchange information are most readily obtained at times of student registration at school or when students first register as patients at the SBHC. Careful explanation of the benefits and potential drawbacks of allowing such information exchange must be provided to students and families. Sharing school records with SBHCs and sharing SBHC records with school staff can raise a number of complex issues. Most notably, some federal and state laws allow some medical information to be protected from the knowledge of parents, but this protection does not apply to information in schools' records. In some states, if a minor has a sexually transmitted disease, the child's clinician (working outside of the school system) does not have to report this to the teen's parent and can refuse to share this information with the teen's parent. Yet educational systems, which operate under another set of district, state, and federal laws and regulations, may require parents to have access to this information. Some districts may even require school personnel to actively notify parents.

School districts and SBHCs must address this issue. Understand your state's laws regarding a minor's consent for health care, protection of health information, and circumstances for breaching confidentiality. Address the right of the student to seek confidential services for prevention and care of pregnancy, sexually transmitted diseases, and mental health services within accepted policies and guidelines. Once specific guidelines, policies, and procedures are in place, students, families, and staff should be alerted to the rationale for them and their implications.

▶ RELATED GUIDELINES

0-03, 1-02

▶ *RELATED LINKS*

http://www.ashaweb.org

http://www.healthinschools.or

http://cms.hhs.gov

http://www.ed.gov/offices/om/fpco/ferpa

http://www.cms.hhs.gov/hipaa

http://www.nasbhc.org

http://www.nasponline.org

4-32–SCHOOL-BASED HEALTH CENTER: QUALITY ASSURANCE[117,118,128–131]

Develop a quality assurance program in school-based health centers (SBHCs) that is in accordance with standards of national certifying bodies and appropriate state regulations.

▶ *RATIONALE*

Quality assurance protocols help SBHCs comply with existing standards of clinical practice, operate comparably to other health care organizations, attain eligibility to be reimbursed for provided services, and continuously improve the quality and safety of the program.

▶ *COMMENTARY*

An SBHC's quality assurance program should be comprehensive and cover all aspects and parameters of care. A written quality assurance plan should establish program goals and objectives and these should be reviewed and updated annually. The quality assurance program should be guided by an interdisciplinary team of clinicians and administrators, with one person designated responsible for the scope of the program (program coordinator or director). The program should have a direct line of reporting to the SBHC clinical director and then to the program governing body.

A quality assurance protocol should include the following components:
- clinician credentialing, recredentialing, and privileging;
- utilization review;
- student (patient) and family satisfaction with review of patient grievances;
- success in coordination of care with community agencies;
- ongoing monitoring of process and of outcome measures;
- staff satisfaction (school staff and SBHC staff);
- clinical protocol and guideline development and monitoring;
- health records review;
- ensuring compliance with appropriate state and federal regulations;
- risk minimization; and
- Clinical Laboratory Improvement Amendments (CLIA) certification.

▶ *RELATED GUIDELINES*

0-13, 0-14

▶ *RELATED LINKS*

http://www.healthinschools.org
http://www.cms.hhs.gov/clia
http://www.nasbhc.org
http://www.uchsc.edu/schoolhealth

4-33—SCHOOL-BASED HEALTH CENTER: FINANCIAL STABILITY[119,132-137]

Require that school-based health centers (SBHCs) establish financial plans that allow them to be sustainable beyond the period covered by start-up funding. Assist SBHCs to establish these plans.

▶ RATIONALE

The establishment of a SBHC is too labor and resource intensive not to plan for long-term sustainability. Financial stability of the SBHC can help establish confidence among students, families, and the community-at-large.

▶ COMMENTARY

Integrated school health service programs require a sound financial base. A long-term funding plan is optimally developed before the integrated school health services program is initiated. Sources of funds may include private health insurance plans, school funds, and various federal funding streams. Advocacy for new mechanisms of health care financing at both state and national levels may be needed to ensure that funding is sustained. Health professionals, parents, educators, and school administrators can be influential spokespersons on behalf of federal, state, and local foundation funding of SBHCs.

Analysis of reimbursement capacity and of stable sources of income should be an inherent part of planning for any school-based health program. Health plans may agree to compensate school-based clinical activities on a fee-for-service basis, while still compensating their community-based providers at the same or a reduced amount. Alternatively, SBHCs may be compensated on the basis of "capitation" by health insurance plans (ie, center is paid a set dollar amount monthly for every one health plan member enrolled in the SBHC). In some communities, health insurance plans do not reimburse SBHCs directly, but expect that the primary care provider officially assigned to a student will pay the SBHC to care for the patient on his or her behalf. This latter model is financially feasible only when a large portion of the student population shares a common medical group or community clinic as the assigned primary care provider and an arrangement is then made between this entity and the SBHC.

Mental health services are sometimes paid differently from other medical services. This varies from one state to another for private insurance, for Medicaid, and for other publicly subsidized health insurance plans. Mental health services may be contracted out or carved out from other systems of payment. Depending on many factors, this can work in schools' favor. Community mental health providers visiting school sites (or mental health providers who are school employees but permitted to bill insurance on behalf of the school) may provide mental health services for students at school and be compensated no differently than those working in traditional clinical office sites for mental health services.

▶ RELATED GUIDELINES

0-08, 1-06

▶ *RELATED LINKS*

http://www.hrsa.gov/financemc

http://www.healthinschools.org

http://cms.hhs.gov

http://www.nasbhc.org

CHAPTER REFERENCES

1. Adelman HS. School-linked mental health interventions: Toward mechanisms for service coordination and integration. *J Comm Psychol.* 1993;21:309–319

2. Rosenblum L, DiCecco M, Taylor L, Adelman H. Upgrading school support programs through collaboration: Resource Coordination Teams. *Soc Work Educ.* 1995;17:117–124

3. Bobo N, Adams VW, Cooper L. Excellence in school nursing practice: developing a national perspective on school nurse competencies. *J Sch Nurs.* 2002;18:277–285

4. National Association of School Nurses. *Professional School Nurse Roles and Responsibilities: Education, Certification, and Licensure.* Scarborough, ME: National Association of School Nurses; 1996

5. National Association of School Nurses. *Scope and Standards of Professional School Nursing Practices.* Scarborough, ME: National Association of School Nurses; 2001

6. National Association of School Nurses. *The School Nurse Role in Delegation of Care: Guidelines and Compendium.* Scarborough, ME: National Association of School Nurses; 1995

7. Schwab NC, Gelfman MHB, eds. *Legal Issues in School Health Services: A Resource for School Administrators, School Attorneys, School Nurses.* North Branch, MN: Sunrise River Press; 2001

8. US Department of Health and Human Services. *Healthy People 2010. 2nd ed. With Understanding and Improving Health and Objectives for Improving Health.* 2 vols. Washington, DC: US Government Printing Office; 2000

9. American Academy of Pediatrics, Committee on School Health. The role of the school nurse in providing school health services. *Pediatrics.* 2001;108:1231–1232

10. National Association of School Nurses. *Position Statement: Caseload Assignments.* Scarborough, ME: National Association of School Nurses; 1995. Available at: http://www.nasn.org/positions/caseload.htm

11. American Academy of Pediatrics, Section on School Health. Residency training and continuing medical education in school health. *Pediatrics.* 1993;92:495–496

12. American Academy of Pediatrics, Section on School Health and Committee on School Health. School Health Leadership Training Kit. Elk Grove Village, IL: American Academy of Pediatrics; 1997. Available at: http://www.schoolhealth.org/trnthtrn/trainmn.html

13. Barnett S, Duncan P, O'Connor KG. Pediatricians' response to the demand for school health programming. *Pediatrics.* 1999;103(4). Available at: http://www.pediatrics.org/cgi/content/full/103/4/e45

14. Fleming M, Allensworth D et al. *How Physicians Work and How to Work with Physicians.* Kent, OH: American School Health Association

15. Zenni EA, Sectish TC, Martin BN, Prober CG. Pediatric resident training in a school environment. A prescription for learning. *Arch Pediatr Adolesc Med.* 1996;150:632–637

16. National Association of School Nurses. *Issue Brief: School Health Nursing Services Role in Health Care: Delegation of Care.* Scarborough, ME. Available at: http://208.5.177.157/briefs/delegation.htm

17. Adelman HS. School counseling. Psychological and social services. In: Marx E, Wooley SF, eds. *Health is Academic: A Guide to Coordinated School Health Programs.* New York, NY: Teachers College Press; 1988:142–168

18. Baruch G. Mental health services in schools: the challenge of locating a psychotherapy service for troubled adolescent pupils in mainstream and special schools. *J Adolesc.* 2001;24:549–570

19. Dryfoos JG. *Safe Passage: Making It Through Adolescence in a Risky Society.* New York, NY: Oxford University Press; 1998

20. Durlak JA: *Successful Prevention Programs for Children and Adolescents.* New York, NY: Plenum Press; 1997

21. Dwyer K, Osher D. *Safeguarding our Children: An Action Guide.* Washington, DC. US Departments of Education and Justice; 2000

22. Elias MJ, Zins JE, Weissberg KS, et al. *Promoting Social and Emotional Learning: Guidelines for Educators.* Alexandria, VA: Association for Supervision and Curriculum Development; 1997

23. Gilliland BE, James RK. *Crisis Intervention Strategies.* 3rd ed. Pacific Grove, CA: Brooks Cole; 1997

24. Greenberg MT, Domitrovich C, Bumbarger B. Prevention of mental disorders in school-aged children. *Prev Treat.* 2001;4:1. Available at: http://journals.apa.org/prevention/volume4/pre0040001a.html

25. Jellinek M, ed. *Bright Futures in Practice: Mental Health.* 2nd ed. Arlington, VA: National Center for Education in Maternal and Child Health, 2002

26. National Institute of Justice. *Conflict Resolution for School Personnel: an Interactive School Safety Training Tool (CD-ROM).* Washington DC: US Department of Justice, Office of Justice Programs: 2002

27. Schinn M, Walker H, Stoner G, eds. *Interventions for Academic and Behavior Problems: Preventive and Remedial Approaches.* Bethesda, MD: National Association of School Psychologists; 2002

28. Thomas A, Grimes J, eds. *Best Practices in School Psychology-IV.* Washington, DC: National Association of School Psychologists; 2002

29. Ohio Chapter American Academy of Pediatrics. *Emergency Guidelines for Schools, 2000.* Available at: http://www.ems-c.org/downloads/pdf/emscguide.pdf

30. Adams RM. *School Nurse's Survival Guide: Ready-to-Use Tips, Techniques and Materials for the School Health Professional.* Englewood Cliffs, NJ: Prentice Hall; 1995

31. American Academy of Pediatrics, Committee on School Health. Guidelines for emergency care in school. *Pediatrics.* 2001;107:435–436

32. American Red Cross. *Community First Aid and Safety.* Washington DC: American Red Cross; 2002

33. Bernardo LM, Anderson L. *Preparing a Response to Emergency Problems: A Self-Study Module.* Scarborough, ME: National Association of School Nurses; 1998.

34. Newton J, Adams R, Marcontel M. *The New School Health Handbook: A Ready Reference for School Nurses and Educators.* 3rd ed. Paramus, NJ: Prentice Hall; 1997

35. Colorado Department of Education. *Child Abuse and Prevention. Guidance for School Personnel.* Denver, CO: Colorado Department of Education; 2002. Available at: http://www.cde.state.co.us/cdeprevention/download/pdf/child_abuse_manual_2002.pdf

36. American Academy of Pediatrics. *A Guide to References and Resources in Child Abuse and Neglect.* 2nd ed. Elk Grove Village, IL: American Academy of Pediatrics; 1998

37. American Nurses Association. *Culturally Competent Assessment for Family Violence.* Washington, DC: American Nurses Association; 1998

38. Ayyub R. Domestic violence in the south Asian Muslim immigrant population in the United States. *J Soc Distress Homeless.* 2000;9:237–248

39. Fukaya M. *The Nurse's Office as Refuge. Monograph Vol. 55.* Okayama, Japan: Benesse Corp, Educational Research Center; 1998

40. Futa KT, Hsu E, Hansen DJ. Child sexual abuse in Asian American families: an examination of cultural factors that influence prevalence, identification, and treatment. *Clin Psychol Sci Pract.* 2001;8:189–209

41. Hong GK, Hong LK. Comparative perspectives on child abuse and neglect: Chinese versus Hispanics and Whites. *Child Welfare.* 1991;70:463–475

42. Iowa Department of Human Services. *Child Abuse: A Guide for Mandatory Reporters.* Des Moines, IA: Iowa Department of Human Services; 1999

43. Jacobson WB. *Safe From the Start: Taking Action on Children Exposed to Violence.* Washington, DC: US Department of Justice; 2000

44. Kernic MA, Holt VL, Wolf ME, McKnight B, Huebner CE, Rivara FP. Academic and school health issues among children exposed to maternal intimate partner abuse. *Arch Pediatr Adolesc Med.* 2002;156:549–555

45. Rouse LP. Abuse in dating relationships: a comparison of Blacks, Whites, and Hispanics. *J Coll Stud Dev.* 1988;29:312–219

46. Struck LM. *Assistance for Special Educators, Law Enforcement, and Child Protective Services in Recognizing and Managing Abuse and Neglect of Children With Disabilities.* Richmond, VA: Virginia Department of Social Services, Child Protective Services Unit; 1999

47. Bednarz PK. The Omaha System: a model for describing school nurse case management. *J Sch Nurs.* 1998;14:24–30

48. National Association of School Nurses. *The School Nurse and Specialized Health Care Services.* Scarborough, ME: National Association of School Nurses; 1996. Available at: http://www.nasn.org/positions/specialized.htm

49. Reel SJ, Morgan-Judge T, Peros DS, Abraham IL. School-based rural case management: a model to prevent and reduce risk. *J Am Acad Nurse Pract.* 2002;14:291–296

50. Scott P. A day in the life of a school health nurse. *Tenn Nurse.* 1998;61:13–15

51. Smith AJ Jr, Armijo EJ, Stowitschek JJ. Current applications of case management in schools to improve children's readiness to learn. *J Case Manag.* 1997;6:105–113

52. Students with chronic illnesses: guidance for families, schools, and students. *J Sch Health.* 2003;73:131–132. Available at: http://www.nhlbi.nih.gov/health/public/lung/asthma/guidfam.pdf

53. Bergren MD. Criteria for software evaluation: legal issues. *J Sch Nurs.* 1999;15:32–33

54. Brener ND, Burstein GR, Dushaw ML, Vernon ME, Wheeler L, Robinson J. health services: results from the School Health Policies and Programs Study 2000. *J Sch Health.* 2001;71:294–304

55. Family Educational Rights and Privacy Act. 20 USC §1232g. 34 CFR Part 99

56. National Task Force on Confidential Student Health Information. *Guidelines for Protecting Confidential Student Health Information.* Kent, OH: American School Health Association; 2000

57. Schwab NC, Panettieri MJ, Bergren MD. *Guidelines for School Nursing Documentation: Standards, Issues, and Models.* Scarborough, ME: National Association of School Nurses; 1998

58. Center for Effective Collaboration and Practice, American Institutes for Research and National Association for School Psychologists. *Safeguarding Our Children: An Action Guide: Implementing Early Warning, Timely Response.* Washington, DC: Department of Education, Department of Justice; 2000

59. US Department of Education, Office of Safe and Drug-Free Schools. *Practical Information on Crisis Planning: A Guide for Schools and Communities.* Washington, DC: 2003. Available at: http://www.ed.gov/offices/OSDFS/emergencyplan/crisisplanning.pdf

60. National Education Association. *Crisis Communication Guide and Toolkit.* Available at: http://www.nea.org/crisis/intro.html

61. Centers for Disease Control and Prevention. School health guidelines to prevent unintentional injuries and violence. *MMWR Morb Mortal Wkly Rep.* 2001;50(RR-22):1–73

62. King KA. Developing a comprehensive school suicide prevention program. *J Sch Health.* 2001;71:132–137

63. Lerner MD, Shelton RD. *A Practical Guide for Crisis Response in Our Schools.* Commack, NY: American Academy of Experts in Traumatic Stress, 2001

64. Lerner MD, Volpe JS, Lindell B. *A Practical Guide for Crisis Response in Our Schools.* 5th ed. Commack, NY: American Academy of Experts in Traumatic Stress, 2003

65. Passarelli C. Are you prepared for an emergency? *J Sch Nurs.* 1995;11:4, 6

66. Pollack I, Sunderman C. Creating safe schools: a comprehensive approach. *Juv Justice.* 2001;8:13–20

67. Reddy M, Borum R, Berglund J, Vossekuil B, Fein R, Modzeleski W. Evaluating risk for targeted violence in schools: comparing risk assessment, threat assessment, and other approaches. *Psych Sch.* 2001;38:157–172

68. Casamassimo PS. *Bright Futures in Practice: Oral Health.* Arlington, VA: National Center for Education in Maternal and Child Health; 1996

69. American Academy of Pediatric Dentistry. Special Issue: Reference Manual 1994–95. *Pediatric Dent.* 1994–1995;16:1–96

70. Casamassimo P. School oral health. *Pediatr Dent.* 1995;17:170

71. Centers for Disease Control and Prevention. Impact of targeted, school-based dental sealant programs in reducing racial and economic disparities in sealant prevalence among schoolchildren—Ohio, 1998–1999. *MMWR Morb Mortal Wkly Rep.* 2001;50:736–738

72. Herman NG, Rosenthal M, Franklin DM. Delivery of comprehensive children's dental services using portable dental clinics in NYC public schools: a six-year analysis. *N Y State Dent J.* 1997;63:36–41

73. Kuthy RA, Siegal MD, Wulf CA. Establishing maternal and child health data collection priorities for state and local oral health programs. *J Public Health Dent.* 1997;57:197–205

74. Simoyan O, Badner V. Implementing a school-based dental health program: the Montefiore model. *J Sch Health.* 2002;72:262–263

75. US Department of Health and Human Services. *Oral Health in America: A Report of the Surgeon General.* Rockville, MD: US Department of Health and Human Services; National Institute of Dental and Craniofacial Research; 2000

76. American Academy of Pediatrics, Committee on School Health. School health assessments. *Pediatrics.* 2000;105:875–877

77. Barrett JR, Kuhlman GS, Stanitski CL, Small E. The pre-participation physical evaluation. In: Sullivan JA, Anderson SJ, eds. *Care of the Young Athlete.* Rosemont, IL: American Academy of Orthopaedic Surgeons/American Academy of Pediatrics; 2000:43–56

78. American Academy of Pediatrics, Committee on Practice and Ambulatory Medicine. Implementation of the immunization policy. *Pediatrics.* 1995;96:360–361

79. American Academy of Pediatrics, Committee on Practice and Ambulatory Medicine. Policy on the development of immunization tracking systems. *Pediatrics.* 1996;97:927

80. American Academy of Pediatrics. *2000 Red Book: Report of the Committee on Infectious Diseases.* Pickering LK, ed. 25th ed. Elk Grove Village, IL: American Academy of Pediatrics; 2003

81. Boyer-Chuanroong L. Roll Up Both Sleeves: *A Comprehensive Immunization Guide for Nurses and Nurse Planners.* Kent OH: American School Health Association; 1999

82. Centers for Disease Control and Prevention. General recommendations on immunization: Recommendations of the Advisory Committee on Immunization Practices (ACIP) and the American Academy of Family Physicians (AAFP). *MMWR Morb Mortal Wkly Rep.* 2002;51(RR-2):1–36

83. Orenstein WA, Hinman AR. The immunization system in the United States: the role of school immunization laws. *Vaccine.* 1999;29;17(Suppl 3):S19–S24

84. Haas MB, ed. *The School Nurse's Source Book of Individualized Healthcare Plans, Volume I.* North Branch, MN: Sunrise River Press; 1993

85. US Department of Education, Office for Civil Rights, Section 504 of the Rehabilitation Act of 1973. Amended 29 USC §794/Section 504

86. Wong DL. *Whaley & Wong's Nursing Care of Infants and Children.* 6th ed. St Louis, MO: Mosby & Co; 1999

87. American School Health Association. *Policy Statement: Scoliosis Screening in Schools.* Kent, OH: American School Health Association; 1997. Available at: http://www.ashaweb.org/resolutions2.html

88. Green M, Palfrey J, eds. *Bright Futures: Guidelines for Health Supervision of Infants, Children and Adolescents.* 2nd ed. Arlington, VA: National Center for Education in Maternal and Child Health; 2000

89. Lewis KD, Bear BJ. *Manual of School Health.* 2nd ed. St. Louis, MO: Saunders-Elsevier Science, 2002

90. List DG, Levy R, Robbins L, Allegrante JP. An information book for a school musculoskeletal screening program. *J Sch Health.* 1994;64:168–170

91. American Academy of Pediatrics, Committee on School Health. *School Health: Policy and Practice.* 5th ed. Nader PR, ed. Elk Grove Village, IL: American Academy of Pediatrics; 1993

92. National Association of School Nurses. *Postural Screening Guidelines for School Nurses.* Scarborough, ME: National Association of School Nurses; 1995

93. National Association of School Nurses. *The Ear and Hearing: A Guide for School Nurses.* Scarborough, ME: National Association of School Nurses; 1998

94. National Association of School Nurses. *Vision Screening Guidelines for School Nurses.* Scarborough, ME: National Association of School Nurses; 1992

95. Velezis MJ, Sturm PF, Cobey J. Scoliosis screening revisited: findings from the District of Columbia. *J Pediatr Orthop.* 2002;22:788–791

96. Vessey JA, Ben-Or K, Mebane DJ, et al. Evaluating the value of screening for hypertension: an evidence-based approach. *J Sch Nurs.* 2001;17:44–49

97. Awbrey LM, Juarez SM. Developing a nursing protocol for over-the-counter medications in high school. *J Sch Nurs.* 2003;19:12–15

98. Massachusetts General Laws Chapter 71, Section 54B; Regulations 105 CMR 210.001 et seq

99. American Academy of Pediatrics, Committee on Children With Disabilities. Provision of educationally-related services for children and adolescents with chronic diseases and disabling conditions. *Pediatrics.* 2000;105:448–451

100. Arnold MJ, Silkworth CK, eds. *The School Nurse's Source Book of Individualized Healthcare Plans, Volume 2.* North Branch, MN: Sunrise River Press; 1999

101. Hootman J. *Quality Nursing Interventions in the School Setting: Procedures, Models, and Guidelines.* Scarborough, ME: National Association of School Nurses; 1996

102. National Association of School Nurses. *Issue Brief: School Nurses and the Individuals with Disabilities Education Act (IDEA).* Scarborough, ME: National Association of School Nurses; 1996

103. American Association of Diabetes Educators. Management of children with diabetes in the school setting. *Diabetes Educ.* 1999;25:873–877

104. Dorsey L, Diehl B. An educational program for school nurses caring for the pediatric client with a tracheostomy. Training the school nurse to care for a child re-entering the public education system with a tracheostomy. *Ostomy Wound Manage.* 1992;38:16–19

105. Pavelka L, McCarthy AM, Denehy J. Nursing interventions used in school nursing practice. *J Sch Nurs.* 1999;15:29–37

106. Taras HL. Too sick to go to school? *Principal.* 2002;81:20–21

107. Williams LK, Reichert A, MacKenzie WR, Hightower AW, Blake PA. Lice, nits, and school policy. *Pediatrics.* 2001;107:1011–1015

108. Selekman J. Attention-deficit/hyperactivity disorder. *J Sch Nurs.* 2002;18:270–276

109. Zimmermann PG. Assessment of abdominal pain in school-age children. *J Sch Nurs.* 2003;19:4–10

110. Benenson AS, ed. *Control of Communicable Diseases Manual.* Washington, DC: American Public Health Association; 1995

111. Centers for Disease Control and Prevention. Recognition of illness associated with the intentional release of a biologic agent. *MMWR Morb Mortal Wkly Rep.* 2001;50(41):893–897

112. Joint Commission on Accreditation of Healthcare Organizations. *Guidance to Health Care Organizations in Preparing for Terrorist Attacks.* Oakbrook Terrace, IL: Joint Commission on Accreditation of Healthcare Organizations; 2001

113. Bergren MD. HIPAA hoopla: privacy and security of identifiable health information. *J Sch Nurs.* 2001;17:336–340

114. Mukherjee S, Lightfoot J, Sloper P. Communicating about pupils in mainstream school with special health needs: the NHS perspective. *Child Care Health Dev.* 2002;28:21–27

115. National Association of School Nurses. *Issue Brief: School Health Nurse's Role in Education: Privacy Standards for Student Health Records.* Scarborough, ME: National Association of School Nurses; 2002. Available at: http://208.5.177.157/briefs/hippa.htm

116. American Academy of Pediatrics, Committee on School Health. Guidelines for the administration of medication in school. *Pediatrics.* 1993;92:499–500

117. Kohn LT, Corrigan JM, Donaldson MS, eds. *To Err is Human: Building a Safer Health System.* Washington, DC: National Academy Press; 2000

118. Silimperi DR, Franco LM, Veldhuyzen van Zanten T, MacAulay C. A framework for institutionalizing quality assurance. *Int J Qual Health Care.* 2002;14(Suppl 1):67–73

119. American Academy of Pediatrics, Committee on School Health. School health centers and other integrated school health services. *Pediatrics.* 2001;107:198–201

120. National Assembly on School-Based Health Care. *Principles and Goals for School-based Health Care.* Washington, DC: National Assembly on School-based Health Care; 2000

121. National Association of School Nurses, National Assembly on School-Based Health Care, and American School Health Association. *Recommendations for Delivery of Comprehensive Primary Health Care to Children and Youth in the School Setting: Joint Statement on the School Nurse/School-Based Health Center Partnership.* Scarborough, ME: National Association of School Nurses; 2001

122. Society for Adolescent Medicine. School-based health centers: position paper of the Society for Adolescent Medicine. *J Adolesc Health.* 2001;29:448–450

123. Duncan P, Igoe JB. School health services. In: Marx E, Wooley SF, eds. *Health is Academic: A Guide to Coordinated School Health Programs.* New York, NY: Teachers College Press; 1988:169–194

124. National Association of School Nurses. *The Role of the School Nurse in School Based Health Care Centers.* Scarborough, ME: National Association of School Nurses; 2001. Available at: http://www.nasn.org/positions/schoolbased.htm

125. Robert Wood Johnson Foundation. *Making the Grade; School-Based Health Centers: Servicing, Operating and Targeting Guidelines.* Princeton, NJ: Robert Wood Johnson Foundation; 1997

126. Hacker K, Wessel GL. School-based health centers and school nurses: cementing the collaboration. *J Sch Health.* 1998;68:409–414

127. Lohrmann DK, Wooley SF. Comprehensive school health education. In: Marx E, Wooley SF, eds. *Health is Academic: A Guide to Coordinated School Health Programs.* New York, NY: Teachers College Press; 1998:43–66

128. Colorado Association of School-Based Health Care. *Certification Standards for School-Based Health Centers: Facilitating Relationships Between School-Based Health Centers and Managed Care Organizations.* Denver, CO: Colorado Association School-Based Health Care: 1998. Available at: http://www.nasbhc.org/Certification.htm

129. National Committee for Quality Assurance. *Standards for the Accreditation of Managed Care Organizations (MCOs).* Washington, DC: National Committee for Quality Assurance; 2001

130. New York State Department of Health. *School-Based Health Centers Principles and Guidelines.* Albany, NY: New York State Department of Health: 1998. Available at: http://www.health.state.ny.us/nysdoh/school/sklcont.htm

131. Shuler PA. Evaluating student services provided by school-based health centers: applying the Shuler Nurse Practitioner Practice model. *J Sch Health.* 2000;70:348–352

132. Asay M, Behrens D, Guernsey BP, et al. *Nine State Strategies To Support School-Based Health Centers: A Making the Grade Monograph.* Washington, DC: George Washington University; 1998

133. Kaplan DW, Calonge BN, Guernsey BP, et al. Managed care and school-based health centers: use of health services. *Arch Pediatr Adolesc Med.* 1998;152:25–33

134. Lear JG, Montgomery LL, Schlitt JJ, Rickett KD. Key issues affecting school-based health centers and Medicaid. *J Sch Health.* 1996;66:83–88

135. Lear JG. School-based health centers: a long road to travel. *Arch Pediatr Adolesc Med.* 2003;157:118–119

136. Making the Grade National Program Office. *Issues in Financing School-Based Health Centers: A Guide for State Officials.* Washington, DC: George Washington University; 1995

137. National Assembly on School-Based Health Care. *Critical Issues in Financing School-Based Health Care.* Washington, DC: National Assembly on School-Based Health Care; 1999

138. Brener ND, Krug EG, Dahlberg LL, Powell KE. Nurses' logs as an evaluation tool for school-based violence prevention programs. *J Sch Health.* 1997;67:171–174

139. National Association of School Nurses. *Position Statement: Case Management.* Scarborough, ME: National Association of School Nurses; 1995. Available at: http://www.nasn.org/positions/casemang.htm

140. Nebraska Department of Health and Human Services. *Emergency Guidelines for School Personnel.* Lincoln, NE: Nebraska Department of Health and Human Services; 1997

141. Vulpitta RT. *On-site Emergency Response Planning Guide.* Itasca, IL: National Safety Council; 2002

142. Waldron NL. Child abuse and disability: the school's role in prevention and intervention. *Prev Sch Fail.* 1996;40:164–168

143. Weist MD, Sander MA, Lever NA, et al. School mental health's response to terrorism and disaster. *J Sch Violence.* 2002;1:5–32

144. Yawn BP, Wollan P, Scanlon P, Kurland M. Are we ready for universal school-based asthma screening? An outcomes evaluation. *Arch Pediatr Adolesc Med.* 2002;156:1256–1262

CHAPTER-RELATED LINKS

American Academy of Allergy, Asthma, and Immunology
http://www.aaaai.org/
Includes a school nurse tool kit for asthma and
    allergy management.

American Academy of Experts in Traumatic Stress
http://www.aaets.org/
Includes practical guidance on acute traumatic stress
    management and on crisis response in schools.

American Academy of Family Physicians
http://www.aafp.org/

American Academy of Pediatric Dentistry
http://www.aapd.org/
Links to articles and publications on preventive dental
    practices and finding local pediatric dentists.

American Academy of Pediatrics School Health Web Site
http://www.schoolhealth.org/
Policy statements, including school health services,
    emergency services in schools, and medication
    administration in schools.

American Academy of Pediatrics
http://www.aap.org/
Includes page with information on "Children, Terrorism,
    and Disaster."

American Association of Suicidology
http://www.suicidology.org

American Dental Association
http://www.ada.org/
Offers information for teachers, students, and parents
    about preventive oral health, how to find local
    dentists, and school intervention programs.

American Diabetes Association
http://www.diabetes.org/

American Heart Association
http://www.americanheart.org/

American Occupational Therapy Association
http://www.aota.org/

American Physical Therapy Association
http://www.apta.org/

American Public Health Organization
http://www.apha.org/

American Red Cross
http://www.redcross.org/

American School Counselor Association
http://www.schoolcounselor.org/

American School Health Association
http://www.ashaweb.org/
Resources for practicing school health professionals
    (Health in Action), and policy resolutions of many
    school health and safety issues.

American Speech-Language-Hearing Association
http://www.asha.org/

Asthma and Allergy Foundation of America
http://www.aafa.org/

Bright Futures
http://brightfutures.aap.org/web
Resources to promote healthy behaviors; reduce
    morbidity and mortality; develop partnerships
    between health professionals, families, and com-
    munities; and improve child health outcomes.

Case Management Society of America
http://www.cmsa.org/
Site includes information on continuing education in
    fields of case management, nursing, social work,
    disease management, and rehabilitation.

Center for Health Services Financing and Managed Care
    (DHHS/HRSA)
http://www.hrsa.gov/financeMC/

Center for Mental Health in Schools.
http://smhp.psych.ucla.edu/
Resources, technical assistance, and continuing education
    on topics related to mental health in schools, with
    a focus on barriers to learning and promotion of
    healthy development.

Center for School Mental Health Assistance
http://csmha.umaryland.edu/
Supports schools and communities in the development
    of programs and provides leadership and technical
    assistance to advance effective interdisciplinary
    school-based mental health programs.

Center for Health and Health Care in Schools
http://www.healthinschools.org/

Centers for Disease Control and Prevention (CDC)
http://www.cdc.gov/

Centers for Disease Control and Prevention (CDC)—
    Guidelines for School Health Programs
http://www.cdc.gov/HealthyYouth/CSHP/index.htm

Centers for Disease Control and Prevention (CDC)—
    Public Health Emergency Preparedness & Response
http://www.bt.cdc.gov/

Centers for Medicare and Medicaid Services

http://cms.hhs.gov/

Formerly Health Care Financing Administration (HCFA), administers federal child insurance programs, HIPAA (Health Insurance Portability and Accountability Act), CLIA (Clinical Laboratory Improvement Amendments), and other federal programs and policies affecting school health services.

Child Health USA

http://www.mchb.hrsa.gov/chusa02/index.htm

Annual report on the health status and service needs of American children.

Children's Bureau

http://www.acf.dhhs.gov/programs/cb/publications/ rpt_abu.htm

A federal Department of Health and Human Services agency, the Children's Bureau's Web site has a "how to report suspected child abuse" page and includes reporting contact information for most of the 50 states.

Clinical Laboratory Improvement Amendments (CLIA)

http://www.cms.hhs.gov/clia/

The objective of the CLIA program is to ensure quality laboratory testing.

Coalition for Community Schools

http://www.communityschools.org/

Coalition to bring together partners to offer a range of supports and opportunities to children, youth, families, and communities — before, during, and after school, 7 days a week.

Connect for Kids

http://www.connectforkids.org/

Resources for teachers and parents with advice from mental health professionals.

Emergency Medical Services for Children (EMS-C)

http://www.ems-c.org/

Family Educational Rights and Privacy Act (FERPA)

http://www.ed.gov/offices/OM/fpco/ferpa/

A US Department of Education Web site that describes a federal law that protects the privacy of student education records.

Federal Emergency Management Agency

http://www.FEMA.gov

Health Insurance Portability and Accountability Act (HIPAA)

http://www.cms.hhs.gov/hipaa/

Addresses the security and privacy of health data and describes national standards for electronic health care transactions and patient identifiers to be used by providers, health plans, and employers.

Healthy People 2010

http://www.healthypeople.gov/

Individuals with Disabilities Education Act (IDEA)

http://www.ed.gov/offices/OSERS/Policy/IDEA/

Massachusetts Department of Education, Department of Public Health; School Health Unit

http://www.state.ma.us/dph/fch/schoolhealth/index.htm

Example of a state resource that provides technical assistance to school health service systems.

Maternal and Child Health Bureau, Health Resources and Services Administration

http://mchb.hrsa.gov/

Includes programs, data, and resources on health and safety issues for school children.

National Assembly on School-Based Health Care

http://www.nasbhc.org/

In relation to school-based health centers, this site provides resources and support regarding advocacy, public policy, technical assistance, training, evaluation, and quality.

National Association of School Nurses

http://www.nasn.org/

Information on delivery of school health services, school nursing protocols, school health policies, federal laws, issues of confidentiality.

National Association of School Psychologists

http://www.nasponline.org/

National Asthma Education and Prevention Program

http://www.nhlbi.nih.gov/about/naepp/

National Coalition for Food Safe Schools

http://www.foodsafeschools.org/

Represents a number of national organizations, associations, and government agencies. Resources for reducing foodborne illness by improving food safety in schools.

National Maternal and Child Oral Health Resource Center

http://www.mchoralhealth.org/

Information on current and emerging public oral health issues.

National School Boards Association

http://www.nsba.org/

Includes sample school policies (including health-related), resources for school attorneys, school governance, and advocacy.

Office of School Health, University of Colorado
http://www.uchsc.edu/schoolhealth/
Includes a School Health Evaluation Services (SHES)
    site that assists schools with school health quality
    assurance issues.

PADRE Foundation
http://www.padrefoundation.org/
Foundation for pediatric and adolescent education and
    research on diabetes. Offers school health protocols.

Robert Wood Johnson Foundation
http://www.rwjf.org/

Safe Child
http://www.safechild.org
Teaches prevention of sexual, emotional, and physical
    abuse of children.

School Social Work Association of America
http://www.sswaa.org/

Society for Adolescent Medicine
http://www.adolescenthealth.org

U Mass-Simmons School Health Institute
http://www.umass.edu/umsshi/
Information on professional development programs
    designed to improve capability of school health
    personnel to deliver comprehensive health and
    human services to students.

US Department of Education
http://www.ed.gov/

US Department of Education—Office of Civil Rights
http://www.ed.gov/about/offices/list/ocr/504faq.html
Provides information on Section 504.

US Department of Education—Emergency Planning
http://www.ed.gov/emergencyplan/
This resource from the Office of Safe and Drug-Free
    Schools provides school leaders with information
    to plan for many emergencies.

◀ **Nutrition and Food Services** ▶

5-01–CLEAN, SAFE, ENJOYABLE MEAL ENVIRONMENT[1-5]

Provide clean, well-lit, and safe food service facilities with adequate space, pleasant surroundings, and supervision that enable students to enjoy the social aspects of eating.

▶ *RATIONALE*

To receive the optimal nutritional and developmental benefits of school nutrition programs and to set a good example for students to establish safe and healthy eating environments in the future, school meal time experiences must be safe and pleasant.

▶ *COMMENTARY*

The school environment has a powerful influence on student behavior. A safe, comfortable, and pleasant dining environment allows students to pay attention to what they are eating and to enjoy the social aspects of a healthy meal. The word "pleasant" is defined in this case to include noise level, which may be controlled by structural and acoustical design. Creative methods can be used to influence noise levels, such as separation from areas with clanking pots and pans, sound-absorbing window coverings that are pleasing to the eye, and encouragement of quiet socialization. Food service stations that accommodate the student population within reasonable time frames should also be provided. Tables and chairs should be of the appropriate size for students, and there should be space designed to accommodate students with special needs (eg, wheel chairs). Tables and floors need to be cleaned between meals. The physical structure of the area must be well maintained and without offensive smells. Rules for safe behavior should be set and enforced. Orders to "eat in silence," whistles, and traffic lights are not appropriate. Adequate supplies of food service equipment, size and location of the dining/kitchen area, the area's lighting, building materials, and open space should be given priority in facility renovations or new construction. Involving students in the design and decoration of the dining area will increase the environmental appeal.

▶ *RELATED GUIDELINES*

6-11, 6-13, 6-16, 7-01

RELATED LINKS

http://www.actionforhealthykids.org
http://www.asfsa.org
http://www.nfsmi.org

5-02–STANDARDS FOR FOOD SERVICE EQUIPMENT, PRACTICES[4,6]

Provide food service equipment that meets the safety and sanitary standards of Underwriter's Laboratories (UL) and NSF International, and use National Food Service Management Institute's guidelines to determine size requirements, specifications, and hygienic precautions.

▶ RATIONALE

For the safety of food service workers and to guarantee food safety, equipment must be appropriate to its purpose and setting, clean and sanitary, and well-maintained. A preventive maintenance and replacement plan also allows the district to make cost-effective, anticipatory decisions about equipment. Good personal hygiene for food service workers must be enforced.

▶ COMMENTARY

Proper equipment enables staff to prepare and serve food in the most safe and healthful manner. Underwriter's Laboratories (http://www.ul.com) is an independent, not-for-profit product safety testing organization that certifies, among other things, commercial electric cooking equipment and drinking water. Equipment, for example steamers or temperature-controlled salad bars, that display the UL label indicate a desired level of safety. All equipment must be regularly maintained so that when it is needed and utilized, it is in proper and safe working condition.

Examples of information provided by NSF International (http://www.nsf.org) and National Food Service Management Institute (http://www.nfsmi.org) are cleaning, inspection (eg, regular checks for gas line leaks in gas-powered kitchen appliances), lubrication, adjustment (eg, refrigerator and vending machine temperatures), and other basic steps to have safe food preparation and to maintain storage equipment. School administrators must hire experienced food service supervisors with knowledge of and training in maintenance of food service equipment, equipment replacement schedules, and food safety through hygienic practices.

▶ RELATED GUIDELINES

0-14, 6-03, 6-14, 6-16

▶ RELATED LINKS

http://www.ashrae.org
http://www.foodsafeschools.org
http://www.nfsmi.org
http://www.nsf.org
http://www.ul.com

5-03–FOOD SERVICES AND HEALTH EDUCATION[2,7]

Coordinate food services with classroom health education lessons to reinforce messages on healthy eating.

▶ *RATIONALE*

Education that encourages students to practice healthful eating for a healthy lifestyle may be more effective if nutrition education messages for students are reinforced within multiple components within the school environment.

▶ *COMMENTARY*

The school cafeteria provides a place for students to practice healthy eating, diet selection, and portion control. Coordinating the dining experience with classroom lessons allows students to apply critical thinking skills taught in the classroom. Nutritious diets that have faith-based restrictions or restrictions because of moral beliefs or special health needs may also be discussed. Address foods available at school cafeterias during classroom nutrition lessons. Another method of coordinating food services with health education is to encourage food service staff (eg, the district dietician) to educate teaching staff or students about healthy aspects of school meals. This may be accomplished by staff visits to classrooms or class visits to the cafeteria. Encourage inclusion of student representatives in planning the menus for school meals. Offer foods that reinforce classroom lessons and display nutrition information in the cafeteria. Student awareness and involvement can help to support the development and enforcement of school policies that make healthy foods available, such as policies described in the Centers for Disease Control and Prevention (CDC) *Guidelines for School Programs*[7] (http://www.cdc.gov), *Guidelines to Promote Lifelong Healthy Eating,* and the *School Health Policy Guide*[2] published by the National Association of State Boards of Education.

▶ *RELATED GUIDELINES*

0-01, 2-06, 2-07, 3-09

5-04–ACCESSIBLE SCHOOL-PROVIDED MEAL PROGRAM[2,5,8–10]

Offer a range of meals and snacks at school that meet the nutritional needs of the student population. Examples include school breakfast, lunch, after-school snacks, and summer food-service programs. Make families aware of food programs offered at school and keep meal programs financially accessible to families.

▶ RATIONALE

Students who miss meals or do not receive adequate nutrition have been shown to have decreased capacity to learn and participate less during class, and they may spend unnecessary time in the health office with complaints of headaches, stomachaches, lightheadedness, and generally not feeling well.

▶ COMMENTARY

School food services are designed to supplement families' efforts. Schools often face cost, space, and scheduling barriers that preclude offering all or most of these meals and snacks. Schools that are able to operate these food programs should ensure that families are aware of all that is offered and that students are linked to any financial assistance programs that may be available for food programs. Outreach efforts to inform families of school meal programs may include descriptions of these programs at open-house events, assistance from parent-teacher associations to disseminate the information, written descriptions mailed or sent home, and translations into multiple languages for parents whose primary language is not English.

If school breakfast is served too early in the morning, it may be inaccessible to some students. To resolve this situation, buses can be scheduled so that students arrive in time to participate in the breakfast program, or breakfast can be served after the beginning of the school day.

▶ RELATED GUIDELINES

1-02, 1-03, 1-06

▶ RELATED LINKS

http://www.eatright.com
http://www.asfsa.org
http://www.cdc.gov
http://www.connectforkids.org
http://www.nfsmi.org
http://www.usda.gov
http://sgreports.nlm.nih.gov/NN

5-05–MEALS: NUTRITION STANDARDS, SPECIAL NEEDS, APPEAL[1,2,7,11–17]

Plan school meal and snack programs so they are appealing and meet the US Department of Agriculture's nutritional standards.

▶ *RATIONALE*

Offering a variety of healthy foods in school meal and snack programs allows students to develop healthy eating habits and to learn to enjoy many different foods. Healthy school meals provide energy and nutrients required by children and adolescents for sound bodies and minds. Schools are required by law to offer school meals and snacks that are consistent with the federal government's Dietary Guidelines for Americans.[11]

▶ *COMMENTARY*

The Dietary Guidelines for Americans[11] stress the importance of choosing a diet that is low in saturated fat and cholesterol and moderate in total fat, choosing a variety of grains daily (especially whole grains), eating a variety of fruits and vegetables daily, and eating some low-fat dairy products each day. Menu planning should provide variety and choices and include input from students, parents, and school personnel on local, cultural, and ethnic favorites of the students. Guidelines for School Programs[7] (Guidelines to Promote Lifelong Healthy Eating) on the Internet site for the Centers for Disease Control and Prevention (CDC [http://www.cdc.gov]) should be referenced for more detailed recommendations. A tool kit for healthy school meals, which is available on the US Department of Agriculture Web site (http://www.usda.gov), includes recipes and training materials.

To the extent possible, accommodate needs of students on special diets (ie, restrictions based on vegetarian or vegan diets, faith, specific food allergies, lactose intolerance) and students whose special care needs or developmental disabilities require a modified food program.

▶ *RELATED GUIDELINES*

0-01, 0-07, 0-13, 1-01, 2-06, 4-15, 4-20, 6-13

▶ *RELATED LINKS*

http://www.actionforhealthykids.org
http://www.eatright.com
http://brightfutures.aap.org/web
http://www.cdc.gov
http://www.nfsmi.org
http://www.usda.gov
http://sgreports.nlm.nih.gov/NN

5-06—DRINKING WATER

Provide safe drinking water for students and encourage them to drink adequate amounts of water throughout the day. Fluoridated water is preferable.

▶ *RATIONALE*

Water is essential for fluid maintenance and good health, and students need access to adequate water supplies throughout the day. The water provided to students and staff must be protected from contamination.

▶ *COMMENTARY*

Water is a "no-calorie" beverage and a great alternative to high-calorie soft drinks that are so widely consumed in school. Students especially need access to water during intense physical activity or when it is very hot.

Cold water, water that tastes good, and drinking fountains that are kept clean and are located in safe areas (ie, to reduce injuries) all encourage water drinking. Fluoridated water is available in many communities' water supply. Where fluoridated water it is not available, schools should consider providing bottled water that is fluoridated (eg, in vending machines or at water coolers) because of the protection it provides against dental caries.

▶ *RELATED GUIDELINES*

3-06, 4-12, 6-03, 6-14

5-07–SCHOOL MEAL SCHEDULING[1,2,5,18]

Allow adequate time for students to eat meals consumed at school and schedule lunch periods as near the middle of the day as possible.

▶ *RATIONALE*

Students need time to eat adequate amounts of food to meet their nutritional needs, which is essential for optimal student health and academic performance. Children will enjoy their food more and may try more healthy options if they can relax, eat, and socialize without feeling rushed. Scheduling lunch at mid-day, instead of morning hours, reduces waste because students are most likely to be hungry. This also prevents transient hunger at other times of the day that can hinder attention and learning.

▶ *COMMENTARY*

Students should be allowed at least 20 minutes of actual eating time for lunch and 10 minutes for breakfast. Actual eating time begins at the time they are seated with their meals. Food served but not eaten does not contribute to nutritional health. Some students with special needs will require more time to eat. In addition to eating time, time allotment for school meal periods needs to reflect other scheduling logistics. This includes the number of students served simultaneously, the number of meal periods and serving stations, and whether meals are brought from home or provided. Schools should avoid scheduling other activities such as assemblies, tutoring, or student club/organization meetings during meal times.

It is important to schedule lunch during the middle of the day when students are most likely to consume the food. There is some evidence that if during the lunch hour, recess were to occur before eating, children would come to lunch less distracted, be hungry, and waste less food.

▶ *RELATED GUIDELINES*

0-05, 0-06, 1-01, 6-16

▶ *RELATED LINKS*

http://www.asfsa.org
http://www.cdc.gov
http://www.usda.gov
http://sgreports.nlm.nih.gov/nn

5-08—ACCESS TO FOODS OUTSIDE OF MEAL PROGRAMS[2,3,5,7,11,19–22]

Restrict or limit the sale of foods and beverages outside of the school meal program in order to promote good dietary practices. Decisions about the sale of competitive foods on campus should be based on nutritional considerations, not solely on potential for profit.

▶ *RATIONALE*

Access to foods that provide little nutritive value undermines schools' nutrition education efforts and the health and educational benefits of school meal programs.

▶ *COMMENTARY*

Places where foods and beverages are sold on school grounds often include the cafeteria, vending machines, snack bars, school stores, concession stands, fund-raising activities, meetings, and celebrations.

Appropriate limitations or even restrictions of food sold outside the school meal program in elementary schools are needed because young children sometimes lack the maturity to make healthy and safe food choices. In secondary schools, limit the sale of foods and beverages outside the school meals program until 30 minutes after the last lunch period. Whole grain foods, fruits, vegetables, water, 100% fruit juice, and milk (low-fat or nonfat; plain or flavored) are examples of foods to favor over those with poorer nutritional content. However, all food purchases outside a school's meal program may have the potential to decrease participation in the program and stigmatize the school meal program as designed for students from low-income families and, therefore, place a school's meal program in jeopardy.

▶ *RELATED GUIDELINES*

0-05, 0-06, 1-01

▶ *RELATED LINKS*

http://www.actionforhealthykids.org
http://www.cdc.gov
http://www.usda.gov

5-09–FOOD CHOICES OUTSIDE OF MEAL PROGRAMS[1,2,5,7,11,20]

Provide and promote nutritious foods and appealing food choices whenever and wherever food is offered at school, outside of school meal programs. Venues include cafeterias, on-campus stores, vending machines, sport events, and food offerings at fundraising projects.

▶ RATIONALE

Providing and encouraging the consumption of nutritious foods can help students improve the quality of their dietary intake, gain experience with a variety of foods, develop healthy eating habits, decrease the prevalence of overweight and obesity, and maximize the contribution that good nutrition has on students' readiness to learn.

▶ COMMENTARY

By establishing nutrition standards or policies for all foods offered on campuses, schools can send consistent messages to students about good nutrition and help shape social norms that influence the dietary habits of students and staff. By expanding choices offered beyond food and beverages high in fat, sodium, or added sugars, a student can practice what he or she has learned in the classroom.

Foods offered should contribute to meeting the dietary needs of students, be consistent with the Dietary Guidelines for Americans,[11] and be from the 5 major food groups of the Food Guide Pyramid (http://www.usda.gov). Restrict or limit the availability of "foods of minimal nutritional value" (FMNV [as defined under National School Lunch Program regulations]) throughout the school, and establish nutrition standards that are stronger than the FMNV definition.

School food services personnel should work with nutrition educators and with vendors to design and implement educational and marketing activities on an ongoing basis to increase students' demands for nutritious snack choices. This may involve manipulating the prices of snacks sold at school to make nutritious choices more attractive. Offer healthy food choices that match the cultural and ethnic diversity of the student population. Education and marketing could also include involving student groups in the development of campaigns to promote nutritious snacks and activities such as sponsoring contests and placing promotional signs around the school building.

▶ RELATED GUIDELINES

0-01, 0-05, 1-01, 1-04

▶ RELATED LINKS

http://www.actionforhealthykids.org
http://www.asfsa.org
http://www.cdc.gov
http://www.usda.gov

5-10–FOODS AS MARKETED ITEMS, REWARDS, PUNISHMENTS[5,7,11,23–25]

Prohibit school practices that encourage students to make unhealthy dietary choices. Such practices include campus advertising, marketing of foods and beverages that are high in fat or sodium or have added sugars, using low-nutritive foods to reward students, or withholding food as punishment.

▶ RATIONALE

Advertising and marketing less healthful food products to students and using food as a reward can encourage overconsumption and relatively unhealthy dietary choices.

▶ COMMENTARY

School-business partnerships should meet identified educational needs, not solely commercial motives. Schools should refrain from promoting products to students that result in consumption of foods that do not conform to the recommendations of the Dietary Guidelines for Americans.[11] To do so risks contradicting healthy eating messages that students receive elsewhere at school and raises ethical questions about advertising and business involvement in the school.

Food should not be used as a reward. By providing food as a reward for good behavior, some children learn to use food for comfort and consolation, which can lead to overeating and obesity.

▶ RELATED GUIDELINES

1-01, 1-04, 7-08

▶ RELATED LINKS

http://www.actionforhealthykids.org
http://www.cdc.gov
http://sgreports.nlm.nih.gov/NN

CHAPTER REFERENCES

1. American School Food Service Association. *Keys to Excellence: Standards of Practice for Nutrition Integrity.* Alexandria, VA: American School Food Service Association; 1995

2. Bogden JF. *Fit, Healthy, and Ready to Learn: A School Health Policy Guide. Part I: Physical Activity, Healthy Eating, and Tobacco-Use Prevention.* Alexandria, VA: National Association of State Boards of Education; 2000

3. Caldwell D, Nestle M, Rogers W. School nutrition services. In: Marx E, Wooley SF, eds. *Health is Academic: A Guide to Coordinated School Health Programs.* New York, NY: Teachers College Press, 1998:195–223

4. Silberberg SC. *The New Design Handbook for School Food Service.* Hattiesburg, MS: National Food Service Management Institute; 1997

5. US Food and Nutrition Service. *Changing the Scene: Improving the School Nutrition Environment. A Guide to Local Action.* Washington, DC: US Department of Agriculture; 2000

6. Nettles MF, Carr DH. *Guidelines for Equipment to Prepare Healthy Meals.* Hattiesburg, MS: National Food Service Management Institute; 1996. Publication NFSMI-R-25–96

7. Centers for Disease Control and Prevention. Guidelines for school health programs to promote lifelong healthy eating. *MMWR Morb Mortal Wkly Rep.* 1996;45(RR-9):1–41

8. 5-Star Child Nutrition Task Force. *School Breakfast for First Class Learning.* University, MS: National Food Service Management Institute, 1999

9. Dairy MAX. *Expanding Breakfast Manual and Video Kit.* Alexandria, VA: American School Food Service Association. Item #4032.

10. Cueto S. Breakfast and performance. *Public Health Nutr.* 2001;4(6A):1429–1431

11. US Department of Agriculture. *Nutrition and Your Health: Dietary Guidelines for Americans 2000.* 5th ed. Washington, DC: US Department of Agriculture; 2000

12. Dairy Council of Wisconsin. *Trimming the Fat: A Step-by-step Guide for Implementing USDA's Food-based Menu System.* Alexandria, VA: American School Food Service Association; 1996

13. Messina V, Mangels AR. Considerations in planning vegan diets: children. *J Am Diet Assoc.* 2001;101:661–669

14. Story M, ed. *Bright Futures in Practice: Nutrition.* 2nd ed. Arlington VA: National Center for Education in Maternal and Child Health; 2002

15. US Department of Agriculture, Food and Nutrition Service, Team Nutrition. *Menu Planner for Healthy School Meals.* Washington, DC: US Department of Agriculture; 1998

16. US Department of Agriculture, Food and Nutrition Service, Team Nutrition. *A Tool Kit for Healthy School Meals: Recipes & Training Materials.* Washington, DC: US Department of Agriculture; 1995

17. US Department of Health and Human Services. *Oral Health in America: A Report of the Surgeon General.* Rockville, MD: US Department of Health and Human Services, National Institute of Dental and Craniofacial Research, National Institute of Health; 2000

18. Getlinger MJ, Laughlin VT, Bell E, Akre C, Arjmandi BH. Food waste is reduced when elementary-school children have recess before lunch. *J Am Diet Assoc.* 1996;96:906–908

19. American Dietetic Association. Local support for nutrition integrity in schools — Position of the American Dietetic Association. *J Am Diet Assoc.* 2000;100:108–111

20. Story M, Neumark-Sztainer D. Competitive foods in schools: issues, trends, and future directions. *Top Clin Nutr.* 1999;15:37–46

21. Stuhldreher WL, Koehler AN, Harrison MK, Deel H. The West Virginia standards for school nutrition. *J Child Nutr Manage.* 1998;22:79–86

22. US Department of Agriculture, Food and Nutrition Information Center. *Food Guide Pyramid.* Washington, DC: US Department of Agriculture; 1997

23. Baxter SD. Are elementary schools teaching children to prefer candy but not vegetables? *J Sch Health.* 1998;68:111–113

24. Robelen EW. Commercialism in schools: supporting students or selling access. Alexandria, VA: Association for Supervision and Curriculum Development; 1998. ASCD Infobrief No. 15

25. US Department of Health and Human Services. *The Surgeon General's Call to Action to Prevent and Decrease Overweight and Obesity.* Rockville, MD: US Department of Health and Human Services, Public Health Service, Office of the Surgeon General; 2001

26. Burt BA. Fluoridation and social equity. *J Public Health Dent.* 2002;62:195–200

CHAPTER-RELATED LINKS

Action for Healthy Kids
http://www.actionforhealthykids.org
Resource for health promotion in schools with an
    emphasis on promotion of sound nutrition and
    increased physical activity.

American Dental Association
http://www.ada.org/
Offers information for teachers, students, and parents
    about preventive oral health, how to find local
    dentists, and school intervention programs.

American Dietetic Association
http://www.eatright.com
Position statements on numerous school nutrition issues.

American School Food Service Association
http://www.asfsa.org/
Information on school nutrition programs; see
    "Emporium" for specific products.

American Society of Heating, Refrigeration, and Air-
    Conditioning Engineers
http://www.ashrae.org

Bright Futures
http://brightfutures.aap.org/web
Resources to promote healthy behaviors; reduce mor-
    bidity and mortality; develop partnerships between
    health professionals, families, and communities;
    and improve child health outcomes.

Centers for Disease Control and Prevention (CDC)
http://www.cdc.gov

Centers for Disease Control and Prevention (CDC)—
    Guidelines for School Health Programs
http://www.cdc.gov/HealthyYouth/CSHP/index.htm

Centers for Disease Control and Prevention (CDC)—
    "School Health Index for Physical Activity
    and Healthy Eating: A Self Assessment &
    Planning Guide"
http://www.cdc.gov/nccdphp/dash/SHI/index.htm

Connect for Kids
http://www.connectforkids.org/
Resources for teachers and parents with advice from
    mental health professionals.

National Coalition for Food Safe Schools
http://www.foodsafeschools.org/
Represents a number of national organizations, asso-
    ciations, and government agencies. Resources
    for reducing foodborne illness by improving food
    safety in schools.

National Food Service Management Institute
http://www.nfsmi.org/
USDA Healthy School Meals Tool Kits and instructions
    on food safety are available at this site.

NSF International (formerly the National Sanitation
    Foundation)
http://www.nsf.org/
Standards development, product certification, education,
    and risk-management for public health and safety.

Society for Nutrition Education
http://www.sne.org/
Innovative strategies for nutrition education.

Underwriter's Laboratories
http://www.ul.com
Product safety testing and certification organization.

US Department of Agriculture
http://www.usda.gov/
US Department of Agriculture—"Child Nutrition
    Policy and Promotion Programs"

US Department of Agriculture—"Team Nutrition.
    A Tool Kit for Healthy School Meals: Recipes &
    Training Materials" (1995)
http://schoolmeals.nal.usda.gov/Training/
    indexexample1.html

US Department of Agriculture—Food Pyramid
http://www.nal.usda.gov/childcare/Resources/
    foodguide_pyramid.html

US Surgeon General Reports
http://sgreports.nlm.nih.gov/NN/
The Surgeon General's Call To Action To Prevent and
    Decrease Overweight and Obesity (2001)
The Surgeon General's Report on Nutrition and Health
    (1988)
The Surgeon General's Report on Nutrition and Health:
    Summary and Recommendations (1988)
Oral Health in America (2000)

◄ Physical Environment ►
and Transportation

GENERAL

6-01—ACCESSIBLE SCHOOL FACILITIES AND PROGRAMS[1-8]

Ensure that school-sponsored programs both on-site and off-site (such as field trips, vocational education work experiences, extracurricular activities, and sporting events) are accessible to all students and staff.

▶ *RATIONALE*

The provision of access to all facilities for students and staff with disabilities is necessary to comply with the Americans with Disabilities Act (ADA)[1] and other federal laws, to enhance safety for those with disabilities, to prevent injury, and to promote an inclusive environment.

▶ *COMMENTARY*

Accessibility to facilities for those with disabilities requires planning for new and renovated buildings and grounds and may require retrofitting of existing facilities. Children's height and other dimensions must be taken into account when designing or purchasing drinking fountains, toilet stalls, lavatories, sinks, and fixed or built-in seats and tables. Include accessible routes for persons to reach buildings and other spaces. Ground surfaces along accessible routes, transportation (drop-off and pick-up sites), getting from one floor to another in multiple-story buildings, and parking spaces must be considered as part of facility planning. Apply these designs to both temporary and permanent facilities—any building that is used for the public.

Public school districts must comply with ADA in all programs, including those that are open to parents or the public. Therefore, aside from classes, events such as graduation exercises, school plays, sporting events, and board of education meetings must be accessible to persons with disabilities.

Technical requirements for accessibility to buildings, facilities, and routes are well defined in the ADA of 1990.[1] The US Departments of Justice (http://www.ada.gov) and of Transportation (http://www.nhtsa.dot.gov) offer guidance and technical assistance for meeting these requirements.

▶ *RELATED GUIDELINES*

0-01, 3-03, 3-05, 3-06, 8-07

▶ *RELATED LINKS*

http://www.access-board.gov
http://www.cefpi.com
http://www.nhtsa.dot.gov
http://www.safetyzone.org
http://www.ada.gov

6-02–COMMUNICATING SAFETY POLICIES[9-12]

Communicate all safety policies to staff, students, and families. Notify parents and staff in advance of physical plant projects and other changes that might affect the health, safety, and well-being of students and staff. Inform staff, students, and families about unplanned incidents such as a chemical and biological exposure or exposure to certain communicable diseases.

▶ *RATIONALE*

Knowledge of safety policies, such as student drop-off and pick-up areas or prohibition of weapons in school, is essential to compliance. Warning parents, students, and staff about projects that affect the physical environment (eg, painting, pesticide spraying) allows persons with unusual sensitivities to be protected from harm. Having a plan to deal with an unforeseen environmental exposure reduces unnecessary delay between exposure and treatment, thereby optimizing health outcomes.

▶ *COMMENTARY*

Involve staff, students, and families in the development and revision of safety policies. Policies without clear parameters may be open to varying interpretation. Policies must be explicit, well-disseminated and explained to all those expected to abide by them. The existence of school health and safety teams with well-defined roles and clear reporting mechanisms can help clarify communication and improve the accuracy, approval, and acceptance of messages.

Projects that benefit from advanced notification include painting, renovation, pesticide application, and removal of mold or asbestos. Schools have a responsibility not only to minimize students' exposure but also to alert their families to the potential for exposure. Students with special health needs such as allergy or asthma who might be unusually susceptible can receive additional protection. When a school cannot predict an unusual environmental event, such as a chemical spill on a nearby highway, the school should consult with emergency personnel about the best ways to protect students (Guideline 4-11). School staff should notify students' families and health professionals of any such exposure and report the substance involved, signs and symptoms to watch for, and how to seek any necessary health care.

Adoption of a plan that addresses environmental concerns will assist the district in responding to them quickly and appropriately. Principles and goals of "risk communication" should be considered when designing a notification mechanism. This helps ensure that heath and safety messages are accurate and clearly understood by families, students, and staff. Parents with limited literacy or limited understanding of the English language must also be considered in this plan. The district should have knowledgeable personnel and/or consultants available to assist with investigations and to assist district personnel in developing the plan. The Agency for Toxic Substances and Disease Registry (http://www.atsdr.cdc.gov) provides information on various toxic substances and on principles to use when communicating the risk of these substances to the public.

▶ *RELATED GUIDELINES*

0-06, 0-09, 1-02, 1-03, 4-11, 4-22, 4-24

▶ *RELATED LINKS*

http://www.atsdr.cdc.gov

http://www.childrenssafetynetwork.org

http://www.ems-c.org

http://www.epa.gov

http://www.mchb.hrsa.gov

http://www.safetyzone.org

◀ Physical Environment ▶ and Transportation

SAFETY PRECAUTIONS BY LOCATION

6-03–BUILDINGS: CONSTRUCTION AND RENOVATION[11,13–19]

Comply with local and state policies that address the design and specifications for new schools and that address construction and renovation projects. Use current professional engineering, public health, scientific, accessibility, and safety guidelines. Plan and implement projects so that workers' and occupants' exposure to environmental hazards is eliminated or minimized and comply with the US Environmental Protection Agency (http://www.cefpi.com) guidelines for air quality and school design.

▶ *RATIONALE*

Designing and building schools as well as improving existing systems and buildings so that they provide a healthy and safe indoor and outdoor environment can prevent health and safety problems for occupants. Schools that are appropriately designed, constructed, and maintained can reduce operations and maintenance costs. Construction and renovation often disturb existing materials or introduce new materials, thereby generating unsafe quantities of particulates, gases, and vapors, which result in poor indoor air quality.

▶ *COMMENTARY*

Safety of a school environment must consider fire, earthquake, and other safety codes (eg, adequate stairways and exits, safety glass), thermal comfort controls, humidification and dehumidification systems, moisture protection measures, and building commissioning. Opt for energy efficiency and environmentally friendly materials and consider the energy absorbing properties of chosen materials. The design and construction of a healthy and safe school environment must also specifically consider school-site selection (based on transportation needs such as walking and biking paths), accessibility standards (ie, accommodating disabilities), safe surfacing (eg, playgrounds, hypoallergenic indoor flooring), and source control measures in areas such as science laboratories and vocational technical areas. Supplies of hot and cold water sources for sinks and toilets should be adequate and located strategically to promote hygiene (eg, near food preparation areas, in rooms where students receive medical procedures, in toileting areas, in classrooms where chemical exposure may require flushing with water). Drinking fountain locations should promote water drinking but be protected from traffic to avoid oral injuries. Design classrooms, media centers, and libraries with good lighting and acoustics. Stairways, hallways, and restrooms should also be well-lit.

In the design stage of a construction and renovation project, strategic plans should be implemented to minimize and eliminate potential exposures to various environmental hazards to workers and occupants. These strategies include but are not limited to: work site isolation, safety practices, indoor air quality-friendly products and materials selection, construction methods, activities scheduling, good housekeeping practices, and project updates and communications. Federal and state regulatory requirements apply to renovations that disturb certain highly regulated substances, such as asbestos-containing materials and lead paint. Renovations in occupied buildings should only be undertaken after the strategic plans have been agreed to by all parties including the school administration, contract administrators, contractors, parents, students, and other interested parties and after obtaining necessary regulatory approval.

▶ *RELATED GUIDELINES*

5-06

▶ *RELATED LINKS*

http://www.aia.org
http://www.ashrae.org
http://www.cehn.org
http://www.csinet.org
http://www.cefpi.rg
http://www.epa.gov
http://www.nist.gov
http://www.safetyzone.org
http://www.cpsc.gov

6-04–BUILDINGS AND GROUNDS: MAINTENANCE[1,3,11,12,15,16,19–28]

Develop and implement comprehensive preventive maintenance procedures to ensure a healthy and safe environment within the building and on school grounds. Include staff training and have procedures that include playgrounds, sports areas, and bathroom facilities.

▶ RATIONALE

A comprehensive preventive maintenance program can avert significant and premature deterioration of the building, its systems, and its playgrounds that could lead to compromised health and safety of students and staff.

▶ COMMENTARY

An environmental safety review of buildings and grounds should be done at least annually. Proper attention to the maintenance of the heating, ventilating, and air-conditioning systems, building envelope (roofs, walls, windows, flooring, subflooring), and housekeeping will improve indoor air quality and energy efficiency and will reduce costs and level of custodial effort to keep the building clean. The maintenance plan should include consideration of weather related problems, such as water on floors in rainy/snowy weather. Maintenance should also include procedures for maintaining safety on school grounds, including playground surfaces and equipment. Have schedules to inspect equipment and repair items not in compliance with US Consumer Product Safety Commission (http://www.cpsc.gov) guidelines.

Cover trash containers to keep out rainwater and remove waste on a regular schedule to prevent noxious odors and environmental reservoirs for disease. Open trash containers with decaying organic materials (scraps of food, for example) attract flies and other vermin that can carry bacteria and viruses to food sources and to humans directly. Cockroaches and rodents can also be vectors of disease.

Toilet facilities must be maintained to be both hygienic and safe. Areas of privacy must be provided (eg, stall doors that are intact and operational). Adequate supplies of soap, toilet tissue, and paper towels must be maintained. Students should not be discouraged from utilizing toilet facilities for reasons of cleanliness or safety.

Require that an experienced maintenance supervisor develop inspection and maintenance procedures, including a detailed preventive maintenance schedule for all equipment, grounds, and facilities. School administrators must be aware of estimated labor-hours to complete all preventive maintenance activities and have a budget to meet those needs.

▶ RELATED GUIDELINES

3-06, 7-01

▶ RELATED LINKS

http://www.ashrae.org
http://www.cehn.org
http://www.epa.gov
http://www.safetyzone.org
http://www.cpsc.gov

6-05—CLASSROOM SAFETY: EQUIPMENT, FACILITIES, STUDENT CONDUCT [3-8,29-35]

Teach students safety practices, ensure safe conduct, and enforce use of applicable safety guards and protection devices in classrooms. Provide appropriate supervision, safe equipment, and safe facilities. Apply these principles to vocational education settings, to youth employment situations, and to all art, science, food preparation, industrial arts, and shop classes.

▶ RATIONALE

Safety education, safe practices, and supervision, when enforced through school policy in science and shop classes, art courses, classes where there is food preparation, and vocational education classes, will prevent serious injuries to staff and students.

▶ COMMENTARY

A coordinated effort to review safety needs as well as to revise and maintain safety protocols in these classes should be implemented through representatives from vocational education, science, and art. Class safety rules should be developed and taught to students. Students should sign a contract at the beginning of the term agreeing to follow the rules. Provide adequate supervision. Inspection checklists should be used in shop and vocational education classes.

Chemicals are of particular concern in classrooms. It is recommended that chemicals be stored by their chemical family rather than alphabetically to minimize dangerous interactions. Dispose of chemicals that are on the banned substance list, are out of date, or are in unlabeled containers. Material safety data sheets (MSDSs) should be available to staff and students for each chemical stored and/or used in the school setting.

Certification programs, continuing education, and educational supplies that pertain to the prevention of injuries in these classes are available.[8] A publication of the American Chemical Society[29] and an Internet site called "The Catalyst" (http://www.thecatalyst.org [a resource for science teachers]) provide detailed safety information pertaining to chemistry, biology, and physics in the school classroom. Guidelines on work space per student, eye protection, fire prevention, and protection from injuries in physics experiments that involve electricity, motion, energy, heat, and sound are available at this Web site. Inspections by the US Occupational Safety and Health Administration (http://www.osha.gov) may be considered in order to verify compliance with meeting safety standards for staff.

Youth who are employed, particularly those who work as part of school-to-work programs or vocational training, require knowledge of safety practices (Guideline 2-06) and the skills to recognize and avoid unsafe work-site situations. Safety issues for students related to sport and physical activity are covered in Guideline 3-05 and Guideline 3-09.

▶ RELATED GUIDELINES

2-06, 3-03, 3-05, 3-09, 3-10, 5-02

▶ *RELATED LINKS*

http://www.thecatalyst.org

http://www.childrenssafetynetwork.org

http://www.keepschoolssafe.org

http://www.nist.gov

http://www.safetyzone.org

http://www.nagcat.org

http://www.osha.gov

▶

6-06—SAFETY ON OUT-OF-SCHOOL TRIPS[3,36–38]

Develop and implement plans to address the safety of students on school-sponsored, out-of-school trips (field trips). Policy should address: supervision of students, transportation to sites, student-specific health information, equipment and expertise required to implement students' individualized health service plans (including administration of medication), and behavioral expectations of students and supervisors.

▶ RATIONALE

Schools are responsible for students and their safety at any school-sponsored event, on or off school grounds.

▶ COMMENTARY

Adequate supervision of students must be planned in advance of each trip and must take into consideration students' health, mental health, and safety needs. This includes having students accompanied by staff who are trained to administer medications, perform first-aid, and observe for health problems (for example, recognizing symptoms of asthma or observing that a student with diabetes has eaten lunch). Arrangements to transport health-related equipment must be made. A responsible adult on the trip should have a copy of each student's emergency information card. Information must include emergency contact information and key health information that will be needed in an emergency.

Encourage the use of school vehicles driven by appropriately trained and licensed school employees, not private vehicles, when the school district provides transportation to school-sponsored events. When private vehicles must be used, require operators to be licensed drivers of the type of vehicle driven, carry insurance for occupants of their vehicles, require occupants to wear safety belts, and follow state regulations for inspection and registration for the vehicle.

Behavioral expectations may include, for example, making one's location known at all times; avoidance of tobacco, alcohol, and illicit drugs (see Guideline 6-11, Guideline 6-12); and housing males and females in separate sleeping quarters.

▶ RELATED GUIDELINES

4-02, 4-07, 4-20

▶ RELATED LINKS

http://www.nhtsa.dot.gov

6-07—SAFE PEDESTRIAN AND VEHICLE TRAFFIC AREAS[3,39-44]

Establish and enforce a plan that is designed to provide safe movement of motorized vehicles, nonmotorized vehicles, and pedestrian traffic on school property. Include all parking, pedestrian, and vehicle traffic areas, bicycle lanes, and student drop-off/pick-up areas. Apply the policy to staff and students driving on campus and to recreational and commercial service vehicles. The plan should encourage walking and/or bicycling to school and include the establishment of safe routes to school.

▶ RATIONALE

Multiple modes of transportation at school as well as transportation to and from school and school-sponsored activities put students and staff at some risk of collision. Proper planning, development and enforcement of standards, and education can decrease risk of collision and injury.

▶ COMMENTARY

Enforce all state and local vehicle regulations (even for school campuses considered to be private property), including occupant protection (safety belts) and helmets for all-terrain vehicles (ATVs) and motorized cycles. Nonmotorized vehicle safety issues are addressed in Guideline 6-19. All motorized vehicles, including motorcycles, ATVs, and trucks, should be operated only by licensed drivers. Prohibit carrying of passengers on motorcycles, ATVs, and in the cargo beds of pickup trucks. Carefully restrict traffic in all loading and unloading zones during school hours.

Route vehicular traffic onto schools' driveways and parking lots to minimize danger to pedestrians. Protect pedestrian paths from bicyclists and students using skates, skate boards, and scooters (eg, separate lanes). Protect users of these nonmotorized recreational vehicles from motorized vehicle traffic. Playgrounds should be located away from traffic. Have clearly marked and separate drop-off and pickup areas for pedestrians, school bus riders, and private vehicle users. Situate them so as to reduce student and staff exposure to vehicle exhaust fumes. Pickup and drop-off points for students should be limited to the curb and preferably at an off-street location that is protected from traffic. Ensure adequate supervision while students are boarding and exiting vehicles. Be certain that crossing guards and members of safety patrols are trained for these roles. Discourage the playing of car radios and public announcement systems in vehicles used to transport students. Communicate all policies to staff, students, and their families.

Conduct a school transportation safety assessment when considering where to build new schools. Assess whether areas have adequate road capacity to handle increased traffic, adequate sidewalks, bicycle lanes, places for school bus stops, and low crime rates that make walking safe. Efforts should be coordinated with appropriate jurisdictional authority to provide well-posted and enforced reduced-speed school zones around campuses. The National Highway Traffic Safety Administration (http://www.nhtsa.dot.gov) and CDC's National Center for Chronic Disease Prevention[39] provide tools and checklists for "walkability" and "bikeability" in communities, as well as suggestions on how to remove barriers that keep students from walking and bicycling to school.

▶ *RELATED GUIDELINES*

0-05, 1-05, 1-06, 3-04

▶ *RELATED LINKS*

http://www.ashrae.org
http://statehighwaysafety.org
http://www.nhtsa.dot.gov
http://www.bicyclinginfo.org

6-08—PLAYGROUND SAFETY[1,3,18,24,45–50]

Use and monitor the use of the most updated US Consumer Product Safety Commission (CPSC) and ASTM International guidelines for playground safety. Use the guidelines to address playground surfacing, the use and maintenance of equipment, and supervision.

▶ RATIONALE

Research has shown that many playgrounds fail to meet CPSC and other safety guidelines and standards. Following guidelines greatly reduces risks of injury to students and others who use the facilities.

▶ COMMENTARY

Students must be taught to play safely. Falling from playground structures and colliding with equipment or other students can result in head, face, oral, and other musculoskeletal injuries. More than 200 000 playground injuries are reported each year in the United States. Approximately 75% of these injuries are attributable to falls, mostly from slides, jungle gyms, and other climbing equipment. Other causes of injury include running into equipment, various collisions, burns from hot surfaces or equipment, and strangulation. Student conduct related to playground safety must be also be addressed (Guideline 3-09).

Schools should follow CPSC (http://www.cpsc.gov) and ASTM International safety guidelines to prevent these types of injuries to students. ASTM International (http://www.astm.org) was formerly known as the American Society for Testing and Materials. Guidelines are fairly specific (eg, do not wear bicycle helmets on play equipment, details on equipment hardware, inspections for sharp edges) and there are multiple ways to retrieve this information (eg, videos, checklists, brochures, instruction books). Major focus areas include separation of playground areas for different age groups, installation and maintenance of safe and developmentally appropriate equipment, use of appropriate surface materials, appropriate fall zone areas, and adequate supervision at all times. Playground equipment and play surfaces should be inspected and maintained. Records should be kept of all playground injuries and reviewed. Injury data should be carefully analyzed and used to guide preventive, intervention, and education strategies. Inspections should take place on at least an annual basis (more often depending on life of equipment and surfaces, such as plastic equipment) and adjustments should be made on the basis of injury cause data, updated guidelines, and repair records.

▶ RELATED GUIDELINES

3-05, 3-06, 3-09, 3-10, 7-07

▶ RELATED LINKS

http://www.access-board.gov
http://www.astm.org
http://www.childrenssafetynetwork.org
http://injuryfree.org/safety.cfm
http://www.uni.edu/playground
http://www.safeusa.org/school/safescho.htm
http://www.cpsc.gov

◀ Physical Environment ▶ and Transportation

PROTECTION FROM SPECIFIC ENVIRONMENTAL AGENTS

6-09—EXPOSURE TO TOXIC/POISONOUS SUBSTANCES IN CLASSROOMS[3,13–15,20,25,29,51,52]

Prohibit the use of toxic and poisonous substances as part of classroom or vocational education unless there is a clearly documented need that cannot be otherwise met and there are protocols and procedures in place to protect students and staff from toxin exposure. Communicate policies on acceptable and unacceptable substances to students, staff, and families.

▶ RATIONALE

Ingestion, inhalation, or other misuse of potentially toxic substances, whether intentional or unintentional, can be prevented. By adopting policies that reduce access, schools and districts can avoid harmful consequences, such as poisoning and burns.

▶ COMMENTARY

Art, theater, shop, vocational courses, science courses, and other courses that require the use of toxic substances, such as paints, solvents, wood dust, and other chemicals, require ventilation systems that are found within the American Conference of Governmental Industrial Hygienists (ACGIH [http://www.acgih.org])[13,51] guidelines. The ACGIH systems, which consider industrial workers' exposures at the "threshold limit value" (TLV), must be designed to meet the American Society of Heating, Refrigerating, and Air-Conditioning Engineers (ASHRAE [http://www.ashrae.org]) standard of 1/10 of the TLV or lower.[14,15,20] Inspections should be performed at least annually for expired chemicals and/or damaged containers, which should be removed and disposed of properly.

Ceramic kilns can be used if they are vented sufficiently and only a teacher or other trained adult is potentially exposed to the heat, kiln wash, etc. Ceramic glazes, either leaded or lead-free, and processes or chemicals requiring ventilation should not be used in elementary schools. For older students in classes such as chemistry, substances should be properly stored and used with supervision. In areas in which students through age 8 may have access, potentially toxic substances should be stored in a locked cabinet.

Poison control and emergency assistance numbers should be clearly posted by all telephones. Poison control and emergency assistance numbers are 800-222-1222 and 911, respectively. Staff and students should be trained in proper response to poisonings and toxic exposures.

▶ RELATED GUIDELINES

0-07, 4-07, 4-11, 4-24

▶ RELATED LINKS

http://www.aapcc.org
http://www.acgih.org
http://www.ashrae.org

6-10—LIVE ANIMALS IN SCHOOL ENVIRONMENT [3,15,28,35,53–56]

Limit exposure to live animals in order to protect the health and safety of students and staff.

▶ *RATIONALE*

Students in schools should not have access to live animals that may pose a threat to safety and health.

▶ *COMMENTARY*

Exposure to live animals places students at risk of animal bites, allergic reactions, and infection from animal vectors. Furred and feathered animals are common triggers for students with allergies and asthma. Reptiles are frequent carriers of infectious diseases. Access to all animals on school property should be limited so that no animal roams freely.

Animals should be eliminated from regular classrooms. Animals necessary for certain curricula, such as biology or animal husbandry/vocational-agricultural programs, should be carefully confined in suitable, sanitary, self-contained enclosures appropriate to the size of the animal. Staff must be responsible for ensuring that enclosures are kept in a sanitary condition. Prior to introducing any animals into the classroom, school staff must verify that students and school personnel have no known allergy to that animal and that animals are free from any diseases or parasites. Animals must present no physical danger to students and contact should be limited to instructional purposes. Students must be fully supervised during all points of animal contact.

▶ *RELATED GUIDELINES*

2-06

RELATED LINKS

http://www.lungusa.org
http://www.epa.gov

6-11—TOBACCO USE POLICY[22,27,57–59]

Develop and enforce policies that prohibit tobacco use on school property by all students, school staff, families, and visitors. This policy should include school vehicles and any school-sponsored indoor or outdoor event.

▶ RATIONALE

Environmental tobacco smoke exposure is a well-recognized health hazard for children and adolescents. Tobacco smoke is associated with serious adverse health effects, including bronchitis, emphysema, exacerbation of asthma, lung cancer, heart disease, and many other illnesses.

▶ COMMENTARY

States and/or school districts typically ban smoking inside schools as well as on school grounds for teachers, staff, and students to minimize students' opportunities to smoke and their exposure to environmental smoke. Studies show that restrictions on smoking may help young persons refrain from starting to smoke. Pipes, cigars, chewing tobacco, and any tobacco product should be included in this policy. Tobacco cessation programs should be offered to all who use tobacco.

▶ RELATED GUIDELINES

2-06, 5-01, 8-03

▶ RELATED LINKS

http://www.lungusa.org
http://www.cdc.gov/tobacco

6-12–DRUG/ALCOHOL-FREE SCHOOL POLICY[60,61]

Develop and enforce alcohol-free and drug-free policies for all school staff, families, students, and visitors at indoor and outdoor school-sponsored events.

▶ RATIONALE

Substances that can impair function and compromise the safety of students and staff must not be allowed on school property or at school-sponsored events. It is illegal for students to purchase, possess, and utilize such substances.

▶ COMMENTARY

An alcohol and drug-free policy still permits staff and students to use prescribed medications during the school day in order to maintain their health. Illicit use of drugs, including tobacco and alcoholic beverages, cannot be tolerated on school property. Failure to comply with these policies should result in disciplinary action and referral to appropriate treatment programs. While expulsion from school may seem to be appropriate, it may aggravate the student's problem rather than help move towards a solution.

Alternate education and therapeutic intervention programs can provide a more acceptable solution and ensure that students receive necessary treatment.

A policy addressing staff using alcohol or other drugs while driving vehicles used to transport students must be in place to ensure the safety of all (Guideline 6-21). Employees found to be using alcohol and illicit drugs must be immediately removed from such duty and appropriate referrals for evaluation and treatment should be made.

▶ RELATED GUIDELINES

2-06, 8-03, 8-05

6-13—INDOOR/OUTDOOR ALLERGENS, IRRITANTS, AIR QUALITY[11,12,17,62-67]

Develop and enforce policies that minimize exposure to indoor and outdoor allergens and irritants for students and staff.

▶ *RATIONALE*

Reducing exposure to allergic triggers is a school's responsibility. Enforcing policies helps to prevent life-threatening events and to keep students and staff with sensitivities free of symptoms and better able to carry out their academic functions.

▶ *COMMENTARY*

Allergies to foods, insect stings, medications, and latex puts approximately 3% of students at risk of severe allergic reactions. Dust mites, pollen, cockroach droppings, molds, animal saliva, urine, and dander are common allergic triggers that cause less severe reactions. Asthma can be exacerbated by these allergens, by tobacco smoke, and by strong odors. Include specific environmental precautions in allergic students' individualized health services plans. On days with high pollen counts and/or pollution levels (eg, smog, ozone), physical activities for sensitive individuals may need to be conducted in a controlled indoor environment (Appendix E). Retrofit buses and reduce idling to minimize students' exposure to vehicle emissions. Use vinyl or nitrile gloves, rather than latex, in handling food, in laboratories, and in caring for special-needs children.

To decrease fungal and pollen exposure in mechanically ventilated buildings, keep windows closed and use efficient filters. Periodically disinfect locker rooms because fungi often grow in moist environments. Regulate the relative humidity of the air (eg, via insulation, dehumidification, source control, temperature control). Unless carpeting is necessary and unless its composition and schedule of maintenance minimize dust, mold, and chemical irritants, consider hard surfaces instead of carpets. Avoid unnecessary accumulation of materials in classrooms and hallways that collect dust and harbor molds.

Limit exposure to animal allergens by minimizing animal presence in classrooms (Guideline 6-10). Weigh risk of allergen exposure against risk of pesticide exposure. Implement pest control strategies (eg, rats, mice, cockroaches, flies, mosquitoes) by controlling food sources and moisture and by using specific pesticides or other "integrated pest management" methods. Recognize that many staff and students are in contact with animals and carry allergens on their clothing to school. Do not require students with certain animal allergies to take field trips to zoos or farms or to be exposed to animals (eg, science projects). Because school renovations that produce dust can aggravate asthma, schedule renovations when students are not present.

Some districts prohibit all students from bringing a food item to school (eg, nuts) when a fellow student is allergic. Although this is one management strategy and proves useful on celebratory occasions when food is brought from homes, it is difficult to enforce, often provides a false sense of security, and is not recommended by the Food Allergy and Anaphylaxis Network (http://www.foodallergy.org). Setting aside a meal table for selected food allergic students is more restrictive but generally safer than relying on all students' parents to read food labels for hidden allergic ingredients. In addition to the allergic child, educate all students, lunch monitors, and other staff on ingredient avoidance. Prohibit sharing of foods and eating on buses. Keep potential allergic foods, such as those with nuts as an ingredient, off of school food service menus and out of vending machines.

▶ *RELATED GUIDELINES*

1-03, 3-06, 5-01, 5-05

▶ *RELATED LINKS*

http://www.cehn.org
http://www.epa.gov
http://www.foodallergy.org
http://www.dehs.umn.edu/iaq/fungus/links.html
http://www.foodsafeschools.org
http://www.dehs.umn.edu/iaq/school

6-14—RESERVOIRS OF INFECTIOUS AGENTS IN PHYSICAL ENVIRONMENT[13,51,68–71]

Control the indoor and outdoor school environment to prevent potential reservoirs for infectious agents from becoming a source of disease (eg, standing water and animal droppings).

▶ RATIONALE

Diseases caused by environmental source infectious agents can be life threatening. Preventive maintenance and control of the environment are relatively straightforward, effective, and essential.

▶ COMMENTARY

Infectious agents (eg, bacteria, fungi) are always present in the air, on environmental surfaces, and as part of contact with other persons. Bioaerosols are microscopic organisms in the air we breathe, are always present in the environment, and pose no problems when kept within reasonable limits. Although bacteria cause many odors in indoor environments (eg, human body odor, locker room odors, sour milk), exposure to such bacteria is rarely harmful.

Rarely, specific infectious agents can become so populous that they pose a particular health risk. When excessively concentrated bioaerosols are inhaled, they can cause disease. The most serious risks are to immunologically compromised individuals. There are many examples: humidifiers may harbor bacteria and cause pneumonia, rhinitis (ie, runny nose), and other respiratory infections; accumulation of bird droppings (feces) can carry infectious fungi (eg, *Histoplasmosis* species, *Cryptococcosis* species); and human contact with rodent droppings can lead to hantavirus infection; human contact with parasites and bacteria in feces of cats, dogs, fowl, and reptiles can cause diseases such as toxoplasmosis and salmonellosis. Untreated water reservoirs can release bioaerosols or attract disease-transmitting insects (eg, mosquitoes), which may increase the risk of West Nile virus infection, legionellosis, and malaria.

Birds, mice, rats, and bats should not be allowed to colonize in attics, air intakes, or other areas near schools where people are likely to be exposed to fecal aerosols. Utilize methods to discourage migrating birds from congregating on school grounds. Any accumulated bird or rodent droppings should be treated to kill disease-causing organisms and then removed when the building is unoccupied.

Regularly clean ventilation systems and carpets. Prevent build-up of dirt and moisture. Immediately attend to unusual situations that could result in bioaerosol problems (eg, wet carpets). Stagnant water should not be allowed to collect in ventilation system drain pans. Aerosol humidifiers should not be used in schools unless specific cleaning protocols are followed for preventing growth of infectious agents. Keep trash cans tightly covered and keep rain gutters clear of obstruction to prevent accumulation of standing water, a breeding ground for mosquitoes.

The National Center for Infectious Diseases Web site (http://www.cdc.gov/ncidod/diseases)[68] has resources that are disease-specific (eg, salmonellosis, West Nile virus infection, etc) and provides tips on disease prevention through management of the physical environment, such as preventing accumulation of standing water and taking caution with animal feces. The American

Conference of Governmental Industrial Hygienists (http://www.acgih.org)[13] has resources targeted to building managers, such as school custodians.

► **RELATED GUIDELINES**

4-22, 4-24, 5-02, 5-06

► **RELATED LINKS**

http://www.acgih.org
http://www.cdc.gov/ncidod/diseases

6-15—UNIVERSAL PRECAUTIONS; BLOODBORNE PATHOGENS[64,65,72–74]

Provide school staff with education on the safe handling of blood, vomit, urine, other body fluids, and fecal material. Provide ample and convenient supplies of gloves, containers for proper disposal of needles and other sharp objects, disinfectants (including bleach), and other equipment in identified, predetermined locations, including classrooms.

▶ RATIONALE

Staff trained in procedures to handle potential exposure to bloodborne pathogens and other infectious agents minimizes risk to students and other staff and alleviates unnecessary anxiety. Transmission of hepatitis B virus, hepatitis C virus, human immunodeficiency virus (HIV), cytomegalovirus, and other viruses is readily preventable through the use of basic protocols. A bloodborne pathogen exposure control plan for schools is mandated by the Occupational Safety and Health Administration (http://www.osha.gov).

▶ COMMENTARY

Sport and playground injuries, severe bites, used needles, and many other occurrences in school can expose students and staff to bloodborne pathogens. "Universal precautions" refers to a set of protocols for handling body fluids properly (ie, blood, saliva, urine, vomit). Body substance isolation (BSI) is an acceptable and alternative set of procedures to universal precautions and differs primarily in that this includes handling of all body fluids and substances.

Universal precautions include: hand washing, avoiding punctures, utilizing gloves when handling body fluids, using containers with plastic liners to dispose of contaminated tissues, having special containers for disposing of contaminated sharp objects, promptly washing blood and other human fluids from skin, and cleaning hard surfaces with a disinfectant (eg, diluted household bleach).

Gloves, disinfectants, and containers to dispose of contaminated materials should be made available throughout the school for easy access. Vinyl and nitril (or nitrile) gloves have less risk than latex for allergic reaction. Nitril gloves have been shown to provide comparable pathogen protection to latex gloves. Masks are required for procedures where splattering to the face is a risk. Good hand washing technique is essential for preventing the spread of disease and should be taught to all staff and students. Adequate facilities for hand washing that should be available throughout all school facilities include warm water, soap or detergent, towels, waste receptacles, and posted signs to instruct on hand washing technique.

▶ RELATED GUIDELINES

4-21, 4-24, 4-26, 5-02, 8-02

▶ RELATED LINKS

http://www.cdc.gov/niosh/sharps1.html
http://www.osha.gov

6-16—HAND WASHING[68,75-77]

Encourage frequent hand washing with warm water and soap for students and staff in order to prevent or reduce the spread of communicable diseases.

▶ **RATIONALE**

Thorough hand washing with warm water and soap is the most effective way to prevent and avoid communicable disease.

▶ **COMMENTARY**

Students and staff should be encouraged to wash their hands with soap and warm water before consuming any food and after the use of the toilet or assisting others with toilet needs. To help prevent disease transmission, health services staff should educate students and staff on the importance of hand washing after nose-wiping, before preparing foods, before eating, and after using the toilet.

Schools should be equipped with adequate facilities and supplies. Adequate facilities for hand washing include warm water, soap, waste receptacles, and posted signs to instruct on hand washing technique. Schools with automatic shutoff water faucets should ensure that water runs for at least 30 seconds to provide adequate time for effective hand washing. Soap dispensers and towel dispensers should be checked daily or more often to be certain they are replenished and functioning.

Waterless hand cleaner should be used when running water is not available but not to replace soap and water when running water is available.

▶ **RELATED GUIDELINES**

2-06, 4-22, 5-02

▶ **RELATED LINKS**

http://www.cdc.gov/ncidod/diseases

◀ Physical Environment ▶ and Transportation

TRANSPORTATION SAFETY

6-17—A PLAN FOR SAFE SCHOOL BUS TRANSPORTATION[1,43,44,78–82]

Develop and implement a plan that promotes safety for bus transportation. Include driver qualifications, student and bus driver transportation equipment, emergency provisions and plans, loading/unloading procedures, staff-child ratios, vehicle maintenance schedules and provisions for special events, special routes, and procedures for children with special needs. Follow legal guidelines as well as local and state regulations and laws.

▶ *RATIONALE*

A transportation plan provides a process for schools to determine needs of students and drivers. Adherence to a transportation plan that is designed to optimize safety will protect staff and students from harm, prevent injuries, and help to avoid delays.

▶ *COMMENTARY*

Federal, state, and local regulations and policies must be implemented, enforced, and augmented by best practices to ensure optimal safety. For loading and unloading, have students do the following: stand at least 10 feet from the edge of the road, wait for driver's permission to load, take caution against catching clothing and drawstrings on bus handrails when exiting, and cross in front of bus where they can be seen by the driver.

Drivers need communication devices so they can communicate to a central dispatcher in the event of an emergency or atypical situation. Provide equipment for students with special health care needs. Safety seats and restraints, wheelchairs, and wheelchair tie-down systems must meet the specific safety needs of students of various heights, weights and positional needs. Inspect these regularly and make needed repairs.

Ensure that transportation needs specified in students' individualized plans are met. Train personnel and familiarize them with procedures necessary to evacuate students in wheelchairs and child restraints as well as students with a range of behavioral and communication problems. School districts should involve police, fire, and emergency medical services personnel in evacuation training exercises. Bus routing schedules should minimize transportation time as excessive hours on a school bus can compromise sleep, study hours, and extracurricular activities. Students picked up first in the morning could be dropped off first in the afternoon.

Use only well-maintained vehicles that have passed regular and consistent inspection and comply with *National School Transportation Specifications and Procedures*.[78] Train transportation staff to address child passenger safety precautions, including use of safety restraints, handling of emergency situations, defensive driving, child supervision responsibilities, and education of students.

Take drivers' age and experience into account when hiring. Laws, rules, regulations, policies and procedures on driver qualifications, including a health and mental health assessment, are determined by each state and addressed by the National Highway Traffic Safety Administration (NHTSA [http://www.nhtsa.dot.gov]). NHTSA offers a training and certification program for child passenger safety (called "NHTSA Standardized Child Passenger Safety Technician Training and Certification Program"), which includes a module for school bus safety. NHTSA also addresses behavior management on the bus; various passenger disabilities and health conditions; securing wheeled mobility devices; transporting infants, toddlers, and preschoolers; emergency evacuation procedures; and routing and scheduling.

RELATED GUIDELINES

4-07, 4-20, 6-06

RELATED LINKS

http://statehighwaysafety.org
http://www.nhtsa.dot.gov

6-18–HEALTH INFORMATION FOR TRANSPORTATION[1,79,83–89]

Provide the transportation department and drivers with access to all health and safety information about students with special health care needs that is relevant to safe transportation, without compromising students' confidentiality.

▶ RATIONALE

Bus drivers spend large amounts of time with and have great responsibility for students with special health care needs, and they must be adequately prepared to meet these needs. Understanding what students with special health care needs may require, including information about their health care and equipment, can reduce staff anxiety and produce a safer environment for the student.

▶ COMMENTARY

Personnel on school buses should be trained in first aid and cardiopulmonary resuscitation (CPR). Health and safety information should be conveyed to the driver by the school nurse who has developed the health services plan for the student with input from the student's family.

School personnel who transport students with special health care needs must also know if certain seating and placement choices within the bus pose a health or safety risk. For example, some students will require a specific type of seat or should not be near an air conditioning vent. Staff requires access to information on management of students' particular behavioral problems (Guideline 6-20).

School personnel who transport students must have the ability to communicate with them in a manner that is comfortable, familiar, and appropriate to the student. Guidelines for staff must be specific to students' language, speech, and hearing-related communication needs so that student and transportation staff can convey relevant health and safety information to each other.

▶ RELATED GUIDELINES

0-03, 0-07, 4-07, 4-13, 4-20, 4-25

RELATED LINKS

http://www.redcross.org
http://www.nhtsa.dot.gov

6-19—BICYCLES, SKATEBOARDS, SKATES, SCOOTERS ON CAMPUS[50,90-93]

Establish and enforce policies for the safe use of all nonmotorized wheeled recreational devices on school property, including appropriate use of protective gear.

▶ RATIONALE

Safety precautions prevent and reduce injury. Head injuries are the most serious type of injury sustained by cyclists of all ages. Approved helmets, when worn properly, save lives and prevent traumatic brain injuries.

▶ COMMENTARY

Many families and schools encourage students to bicycle to school because of the benefits of regular exercise. Nonmotorized wheeled devices that students (and staff) use for transportation or recreation include bicycles, tricycles, skateboards, skates, and scooters. Safety policies need to be communicated to families, staff, and students (Guideline 6-02). Policies must include the required use of properly fitted, approved helmets and prohibitions on the carrying of passengers. In addition to helmets, require the use of other personal protection equipment such as wrist guards and knee and elbow pads. Helmets and other protective gear must be worn properly to prevent injuries.

Allow the use of wheeled nonmotorized devices on specific areas of campus and on crosswalks leading to and from the facility. Avoid use in loading and unloading zones during school hours. Wheeled nonmotorized devices should be walked, not ridden, in areas of heavy pedestrian traffic. School staff should help establish the safest routes for staff and students on bicycles (and other such vehicles) to get to school. Secure storage space should be provided for these nonmotorized wheeled devices and for helmets.

▶ RELATED GUIDELINES

2-06, 3-06, 3-10

▶ RELATED LINKS

http://www.ashrae.org
http://statehighwaysafety.org
http://injuryfree.org/safety.cfm
http://www.iisa.org
http://www.nhtsa.dot.gov
http://www.bicyclinginfo.org
http://www.cpsc.gov

6-20–SAFE STUDENT CONDUCT DURING TRANSPORTATION[3,44,94–98]

Establish and implement comprehensive training programs for staff and for students so that students demonstrate acceptable behavior during transportation and during drop-off and pickup.

▶ RATIONALE

Training transportation staff to manage student behavior can prevent serious injuries that originate with or are exacerbated by poor student conduct. Behavior management techniques, interaction with students' families, and collaboration with students' regular school programs can enhance transportation safety.

▶ COMMENTARY

Managing student behavior and having appropriate discipline are unusually challenging when students are being transported. Poor conduct can lead to vandalism, injury, and death. Transportation staff must address behavior management issues of all students who share the same vehicle, including those with special needs. Students and families must understand the rules and expectations. Safety should be the focus of student conduct, which includes: keeping passengers seated, using safety belts when available, and keeping arms and heads inside windows. Excessive noise and unsafe student behavior can distract or harm the driver, increasing the risk of a crash.

One way to enforce safe student conduct on school buses is to have additional staffing on the bus. Teach school transportation staff basic behavior management techniques (eg, how to give positive reinforcement for good behavior and discourage bad behavior). Transportation staff should have rules that are simple, realistic, and enforced fairly. Transportation staff should monitor student behavior, be consistent with their responses, and take a positive attitude and approach with students. Strong and consistent enforcement of discipline in accordance with district policy must be maintained.

Students with special health, mental health, and educational needs (including but not limited to students with primarily mental and emotional disabilities) can have individualized transportation behavior protocols written into their individualized education program. Arrange this if behavior problems are anticipated when the student's individualized education program is developed or as they arise. Individualized behavioral protocols designed to promote acceptable conduct during transportation should be developed together with students' families and with the multidisciplinary teams that are involved with students' on-site education and support. School personnel who transport students with special health care needs and behavior management problems must follow all federal regulations and school district policies related to students with special needs.

▶ RELATED GUIDELINES

0-07, 2-07, 4-20, 7-01, 7-07, 7-08, 8-06

▶ RELATED LINKS

http://www.nasponline.org
http://www.nhtsa.dot.gov

6-21—BUS DRIVERS AND ALCOHOL/DRUG USE[2,3,44,82]

Adopt and enforce a zero-tolerance, alcohol-free, and other drug-free policy for school bus drivers.

▶ RATIONALE

High rates of motor vehicle crashes are associated with alcohol and other drug impairment. School bus drivers must not be impaired by alcohol or other drugs that can affect their driving abilities and compromise the safety of students.

▶ COMMENTARY

More than 50% of all motor vehicle crashes involve alcohol. School bus drivers should be regularly tested for drugs and alcohol, and if they are found to be under the influence of alcohol or other drugs, they should immediately be fired.

Specific regulations regarding the operation of a school bus when taking medications (eg, antidepressant agents, antihypertensive agents, antihistamines) are determined at the state level. At the very least, bus drivers should be instructed not to operate school buses if initiating any medication, any new dose of a medication, or initiating any new combination of medications which may result in drowsiness, lightheadedness, or other adverse reaction that could impair ability to safely operate a school bus. If any previous experience with a medication or combination of medications has resulted in such an adverse reaction, it must not be taken within 24 hours of operating a school bus. A bus driver on a medication (over-the-counter and prescribed) should report this immediately to his/her supervisor.

▶ RELATED GUIDELINES

0-02, 8-03, 8-05

▶ RELATED LINKS

http://statehighwaysafety.org
http://www.nhtsa.dot.gov

◀ Physical Environment ▶
and Transportation

EMERGENCY PREPAREDNESS

6-22–EMERGENCY SUPPLIES AND EQUIPMENT [38,99,100–102]

Provide and maintain emergency supplies (such as first aid equipment, posted signs, and communication equipment) in identified, predetermined locations, including in all buildings and buses. Emergency supplies should also be available at all indoor and outdoor school-sponsored events.

▶ **RATIONALE**

Emergencies can occur at any time or at any place, and supplies need to be available to treat less severe injuries and to stabilize more severe injuries until appropriate help arrives.

▶ **COMMENTARY**

The Ohio Chapter of the American Academy of Pediatrics together with Emergency Medical Services for Children (EMS-C [http://www.ems-c.org]) have created emergency guidelines for schools that include recommended first aid supplies.[99] Ensure that supplies are accessible and inspected at least monthly and resupplied after each use. Written guidelines should identify members of the staff responsible for inspecting and maintaining emergency equipment as well as those who are trained in first aid and cardiopulmonary resuscitation (CPR). Epinephrine injector pens, gloves, and other supplies should be included. Automated external defibrillators (AEDs) have electric paddles to resuscitate a person with cardiac arrest. Because of the low mean age of students and staff, these devices are required on fewer occasions per capita in schools as compared with many other settings. But when AEDs have been available in schools, they have successfully saved lives and so they may also be considered as desired emergency equipment for the school environment.

Special emergency equipment required for any student with a special health care need must also be accessible and in ample supply (eg, glucagon for students with diabetes). Schools need to be prepared for emergencies on campus and at all school-sponsored events (eg, field trips, sporting events, and outdoor education). Therefore, equipment should include some means of communicating rapidly if emergency medical services are needed (eg, walkie-talkies, telephones). Emergency assistance numbers should be posted in strategic places (eg, near telephones). Poison control and emergency assistance numbers are 800/222-1222 and 911, respectively.

▶ **RELATED GUIDELINES**

4-07, 4-11, 4-19, 4-20, 4-26

▶ **RELATED LINKS**

http://www.americanheart.org
http://www.ems-c.org
http://www.foodallergy.org
http://www.ed.gov/emergencyplan

6-23—FACILITY PREPARATION FOR EVACUATION, LOCKDOWN, DISASTERS[3,26,88,100,103–107]

Establish physical environment and ground security measures that will prepare each school to respond to fire, natural disasters, attacks, and other crises.

▶ **RATIONALE**

By preparing the school environment and personnel for crises well in advance, lives can be saved, injuries can be reduced, and school property can be preserved.

▶ **COMMENTARY**

Schools must have a system for which evacuation, lockdown, and other responses to situations are decided. Establish the safest areas on or near campus to evacuate students and staff for various types of disasters (eg, hurricanes, flood, earthquake, fire, loss of electricity). Have a plan to safely transport students in cases where hazardous chemical or biological exposure requires evacuation that is distant from the school site. In addition to regular assessments of school buildings and grounds (eg, for fire hazards), provide opportunities for students and staff to practice evacuations (eg, fire drills).

Plans need to define how each school will be closed to outsiders and how to secure the campus perimeter and protect the building against vandalism. Methods for effective enforcement must be considered, including the presence of law enforcement on campus. Some schools must also prepare to accept people who are evacuated for disasters that occur elsewhere.

Educate staff and students on disaster plans, make the information known and accessible, and preassign tasks to members of the staff. This includes training staff how to use fire extinguishers, use communication equipment, and implement other aspects of disaster plans. Develop a system to report violent incidents; to deal with the media; to reach staff, students, and families; and to respond to the aftermath (both physical and emotional). Partnerships with various community agencies (eg, public utilities, fire, law enforcement, emergency medical services, and health, mental health, and social service agencies) and parents are necessary to develop these plans.

Guidelines for schools regarding crisis preparedness have been developed by the US Department of Education (http://www.ed.gov/emergencyplan).[103] The National Education Association provides a useful tool kit[88] designed to prepare schools for such crises.

▶ **RELATED GUIDELINES**

4-11

▶ **RELATED LINKS**

http://www.ems-c.org
http://www.FEMA.gov
http://www.nasponline.org
http://www.safetyzone.org
http://www.ed.gov/emergencyplan

CHAPTER REFERENCES

1. Americans With Disabilities Act of 1990. Pub L No. 101-336 (1990). Available at: http://www.usdoj.gov/crt/ada/pubs/ada.txt

2. American Academy of Pediatrics, Committee on School Health and Committee on Injury and Poison Prevention. School transportation safety. *Pediatrics.* 1996;97:754–757

3. Centers for Disease Control and Prevention. School health guidelines to prevent unintentional injuries and violence. *MMWR Recomm Rep.* 2001;50(RR-22):1–73

4. Children's Safety Network. *Protecting Working Teens: A Public Health Resource Guide.* Newton, MA: Children's Safety Network; 1995

5. Massachusetts Department of Public Health. *Teens at Work: Injury Surveillance and Intervention Project.* Boston, MA: Occupational Health Surveillance Program; 2000. Available at: http://www.state.ma.us/dph/bhsre/ohsp/ohsp.htm

6. National Institute for Occupational Safety and Health. *Promoting Safe Work for Young Workers: A Community-based Approach.* Cincinnati, OH: National Institute for Occupational Safety and Health; 1999

7. National Research Council and Institute of Medicine, Committee on the Health and Safety Implications of Child Labor. *Protecting Youth at Work: Health, Safety, and Development of Working Children and Adolescents in the United States.* Washington, DC: National Academy Press; 1998

8. Posner M. *Preventing School Injuries: A Comprehensive Guide for School Administrators, Teachers, and Staff.* New Brunswick, NJ: Rutgers University Press; 2000

9. American Public Health Association. Creating healthier school facilities. *Am J Public Health.* 2001;91:494–495

10. Etzel RA. Indoor air pollutants in homes and schools. *Pediatr Clin North Am.* 2001;48:1153–1165

11. US Environmental Protection Agency. *IAQ Tools for School Kits.* Washington, DC: US Environmental Protection Agency; 2000. Available at: http://www.epa.gov/iaq/schools/pubs.html

12. US Environmental Protection Agency. *Mold Remediation in Schools and Commercial Buildings.* Washington DC: US Environmental Protection Agency; 2001. Available at: http://www.epa.gov/iaq/molds/images/moldremediation.pdf

13. American Conference of Governmental Industrial Hygienists. *Guidelines for the Assessment of Bioaerosols in the Indoor Environment.* Cincinnati, OH: American Conference of Governmental Industrial Hygienists; 1989

14. American Society of Heating, Refrigerating, and Air-Conditioning Engineers. *Ventilation for Acceptable Indoor Air Quality, 62-1989 (Including ANSI/ASHRAE Addendum 62a-1990).* Atlanta, GA: American Society of Heating, Refrigerating, and Air-Conditioning Engineers; 1990

15. American Society of Heating, Refrigerating, and Air-Conditioning Engineers. Operation and maintenance management. In: *1999 ASHRAE Handbook: Heating, Ventilating, and Air-Conditioning Applications.* Atlanta, GA: American Society of Heating, Refrigerating, and Air-Conditioning Engineers; 1999:37.1–37.5

16. California Electric and Magnetic Fields Program. *General Information: Site Planning.* Oakland, CA: California Electric and Magnetic Fields Program; 1997–1999

17. Taras H, Campana J. How one school district decided on a carpet policy. *J Sch Health.* 2003;73:45

18. US Consumer Product Safety Commission. *Handbook for Public Playground Safety.* Washington, DC: US Consumer Product Safety Commission; 1997

19. US Environmental Protection Agency. *Indoor Air Quality Tools for Schools: Renovation and Repairs Checklist.* Washington, DC: US Environmental Protection Agency; 2001. Available at: http://www.epa.gov/iaq/schools/tfs/renovate.html

20. American Society of Heating, Refrigerating, and Air-Conditioning Engineers. *ASHRAE Standard 62-1999. Ventilation for Acceptable Indoor Air Quality.* Atlanta, GA: American Society of Heating, Refrigerating, and Air-Conditioning Engineers; 1999

21. American Veterinary Medical Association, Task Force on Canine Aggression and Human-Canine Interactions. A community approach to dog bite prevention. *J Am Vet Med Assoc.* 2001;218:1732–1749

22. Bogden JF. *Fit, Healthy, and Ready to Learn: A School Health Policy Guide. Part I: Physical Activity, Healthy Eating, and Tobacco-Use Prevention.* Alexandria, VA: National Association of State Boards of Education; 2000

23. Bowers L, Gabbard C. How safe is your playground? Risk factor two: age-appropriate design of safe playgrounds. *J Phys Educ Recreation Dance.* 2000;71:23–25

24. Bruya L. How safe is your playground? Risk factor one: supervision on a safe playground. *J Phys Educ Recreation Dance.* 2000;71:20–22

25. Burgess JL, Kovalchick DF, Lymp JF, Kyes KB, Robertson WO. Health effects of hazardous materials exposures. *J Toxicol Clin Toxicol.* 2000;38:542–543

26. Center for Effective Collaboration and Practice, American Institutes for Research and National Association for School Psychologists. *Safeguarding Our Children: An Action Guide: Implementing Early Warning, Timely Response.* Washington, DC: Department of Education, Department of Justice; 2000

27. Centers for Disease Control and Prevention. Cigarette smoking among high school students-11 States, 1991– 1999. *MMWR Morb Mortal Wkly Rep.* 1999;48:686–692

28. Centers for Disease Control and Prevention. Dog-bite-related fatalities-United States, 1995–1996. *MMWR Morb Mortal Wkly Rep.* 1997;46:463–467

29. American Chemical Society, Committee on Chemical Safety. *Safety in Academic Chemistry Laboratories.* Washington, DC: American Chemical Society; 1995

30. American Academy of Pediatrics, Committee on Injury and Poison Prevention and Committee on Community Health Services. Prevention of agricultural injuries among children and adolescents. *Pediatrics.* 2001;108:1016–1019

31. Dean RA, Gerlovich JA. *Safety in the Elementary Science Classroom.* Washington, DC: National Science Teachers Association; 1997

32. Knight S, Junkins EP Jr, Lightfoot AC, Cazier CF, Olson LM. Injuries sustained in shop class. *Pediatrics.* 2000;106:10–13

33. Laflamme L, Eilert-Petersson E. School-injury patterns: a tool for safety planning at the school and community levels. *Accid Anal Prev.* 1998;30:277–283

34. McCann M. *Art Safety Procedures: A Health and Safety Manual for Art Schools and Art Departments.* New York: Center for Safety in the Arts; 1992

35. National Science Teachers Association. *Safety in the Elementary Science Classroom.* Arlington, VA: National Science Teachers Association; 1997

36. Hootman J, Schwab NC, Gelfman MHB, Gregory EK, Pohlman KJ. School nursing practice: clinical performance issues. In: Schwab ND, Gelfman MHB, eds. *Legal Issues in School Health Services.* North Branch, MN: Sunrise River Press; 2001:167–230

37. National Association of School Nurses. *Position Statement: Out-of-School Education Field Trips and Camps.* Scarborough, ME: National Association of School Nurses; 2000. Available at: http://www.nasn.org/positions/outofschool.htm

38. National Association of School Nurses. *Position Statement: School Nurse Role in Emergency Preparedness.* Scarborough, ME: National Association of School Nurses; 2001. Available at: http://www.nasn.org/positions/emergencyprep.htm

39. National Center for Chronic Disease Prevention and Health Promotion, Division of Nutrition and Physical Activity, Centers for Disease Control and Prevention. *Kids Walk-to-School: A Guide to Promote Walking to School.* Atlanta, GA. 2000. Available at: http://www.bikewalk.org/assets/pdf/kidswalk.pdf

40. American Academy of Pediatrics, Committee on Injury and Poison Prevention. All-terrain vehicle injury prevention: two-, three-, and four-wheeled unlicensed motor vehicles. *Pediatrics.* 2000;105:1352–1354

41. National School Transportation Association. *National School Bus Loading Zone Fatalities.* Alexandria, VA: National School Transportation Association; 2001

42. Russell A, Boop FA, Cherny WB, Ligon BL. Neurologic injuries associated with all-terrain vehicles and recommendations for protective measures for the pediatric population. *Pediatr Emerg Care.* 1998;14:31–35

43. US Department of Transportation, National Highway Traffic Safety Administration. *Federal Motor Vehicle Safety Standards and Regulations.* Washington, DC: National Highway Traffic Safety Administration; 1999. Available at: http://www.nhtsa.dot.gov/cars/rules/import/FMVSS

44. US Department of Transportation, National Highway Traffic Safety Administration. Highway safety guideline No. 17-pupil transportation safety. In: *Uniform Guidelines for State Highway Safety Programs: Highway Safety Program Guideline Numbers and Titles.* Washington, DC: National Highway Traffic Safety Administration; 2001. Available at: http://www.nhtsa.dot.gov/nhtsa/whatsup/tea21/tea21programs/402Guide.html

45. American Society for Testing and Materials. *Annual Book of ASTM Standards.* Vol 15.07. Conshohocken, PA: American Society for Testing and Materials; 2001:472–526, 861–867

46. Kalinowski LB, Bowler T. Risk factor four: equipment and surfacing maintenance on safe playgrounds. *J Phys Educ Recreation.* 2000;71:20–24

47. Laforest S, Robitaille Y, Dorval D, Lesage D, Pless B. Severity of fall injuries on sand or grass in playgrounds. *J Epidemiol Community Health.* 2000;54:475–477

48. Mack MG, Henderson W. How safe is your playground? Risk factor three: fall surfacing on safe playgrounds. *J Phys Educ Recreation Dance.* 2000;71:17–19

49. National Program for Playground Safety. *Summary of Action Steps: Local Level; State Level; National Level.* Cedar Falls, IA: University of Northern Iowa; 2001

50. Powell, EC, Tanz RR. Cycling injuries treated in emergency departments: need for bicycle helmets among preschoolers. *Arch Pediatr Adolesc Med.* 2000;154:1096–1100

51. American Conference of Governmental Industrial Hygienists. *School Workers Health and Safety Guide.* 3rd ed. Cincinnati, OH: American Conference of Governmental Industrial Hygienists; 2001

52. Children's Environmental Health Network. *Training Manual on Pediatric Environmental Health: Putting it Into Practice.* Oakland, CA: Children's Environmental Health Network; 1999

53. National Science Teachers Association. *Guidelines for Responsible Use of Animals in the Classroom.* Arlington VA: National Science Teachers Association; 1991. Available at: http://www.nsta.org/position#list

54. Patrick GR, O'Rourke KM. Dog and cat bites: epidemiologic analyses suggest different prevention strategies. *Public Health Rep.* 1998;113:252–257

55. Quinlan KP, Sacks JJ, Kresnow M. Exposure to and compliance with pediatric injury prevention counseling—United States, 1994. *Pediatrics.* 1998;102(5). Available at: http://www.pediatrics.org/cgi/content/full/102/5/e55

56. Robinson RA, Pugh RN. Dogs, zoonoses and immunosuppression. *J R Soc Health.* 2002;122:95–98

57. Hopper JA, Craig KA. Environmental tobacco smoke exposure among urban children. *Pediatrics.* 2000;106(4). Available at: http://www.pediatrics.org/cgi/content/full/106/4/e47

58. Joad JP. Smoking and pediatric respiratory health. *Clin Chest Med.* 2000;21:37–46

59. Wakefield MA, Chaloupka FJ, Kaufman NJ, Orleans CT, Barker DC, Ruel EE. Effect of restrictions on smoking at home, at school, and in public places on teenage smoking: cross sectional study. *BMJ.* 2000;321:333–337

60. Lowry R, Cohen LR, Modzeleski W, Kann L, Collins JL, Kolbe LJ. School violence, substance use, and availability of illegal drugs on school property among US high school students. *J Sch Health.* 1999;69:347–355

61. Modzeleski W, Small ML, Kann LK. Alcohol and other drug prevention policies and education in the United States. *J Health Educ.* 1999;30:S42–S49

62. American Academy of Allergy, Asthma and Immunology Board of Directors. Anaphylaxis in schools and other childcare settings: position statement. *J Allergy Clin Immunol.* 1998;102:173–176

63. Institute of Medicine, Committee on the Assessment of Asthma and Indoor Air. *Clearing the Air: Asthma and Indoor Air Exposures.* Washington, DC; National Academy Press; 2000

64. Korniewicz DM, El-Masri M, Broyles JM, Martin CD, O'Connell KP. Performance of latex and nonlatex medical examination gloves during simulated use. *Am J Infect Control.* 2002;30:133–138

65. Rego A, Roley L. In-use barrier integrity of gloves: latex and nitrile superior to vinyl. *Am J Infect Control.* 1999;27:405–410

66. Smedje G, Norback D. Irritants and allergens at school in relation to furnishings and cleaning. *Indoor Air.* 2001;11:127–133

67. Tortolera SR, Bartholomew LK, Tyrrell S, et al. Environmental allergens and irritants in schools: a focus on asthma. *J Sch Health.* 2002;72:33–38

68. National Center for Infectious Diseases. *An Ounce of Prevention: Keeps the Germs Away.* Atlanta, GA: Centers for Disease Control and Prevention. Available at: http://www.cdc.gov/ncidod/op/handwashing.htm

69. American Conference of Governmental Industrial Hygienists. *Industrial Ventilation: A Manual of Recommended Practice.* 24th ed. Cincinnati, OH: American Conference of Governmental Industrial Hygienists; 2001

70. Emmons CW. Saprophytic sources of *Cryptococcus neoformans* associated with the pigeon *(Columba livia).* *Am J Hyg.* 1995;62:227–232

71. Michel O, Ginanni R, Duchateau J, Vertongen F, LeBon B, Sergysels R. Domestic endotoxin exposure and clinical severity of asthma. *Clin Exp Allergy.* 1991;21:441–448

72. American Academy of Pediatrics, Committee on Sports Medicine and Fitness. Human immunodeficiency virus and other blood-borne viral pathogens in the athletic setting. *Pediatrics.* 1999;104:1400–1403

73. Friedland LR. Universal precautions and safety devices which reduce the risk of occupational exposure to blood-borne pathogens: a review for emergency health care workers. *Pediatr Emerg Care.* 1991;7:356–362

74. Riddell LA, Sherrard J. Blood-borne virus infection: the occupational risks. *Int J STD AIDS.* 2000;11:632–639

75. Grosse SJ. *Educating Children and Youth To Prevent Contagious Disease.* Washington, DC: ERIC Clearinghouse on Teaching and Teacher Education; 1999

76. Rodriguez S. The importance of school-based handwashing programs. *J Sch Nurs.* 2002;Oct(Suppl):19–22

77. White CG, Shinder FS, Shinder AL, Dyer DL. Reduction of illness absenteeism in elementary schools using an alcohol-free instant hand sanitizer. *J Sch Nurs.* 2001;17:258–265

78. National School Transportation Association. *Specifications and Procedures: 2000 Revised Edition.* Central Warrensburg, MO: Missouri Safety Center; 2000

79. American Academy of Pediatrics, Committee on Injury and Poison Prevention. School bus transportation of children with special health care needs. *Pediatrics.* 2001;108:516–518

80. American College of Emergency Physicians, Trauma Care and Injury Control Committee. School bus safety. *Ann Emerg Med.* 2000;36:179–180

81. National Highway Traffic Safety Administration. *Guideline for the Safe Transportation of Pre-school Age Children in School Buses.* 1999. Available at: http://www.nhtsa.dot.gov/people/injury/buses/Guide1999/prekfinal.htm

82. National Transportation Safety Board. *Pupil Transportation in Vehicles Not Meeting Federal School Bus Standards.* Washington, DC: National Transportation Safety Board; 1999

83. American Academy of Pediatrics, Committee on Injury and Poison Prevention. Transporting children with special health care needs. *Pediatrics.* 1999;104(4 Pt 1):988–992

84. American Red Cross. *Community First Aid and Safety.* Washington DC: American Red Cross; 2002

85. Family Educational Rights and Privacy Act, 20 USC 1232g, 34 CFR 99

108. *Federal School Bus Standards.* Washington, DC: National Transportation Safety Board; 1999

86. National Association of School Nurses. *Issue Brief: School Health Nursing Services Role in Health Care Inclusion.* Scarborough, ME: National Association of School Nurses; 2001. Available at: http://www.nasn.org/briefs/inclusion.htm

87. National Association of School Nurses. *Issue Brief: School Health Nursing Services Role in Health Care. School Health Nurses and the Individuals With Disabilities Education Act (IDEA).* Scarborough, ME: National Association of School Nurses; 2001. Available at: http://www.nasn.org/briefs/idea.htm

88. National Education Association. *Crisis Communication Guide and Toolkit.* Available at: http://www.nea.org/crisis/intro.html

89. National Task Force on Confidential Student Health Information. *Guidelines for Protecting Confidential Student Health Information.* Kent, OH: American School Health Association, 2000

90. American Academy of Pediatrics, Committee on Injury and Poison Prevention. Skateboard injuries. *Pediatrics.* 1995;95:611–612

91. American Academy of Pediatrics, Committee on Injury and Poison Prevention. Bicycle helmets. *Pediatrics.* 2001;108:1030–1032

92. American Academy of Pediatrics, Committee on Injury and Poison Prevention and Committee on Sports Medicine and Fitness. In-line skating injuries in children and adolescents. *Pediatrics.* 1998;101:720–722

93. US Department of Transportation, National Highway Traffic Safety Administration. *National Strategies for Advancing Bicycle Safety.* Washington, DC: National Highway Traffic Safety Administration; 2001. Available at: http://www.nhtsa.dot.gov/people/injury/pedbimot/bike/bicycle_safety/strategies.htm

94. Ellis J. *Bus Attendant: Training and Resource Manual.* Syracuse, NY: Pupil Transportation Safety Institute, 1995

95. Illinois State Board of Education. *Student Management. Illinois School Bus Driver Training Curriculum.* Springfield, IL: Illinois State Board of Education; 1995:52–59

96. Iowa Department of Education. *Student Transportation: Behavior Management on the Bus.* Des Moines, IA: Iowa Department of Education. Available at: http://www.state.ia.us/educate/ecese/asis/trans/behavmod.html

97. US Department of Transportation, National Highway Traffic Safety Administration. *Developing a School Transportation Safety Program.* Washington, DC: National Highway Traffic Safety Administration; 2001. Available at: http://www.nhtsa.dot.gov/people/injury/buses/GTSS/program.html

98. US Department of Transportation, National Highway Traffic Safety Administration. Student management. In: *School Bus Driver In-Service Safety Series.* Washington, DC: National Highway Traffic Safety Administration; 2001. Available at: http://www.nhtsa.dot.gov/people/injury/buses/schbus/schoolbus_drivers/topic_2/index.html

99. Ohio Chapter American Academy of Pediatrics. *Emergency Guidelines for Schools.* Worthington, OH: Ohio Chapter American Academy of Pediatrics; 2000. Available at: http://www.ems-c.org/downloads/pdf/emscguide.pdf

100. American Academy of Pediatrics, Committee on School Health. Guidelines for emergency medical care in school. *Pediatrics.* 2001;107:435–436

101. Passarelli C. Are you prepared for an emergency? *J Sch Nurs.* 1995;11:4, 6

102. US Department of Education, Office of Safe and Drug-Free Schools. *Practical Information on Crisis Planning: A Guide for Schools and Communities,* Washington, DC: US Department of Education; 2003. Available at: http://www.ed.gov/offices/OSDFS/emergencyplan/crisisplanning.pdf

103. Dwyer K, Osher D, Warger C. *Early Warning, Timely Response: A Guide to Safe Schools*. Washington, DC: US Department of Education; 1998

104. King KA. Developing a comprehensive school suicide prevention program. *J Sch Health*. 2001;71:132–137

105. Pollack I, Sunderman C. Creating safe schools: a comprehensive approach. *Juv Justice*. 2001;8:13–20

106. Reddy M, Borum R, Berglund J, Vossekuil B, Fein R, Modzeleski W. Evaluating risk for targeted violence in schools: comparing risk assessment, threat assessment, and other approaches. *Psych Sch*. 2001;38:157–172

107. Vulpitta RT. *On-site Emergency Response Planning Guide*. Itasca, IL: National Safety Council; 2002

CHAPTER-RELATED LINKS

Access Board
http://www.access-board.gov/
Federal agency committed to accessible design.

Agency for Toxic Substances and Disease Registry
http://www.atsdr.cdc.gov/
This agency of the US Department of Health And Human Services provides health information to prevent harmful exposures and disease related to toxic substances.

American Association of Poison Control Centers
http://www.aapcc.org/

American Conference of Governmental Industrial Hygienists (ACGIH)
http://www.acgih.org/
Information for school custodians on air sampling, bioaerosols, infectious agents, and industrial ventilation.

American Heart Association
http://www.americanheart.org/

American Institute of Architects
http://www.aia.org

American Lung Association
http://www.lungusa.org
School-specific resources address air quality, tobacco prevention, and asthma management (1-800-LUNGUSA). Tobacco Control Web page: http://www.lungusa.org/tobacco

American Red Cross
http://www.redcross.org/

American Society of Heating, Refrigeration, and Air-Conditioning Engineers
http://www.ashrae.org

ASTM International (formerly known as American Society for Testing and Materials)
http://www.astm.org/
Provides consensus standards and related technical information in order to promote public health and safety as well as contribute to the reliability of materials, products, systems, and services. This includes anything from art materials and sports equipment to construction supplies and playground equipment/surfaces.

The Catalyst
http://www.thecatalyst.org/
A site developed for secondary school teachers as a resource for finding relevant information for teaching chemistry. Includes safety measures to be taken in biology, chemistry, and physics classes.

Children's Environmental Health Network
http://www.cehn.org/
Provides a resource guide for children's environmental health.

Children's Safety Network
http://www.childrenssafetynetwork.org
Resources on building core capacity (infrastructure, data, interventions, policy, training) for prevention of youth violence, suicide, and injuries (including rural, agricultural); also, resources on safety related to the school environment, young workers, and transportation.

Construction Specifications Institute
http://www.csinet.org/

Council of Educational Facility Planners
http://www.cefpi.com/
Professional association of those involved in planning, designing, building, and equipping schools; resources on advocacy, education on the efficacy of school design and student outcomes; training and professional development, research.

Emergency Medical Services for Children (EMS-C)
http://www.ems-c.org/

Environmental Protection Agency
http://www.epa.gov/

Environmental Protection Agency—Indoor air quality:
"AirNow" (ground-level ozone or "smog")
http://www.epa.gov/airnow/

Environmental Protection Agency—"Tools for Schools"
including renovations
http://www.epa.gov/iaq/schools/

Environmental Protection Agency—"Keeping Kids Safe
from Sun and Smog"
http://www.epa.gov/sunwise/doc/summertime.pdf
Includes a color-coded air quality index that relate
to ozone levels and a UV index that relates to
harmful effects of sun.

Environmental Protection Agency—School Buses
http://www.epa.gov/cleanschoolbus/

Environmental Protection Agency—Exhaust Fumes
http://www.epa.gov/otaq/retrofit/

Environmental Protection Agency—Additional School-
Specific Matters and Resources
http://epa.gov/schools

Federal Emergency Management Agency
http://www.FEMA.gov

Food Allergy and Anaphylaxis Network
http://www.foodallergy.org/
Information on managing food allergies in schools.

Governors Highway Safety Association
http://statehighwaysafety.org
Promotes occupant protection; addresses impaired
driving; speed enforcement; and school bus,
pedestrian, and bicycle safety.

Injury Free Coalition for Kids
http://injuryfree.org/safety.cfm
Safety tips and resources.

Inline Skating Association
http://www.iisa.org
Safety tips on equipment.

Keep Schools Safe
http://www.keepschoolssafe.org
Information on violence and unintentional injury
prevention in schools.

Maternal and Child Health Bureau; Health Resources
and Services Administration
http://www.mchb.hrsa.gov/
Links to federal programs that strengthen health and
safety of mothers, infants, children, adolescents, and
their families—many of which are school related.

Mycological Aspects of Indoor Environmental Quality
http://www.dehs.umn.edu/iaq/fungus/links.html

National Association of School Psychologists
http://www.nasponline.org/

National Center for Infectious Diseases (CDC)
http://www.cdc.gov/ncidod/diseases/
Access to division of Vector-Borne Infectious Diseases
and of Bacterial and Mycotic Diseases. Brochures
and resources for the public and professionals
include tips on disease prevention through
management of the physical environment,
such as preventing accumulation of standing
water and taking caution with animal feces.

National Coalition for Food Safe Schools
http://www.foodsafeschools.org/
Represents a number of national organizations,
associations, and government agencies.
Resources for reducing foodborne illness
by improving food safety in schools.

National Highway Traffic Safety Administration
(US Department of Transportation)
http://www.nhtsa.dot.gov
Information on child safety restraint systems, training
for child passenger safety technicians, and on laws
and regulations governing transporting children
and proper helmet use. "Child Passenger Safety"
pages include information on transporting children
with disabilities and school bus safety.

National Institute for Occupational Safety and Health
(NIOSH) Sharps Disposal Containers
http://www.cdc.gov/niosh/sharps1.html
Information on selecting, evaluating, and using sharps
disposal containers.

National Institute of Standards and Technology
http://www.nist.gov

National Program for Playground Safety
http://www.uni.edu/playground

National Resource Center for Safe Schools
http://www.safetyzone.org

North American Guidelines for Children's Agricultural
Tasks
http://www.nagcat.org

Occupational Safety and Health Administration
http://www.osha.gov/

Pedestrian and Bicycle Information Center
http://www.bicyclinginfo.org

Safe USA

http://www.safeusa.org/school/safescho.htm

Resources for safety on playgrounds and in sports
and for violence prevention.

School Indoor Air Quality Questions and Answers
Web site

http://www.dehs.umn.edu/iaq/school/

Tobacco Information and Prevention Source (TIPS),
National Center for Chronic Disease Prevention
and Health Promotion

http://www.cdc.gov/tobacco

US Consumer Product Safety Commission

http://www.cpsc.gov

US Department of Education, Emergency Planning

http://www.ed.gov/emergencyplan/

This resource from the Office of Safe and Drug-Free
Schools provides school leaders with information
to plan for any emergency.

US Department of Justice, Americans with Disabilities Act

http://www.ada.gov/

Information and technical assistance on compliance
with the Americans with Disabilities Act.

◄ Social Environment ►

7-01—HEALTHY AND SAFE SOCIAL ENVIRONMENT[1-10]

Establish a safe, healthy social environment at school for students and staff. Each day, provide each student with at least one meaningful and positive interaction with a staffperson (or other adult). Have policies that are clearly understood by students, staff, and families.

▶ RATIONALE

A school environment that promotes "prosocial" student behavior, has high expectations and standards for academic achievement and behavior, and engages students in positive relationships with adults will encourage successful learning and reduce negative, antisocial behaviors.

▶ COMMENTARY

Students need environments with a clear structure and a sense of safety. When students feel afraid and unprotected, they often take matters into their own hands and display risky and dangerous behaviors as a means of self-protection. Provide an environment that allows students and staff an opportunity to express their feelings, fears, and anxieties about issues that concern them. Develop and fairly enforce rules for bullying, hazing, harassment, or discrimination with student, staff, and family input. Expectations and consequences must be adequately and properly publicized. Arrange for professionally trained staff and student leaders to monitor nonclassroom areas (eg, hallways, restrooms, lunch and recess) and provide social guidance and safety for all individuals.

A daily, meaningful and positive interaction with an adult at school who is capable of having positive expectations for each student's ability to succeed will help each student feel valued. Schools can achieve this in various ways. For example, schools may match each student to a counselor, teacher, administrator, coach, or other adult to be their mentor. Some schools have adult volunteers who visit the school on a regular basis in order to read to, mentor, or tutor students. Positive interactions with adults need not be academic. Involve students in various decision-making processes. Help students find opportunities in the community where they can engage in positive roles, perhaps as part of community service, recreation, or other enrichment experiences. By having a range of nonacademic activities at school (eg, athletics, arts, special interest clubs, Reserve Officers Training Corps, vocational training), schools create excellent additional opportunities for students to feel successful and develop a sense of accomplishment. The development of positive self-esteem comes from a sense of being connected to valued people, places, and things; a sense of uniqueness.

A school's infrastructure can provide students with opportunities to learn and practice social skills, such as communication, problem solving, anger management, mediation, leadership, management, and planning skills. Each student should have a sense of ownership, attachment, responsibility, and input into school life (eg, school government, peer mediation, involvement of students in formal school committees and activities).

Emphasize acceptance, tolerance, respect, and enjoyment of what individual differences bring to a school and community, including staff and student differences in ethnicity, age, gender, sexual orientation, culture, and special needs. Communicate with parents for purposes of recognition of student accomplishments, awareness of behavioral and emotional issues and stresses, and referrals to community resources (eg, social services and those that address substance abuse, violence, or special needs).

▶ ***RELATED GUIDELINES***

0-01, 0-07, 1-03, 5-01, 5-10, 6-01, 6-20

▶ ***RELATED LINKS***

http://smhp.psych.ucla.edu
http://csmha.umaryland.edu
http://www.childrenssafetynetwork.org
http://www.casel.org
http://www.connectforkids.org
http://www.keepschoolssafe.org
http://www.nasponline.org
http://www.nimh.nih.gov
http://www.mentalhealth.org
http://www.safetyzone.org
http://www.saddonline.com
http://www.pledge.org
http://www.ed.gov
http://sgreports.nlm.nih.gov/NN

7-02–SOCIAL SERVICES, MENTAL HEALTH SUPPORT[9-20]

Ensure that social services and mental health support are available to all students and staff in the school setting and integrate this support into other school programs.

▶ RATIONALE

Staff and students who function well socially and emotionally are apt to perform better academically. Part of schools' educational mission is to promote social and emotional functioning as well as academic achievement.

▶ COMMENTARY

Support for a student might include providing the student with additional counseling time with a member of the school health and safety team, steering a student to a staff-facilitated support group meeting with peers and assigning students whom are new to a school with a student ambassador or "buddy." When possible, make services such as tutoring and mentoring available within the school setting. This may be provided by the school system or by trained persons invited into the school. Because there will always be a level of service that is unrealistic to provide within the school, having facilitated linkages to specialized services in the community is essential.

School programs and services that address mental health and psychosocial concerns are frequently not adequately integrated into schools' daily instructional efforts. Yet, mental health promotion can be integrated successfully into many school programs. During daily classroom instruction and other school activities, students can be taught that both appropriate and inappropriate behaviors can stem from one's feelings. Once students understand this, many will be more likely to use introspection and subsequent verbalization strategies as substitutes to acting out or withdrawal. They may be more likely to seek help when they are troubled. Provide staff development so that staff members understand how to support students in this manner. Staff development in the area of developmental psychology will help staff form expectations of students that are appropriately adjusted to students' developmental stages. Integration can be improved by having members of the counseling, psychological, health, and social services staff communicate with classroom teachers and recess monitors, observe students during instruction and recreation, and assist staff with how they can respond to individual students and with the class as a whole. Such integration should be specified in the district's guiding principles (eg, vision statement, policy statement, or school improvement plan). Staff need to recognize that they are role models for students at school.

▶ RELATED GUIDELINES

0-08, 1-01, 2-07, 4-01, 4-06, 4-09, 4-11, 4-16, 4-17, 4-25, 8-05

▶ RELATED LINKS

http://smhp.psych.ucla.edu
http://csmha.umaryland.edu
http://www.casel.org
http://www.nasponline.org
http://www.safetyzone.org
http://www.ed.gov

7-03—RECOGNITION AND REFERRAL OF STUDENTS UNDER STRESS[12,15,21-31]

Implement prevention programs that focus on recognition of stressful life situations and interventions to help students deal with these stresses.

▶ RATIONALE

Early detection of the most common psychosocial and educational stresses can lead to fewer problems with learning and school performance when these issues are dealt with expediently at school. Engagement in high-risk behavior may be decreased if prevention programs are designed for early identification of and interventions for students needing support.

▶ COMMENTARY

Research has identified a variety of commonplace educational and psychosocial problems and external stressors that interfere with students' learning and teachers' teaching.

A variety of problems affect the ability of many students to be successful in the classroom. Examples of stresses that affect achievement are: school adjustment difficulties, language problems, school and life transitions, substance and alcohol use, and trauma. Social, interpersonal, and family stresses also affect learning. They include recent loss, isolation, psychological reactions to sexual activity, concerns with sexual identity, abuse and neglect (physical, mental, and sexual), other forms of victimization, and exposure to various forms of violence, including witnessing or learning about a violent situation or suicide. Difficulties with learning or attention are also stressors.

School staff members are often in a position to learn of such life stresses that affect students soon after they occur. They may present to school staff as high-risk behaviors (eg, poor attendance, delinquency, gang-related activities, conduct, and behavior problems). School staff can help ensure that students who might need assistance are referred to school mental health professionals for further assessment. Some students may require referral outside of the school setting for additional assessment and/or intervention. Provide staff development so that all staff members are aware of the potential consequences of such stresses. Staff must also know where to refer students and how to approach a student who requires a referral. Appendix F lists stressors that are often associated with violence and suicide.

▶ RELATED GUIDELINES

0-07, 0-08, 1-02, 4-06, 4-11, 4-23, 8-05

▶ RELATED LINKS

http://www.suicidology.org
http://cecp.air.org
http://smhp.psych.ucla.edu
http://csmha.umaryland.edu
http://www.nasponline.org
http://www.nimh.nih.gov
http://www.mentalhealth.org
http://www.ed.gov
http://sgreports.nlm.nih.gov/NN

7-04—SUICIDE PREVENTION STRATEGIES[3,22,24,26,32-42]

Actively prevent suicidal behavior by training staff and having programs that identify high-risk students and then link them to therapeutic and preventive community services.

▶ *RATIONALE*

Early identification and intervention offer the potential of preventing suicide. School personnel are in an excellent position to identify students at risk of suicide and, as a result, need to know both what to look for and how to respond.

▶ *COMMENTARY*

Students who have mental disorders (eg, depression, schizophrenia, alcoholism, substance abuse, conduct disorders), who have had a prior attempt of suicide, or who have been exposed to suicide behaviors have a heightened risk of suicide. Victimization, bullying, isolation, trauma, hopelessness, recent loss, and having difficulty with issues of sexual identity are other risks for suicide. Teachers and other staff are well positioned to detect these risks and take action. School personnel must consider any talk about suicide a serious warning sign.

School protocols, when there is a suicide or attempted suicide, must focus on both the involved individual (ie, linkage to mental health services and monitoring of continued participation) and on the school population (ie, interventions to address stresses that are related to the exposure, identification of students at risk of copy behavior, and referrals as necessary for evaluation and services). Develop data collection and data analysis systems that provide for tracking cases, feedback to the school and the community and allow for evaluation of schools' prevention programs.

Appendix F and the Centers for Disease Control and Prevention guidelines[3] describe factors indicative of increased risk of suicide, strategies that schools could adopt to prevent and confront these risks, and methods of tracking incidents.

▶ *RELATED GUIDELINES*

0-03, 0-08, 0-09, 0-13, 0-14, 4-06, 4-07, 4-08, 4-09, 4-10, 4-11

▶ *RELATED LINKS*

http://www.afsp.org
http://www.suicidology.org
http://www.keepschoolsafe.org
http://smhp.psych.ucla.edu
http://csmha.umaryland.edu
http://www.childrenssafetynetwork.org
http://www.nes.org
http://www.nimh.nih.gov
http://www.mentalhealth.org
http://www.save.org
http://www.sprc.org
http://www.ed.gov

7-05–VIOLENCE PREVENTION STRATEGIES[1,3,4,13,22,24,26,32–37,39,43–46]

Provide the following violence prevention and management services: (a) rules prohibiting violent and disrespectful behaviors; (b) protocols to deal with violent events; (c) links to mediation, mentoring, and therapeutic services; (d) strategies to identify students at high risk of engaging in violence; (e) staff education; and (f) evaluation of violence policies and programs.

▶ RATIONALE

An environment that makes students feel safe will also reduce students' motivation to take matters into their own hands and prevent the escalation of aggressive behaviors. School policies, rules, and resources aimed at violent behavior that are therapeutic, not simply punitive, diminish chances for long-term emotional, spiritual, and physical sequelae. Linking students to assistance programs prevents criminalization of students with correctable difficulties.

▶ COMMENTARY

A safe social environment provides many good role models for students and has opportunities for them to learn and enhance communication skills, problem-solving, and anger management. The physical environment can also be designed to be reassuring to students and reduce chances for violence. Provide adequate lighting and presence of adults (ie, staff, parents, safety officers) in school hallways, rest rooms, and playgrounds. Students need to feel that the environment is safe for them to communicate their needs. Culturally competent teachers are more likely to be good role models and more capable of communicating effectively. Guidelines on developing cultural competency are provided in Appendix B. Detailed school guidelines to prevent and manage violence are available.[3,43]

Categories of programs that have shown to be either effective or encouraging to reduce violence are: mentoring, tutoring students with academic difficulties, home visitation (particularly in elementary grades), parenting training and support, therapeutic foster care, and programs or curricula addressing bullying, conflict resolution, anger management, mediation, and refusal skills. Peer mediation programs are often appropriate. Leadership skills, connectedness, and a sense of ownership and responsibility for aspects of school life can reduce violence (eg, student government or peer mediation). Provide numerous venues where students can achieve success (eg, athletics, arts, vocational training) and communicate that each student is expected to succeed. Develop data collection and analysis systems that provide for tracking cases, feedback to the school and the community, and evaluation of prevention programs in the schools.

Labeling students based on race, socioeconomic status, gender, and similar general descriptors has a detrimental effect on academic performance as well as on social and emotional well-being. These demographic attributes should not be used to select students for participation in a violence prevention program. However, knowing risk factors for violence can help when working with an entire student population. While most students who have risk factors for violence do well (eg, those exposed to violence at home early in life), most will benefit from the opportunity to address their issues. See Appendix F for lists of risk factors for violence, school preventive strategies, and program evaluation methods.

▶ **RELATED GUIDELINES**

0-01, 0-08, 0-13, 1-01, 2-06, 2-07, 4-01, 4-08, 4-11, 6-03

▶ **RELATED LINKS**

http://smhp.psych.ucla.edu
http://csmha.umaryland.edu
http://www.childrenssafetynetwork.org
http://www.no-bully.com
http://www.connectforkids.org
http://www.keepschoolssafe.org
http://www.nes.org
http://www.nimh.nih.gov
http://www.mentalhealth.org
http://www.safeusa.org/school/safescho.htm
http://www.ed.gov
http://ojjdp.ncjrs.org
http://sgreports.nlm.nih.gov/NN

7-06–ADJUSTMENTS TO PSYCHOLOGICAL TRAUMA AND LOSS[34,44,47–55]

Make accommodations and/or adjustments for students during and after experiences of psychological trauma or loss.

▶ RATIONALE

Students who are coping with trauma or loss bear a heavy burden and may have difficulty focusing on academic work until they have dealt with trauma or loss issues.

▶ COMMENTARY

Surveys of adolescents who have suffered trauma or loss indicate that they perceived their teachers to be helpful when they adjusted expectations about deadlines, rescheduled examinations, or extended due dates. Teachers were perceived as not helpful when they told students to focus on their schoolwork following trauma or loss or drew unnecessary attention to the students.

Accommodations for a student might include the following: (a) allowing the student time out of the classroom to meet with the school counselor, nurse, psychologist, or social worker; (b) extending due dates for assignments and rescheduling examinations; (c) providing classroom discussion appropriate to the situation; and (d) acting discreetly, as necessary.

Take school-wide actions when many students share a sense of loss or of trauma. Make all students aware that doors are open for communication. Invite the school or district crisis team to the site so that they may identify strategies to help students who are experiencing loss. Be sure teachers have ready access to those strategies. Ensure that staff has easy access to lists of mental health resources in the school, district, and community. Teachers and other staff coordinate their efforts as they identify and offer accommodations to students.

▶ RELATED GUIDELINES

4-06, 4-11, 8-05

▶ RELATED LINKS

http://smhp.psych.ucla.edu
http://csmha.umaryland.edu
http://www.nasponline.org
http://www.ed.gov

7-07—ACTIONS AGAINST BULLYING[31,43,56–62]

Establish and enforce policies that prohibit bullying, hazing, teasing, harassment, and discrimination.

▶ *RATIONALE*

Bullying, hazing, and discrimination are often precursors to escalated violent behavior and associated with psychosomatic problems and future psychiatric problems in certain persons. Prevention of bullying and discrimination provides for a more conducive learning environment for students and a safer environment for all.

▶ *COMMENTARY*

Bullying is the repeated and deliberate use of aggression and power to cause physical pain and/or emotional distress. Bullying can be verbal, physical, unpleasant gestures, social coercion, social exclusion, or any combination of these. Although in most bullying situations at school, students are in the roles of bullies and victims, staff members can be bullies and victims of bullying as well. Physical appearance (including facial and dental appearance, obesity, short stature, and racial characteristics), perceived sexual orientation, having a homosexual parent, and stuttering have been shown to be associated with victimization. Harassment of those with disabilities, including developmental delay, attention-deficit disorders, and conduct disorders; and gender-based harassment (eg, sexual remarks) are not uncommon. Some approaches to dealing with bullying at school have shown promise. They deal with the victim and the bully as individuals as well as with system-wide programs. Internet resources (see "Related Links") provide some useful strategies.

Have clearly understood, well-publicized, and universally enforced rules about bullying, harassment, and discrimination. Supervision is critically important because most bullying takes place when usual supervision is at its lowest. Identify high-risk areas and particular times of the day when bullying is likely to occur. Spot checks can help deal with difficult staffing issues. When bullying occurs, aggressive and angry punishments may be ineffective responses. Instead, defuse the situation by immediately removing the victim and bully from the scene. Consider a policy whereby the bully must make amends for the distress that has been caused, perhaps through an apology (eg, public, face-to-face, written, a gift given to victim by the bully). Link the bully and the victim to social and health professional staff at school. Underlying emotional, mental health, and social stresses may contribute to being a bully or a victim. Initiate assessment of such factors and follow this by referring students for further assessment and/or management, as necessary. Teaching victims new reaction skills (ie, demonstrating indifference, not being counteraggressive, and learning how to avoid an appearance of being helpless) may be helpful.

Consider programs that redirect aggressive behaviors of all students towards other activities. Sports and competitive games are examples. Alternatively, activities that are incompatible with aggression, such as caring for plants or people, may also be tried. Because empathetic support that victims receive from peers is as important as support received from adults, consider educating all students about peer support. Teach students to mentor, befriend, and advocate for their bullied peers through group discussion, videos, drama, and role-play. Bystanders have the power to modify a bullying situation if they become active, rather than passive. This can generate skills, interest, and willingness among students to intervene when bullying and harassment occur.

▶ *RELATED GUIDELINES*

0-01, 2-07, 3-09, 4-08, 7-01

▶ *RELATED LINKS*

http://smhp.psych.ucla.edu
http://csmha.umaryland.edu
http://www.no-bully.com
http://www.keepschoolssafe.org
http://www.nes.org
http://www.safetyzone.org
http://www.ed.gov

7-08–POLICIES ON STUDENT DISCIPLINE[63-67]

Utilize disciplinary actions that do not jeopardize students' physical health or safety, that do not harm emotional well-being, and do not discourage physical activity or other healthful behaviors. Prohibit use of food as a reward or punishment.

▶ RATIONALE

Corporal punishment increases chances for violent behavior in susceptible youth. When suspended or expelled students are out of school, they are often exposed to safety and health risks. Denial of recess or forced physical activity (running laps, doing extra push-ups) as a disciplinary action can send a message that physical activity is a luxury or a punishment. Both can discourage enjoyment in lifelong physical activity.

▶ COMMENTARY

Acceptable forms of disciplinary actions include time out, staying after school, performing services, and reduction in grades. Unacceptable forms include verbal abuse, corporal punishment, and actions likely to humiliate students. When a student's actions threaten injury to the student or someone else, physical restraint is sometimes necessary. Schools can use incentives (or their withdrawal) as behavior management tools. Examples of incentives are: stars on a chart hung on classroom wall, extra free-time, extra recess, participation in special events (eg, field trips), points students can use to purchase books or merchandise, student's name in the school newspaper, featuring a "student of the week," and choosing student to make public announcements.

Proponents of expulsion and suspension find that these actions not only punish students, but alert parents and protect other students and school staff. But there are unintended health, mental health, and safety consequences. Suspension and expulsion are often reserved for students who use illicit substances, commit crimes, disobey rules, and threaten violence. These students are most likely to be victims of abuse or to be depressed or otherwise mentally ill. For students with major home-life stresses, suspension compounds current stresses and predisposes them to even higher risks of behavioral problems. Adolescents are more likely to smoke, use alcohol and other drugs, commit crimes, and engage in sexual intercourse when out of school. Suicidal ideation and behavior may be expected to occur more frequently at such times of isolation among susceptible youth. Students face greater risks of dropping out permanently and becoming entangled in the courts when they are excluded from school.

Students who are suspended or expelled should have immediate professional support and continuous adult supervision during school hours. Suspension and expulsion should always be accompanied by a referral to a health and/or mental health professional to identify any underlying problems. Innovative disciplinary actions schools have taken include: immediate transfer of students to supervised "suspension classrooms" (until they are either moved to an alternate setting or readmitted to regular school site), having parents accompany students to school for a portion of the school day, and having students provide community service on school grounds during nonschool hours.

Schools are required to provide educational services to students receiving services under the Individuals with Disabilities Education Act, even when they are expelled, if the offending behavior is related to their disability. Schools must do pre-expulsion assessments and demonstrate reasonable efforts to minimize the risk of harm in these students' educational placement. Modifications of these students' individualized education programs (IEPs) are often specifically redesigned to address and prevent recurrence of inappropriate behavior. This is a promising model for managing disciplinary problems of all students (ie, both regular and special education).

▶ **RELATED GUIDELINES**

4-01, 4-06, 4-17, 4-23, 5-10

▶ **RELATED LINKS**

http://smhp.psych.ucla.edu
http://csmha.umaryland.edu
http://www.nasponline.org
http://www.ed.gov
http://ojjdp.ncjrs.org

CHAPTER REFERENCES

1. Bell CC, Gamm S, Vallas P, Jackson P. Strategies for the prevention of youth violence in Chicago public schools. In: Shafii M, Shafii SL, eds. *School Violence: Assessment, Management, Prevention.* Washington, DC: American Psychiatric Publishing; 2001:251–272

2. Bogden JF. *Fit, Healthy, and Ready to Learn: A School Health Policy Guide. Part 1. Physical Activity, Healthy Eating, and Tobacco-Use Prevention.* Alexandria, VA: National Association of State Boards of Education; 2000

3. Centers for Disease Control and Prevention. School health guidelines to prevent unintentional injuries and violence. *MMWR Recomm Rep.* 2001;50(RR-22):1–73

4. Dwyer K, Osher D. *Safeguarding Our Children: An Action Guide.* Washington, DC: US Departments of Education and Justice, American Institutes for Research; 2000

5. Haynes NM, Comer JP. Integrating schools, families, and communities through successful school reform: The School Development Program. *School Psychol Rev.* 1996;25:501–506

6. Henderson AC. The importance of a healthy school environment. In: Cortese P, Middleton K, eds. *The Comprehensive School Health Challenge: Promoting Health Through Education.* Santa Cruz, CA: ETR Associates; 1994:145–178

7. Henderson AC, Rowe DE. A Healthy school environment. In: Marx E, Wooley SF, eds. *Health is Academic: A Guide to Coordinated School Health Programs.* New York, NY: Teachers College Press; 1988:96–115

8. Los Angeles County Office of Education. *Classroom Management: A California Resource Guide for Teachers and Administrators of Elementary and Secondary Schools.* Downey, CA: Los Angeles County Office of Education; 2000. Available at: http://www.lacoe.edu/lacoeweb/DocsForms/20010719021044_classroom_mgmt.pdf

9. National Association of State Mental Health Program Directors and National Association of State Directors of Special Education. *Mental Health, Schools and Families Working Together for All Children and Youth: Toward a Shared Agenda.* Alexandria, VA: National Association of State Mental Health Program Directors and National Association of State Directors of Special Education; 2002

10. Weissberg RP, Elias MJ. Enhancing young people's social competence and health behavior: an important challenge for educators, scientists, policymakers, and funders. *Appl Prev Psychol.* 1993;2:179–190

11. Adelman H. School counseling, psychological and social services. In: Marx E, Wooley SF, eds. *Health is Academic: A Guide to Coordinated School Health Programs.* New York, NY: Teachers College Press; 1988:142–168

12. Carnegie Council on Adolescent Development. *Great Transitions: Preparing Adolescents for a New Century.* New York, NY: Carnegie Corporation of New York; 1995

13. Center for Mental Health in Schools. *Mental Health in Schools: Guidelines, Models, Resources, and Policy Considerations.* Los Angeles, CA: Center for Mental Health in Schools; 2001

14. Consortium on the School-Based Promotion of Social Competence. The school-based promotion of social competence: theory, research, practice, and policy. In: Haggerty RJ, Sherrod LR, Garmezy N, Rutter M, eds. *Stress, Risk, and Resilience in Children and Adolescents: Processes, Mechanisms, and Interventions.* New York, NY: Cambridge University Press; 1994:268–316

15. Drug Strategies. *Making the Grade: A Guide to School Drug Prevention Programs.* Washington, DC: Drug Strategies; 1999

16. Garmezy N. Resilience and vulnerability to adverse developmental outcomes associated with poverty. *Am Behav Sci.* 1991;34:416–430

17. Rosenblum L, DiCecco M, Taylor L, Adelman H. Upgrading school support programs through collaboration: resource coordinating teams. *Soc Work Educ.* 1995;17:117–124

18. Weist MD, Myers CP, Hastings E, Ghuman H, Han Y. Psychosocial functioning of youth receiving mental health services in the schools vs. community mental health centers. *Comm Mental Health J.* 1999;35:69–81

19. Weist MD. Expanded school mental health services: a national movement in progress. In: Ollendick TH, Prinz RJ, eds. *Advances in Clinical Child Psychology.* Philadelphia, PA: Brunner/Mazel; 1997;319–352

20. Weist MD. Toward a public mental health promotion and intervention system for youth. *J Sch Health.* 2001;71:101–104

21. American Academy of Pediatrics, Committee on Substance Abuse. The role of schools in combating substance abuse. *Pediatrics.* 1995;95:784–785

22. Bell CC, Clark DC. Adolescent suicide. *Pediatr Clin North Am.* 1998;45:365–380

23. Friesen BJ, Poertner J. *From Case Management to Service Coordination for Children With Emotional, Behavioral, or Mental Disorders: Building on Family Strengths.* Baltimore, MD: Paul H. Brookes; 1995

24. Gilliland BE, James RK. *Crisis Intervention Strategies.* 3rd ed. Pacific Grove, CA: Brooks Cole; 1997

25. Hooper K, Lawson HA. *Serving Children, Youth and Families Through Interprofessional Collaboration and Service Integration: A Framework for Action.* Oxford, OH: The Danforth Foundation and the Institute for Educational Renewal at Miami University; 1994

26. Mazza J. School-based suicide prevention programs: are they effective? *School Psychol Rev.* 1997;26:382–396

27. National Institute on Drug Abuse. *Drug Abuse Prevention: What Works.* Rockville, MD: US Department of Health and Human Services; 1997

28. O'Carroll PW, Mercy JA, Steward JA. CDC recommendations for a community plan for the prevention and containment of suicide clusters. *MMWR Morb Mortal Wkly Rep.* 1988;37(S-6):1–12

29. Pumariega AJ, Vance HR. School-based mental health services: the foundation for systems of care for children's mental health. *Psychol Sch.* 1999;36:371–378

30. Ross JG, Eihaus KE, Hohenemser LK, Green B. School health policy prohibiting tobacco use, alcohol and other drug use, and violence. *J Sch Health.* 1995;65:333–338

31. Tobler NS, Stratton HH. Effectiveness of school-based drug prevention programs: a meta-analysis of the research. *J Prim Prev.* 1997;18:71–128

32. Barrios L. Special report. Federal activities addressing violence in schools. *J Sch Health.* 2000;70:119–140

33. Davis J, Brods S. Suicide. In: Sandoval J, ed. *Handbook of Crisis Counseling Intervention and Prevention in the Schools.* 2nd ed. Hillsdale, NY: Lawrence Erlbaum Associates; 2001:273–299

34. Dwyer K, Osher D, Warger C. *Early Warning, Timely Response: A Guide to Safe Schools.* Washington, DC: US Department of Education; 1998

35. Eggert LL, Thompson EA, Herting JR, Nicholas LJ. Reducing suicide potential among high-risk youth: tests of a school-based prevention program. *Suicide Life Threatening Behav.* 1995;25:276–296

36. Forjuoh SN, Zwi AB. Violence against children and adolescents. International perspectives. *Pediatr Clin North Am.* 1998;45:415–426

37. Kalafat J, Elias M. An evaluation of a school-based suicide awareness intervention. *Suicide Life Threatening Behav.* 1994;24:224–233

38. King RA, Schwab-Stone M, Flisher AJ, Greenwald S, Kramer RA, Goodman SH, Lahey BB, Shaffer D, Gould MS. Psychosocial and risk behavior correlates of youth suicide attempts and suicidal ideation. *J Am Acad Child Adolesc Psychiatry.* 2001;40:837–846

39. Lieberman R, Davis J. Suicide intervention. In: Brock S, Lazarus P, Jimerson S. *Best Practices in School Crisis Prevention and Intervention.* Bethesda, MD. National Association of School Psychologists; 2002

40. McCarthy AR. *Healthy Teens: Facing the Challenges of Young Lives.* 3rd ed. Birmingham, MI: Bridge Communications Inc; 2000

41. National Institute of Justice. *Conflict Resolution for School Personnel: An Interactive School Safety Training Tool* (CD-ROM). Washington, DC: US Department of Justice, Office of Justice Programs; 2002

42. Shaffer D, Craft L. Methods of adolescent suicide prevention. *J Clin Psychiatry.* 1999;60(Suppl 2):70–76, 113–116

43. Drug Strategies. *Safe Schools, Safe Students: A Guide to Violence Prevention Strategies.* Washington, DC: Drug Strategies; 1998

44. Gray RE. The role of school counselors with bereaved teenagers: with and without peer support groups. *Sch Couns.* 1998;35:185–193

45. King MA, Sims A, Osher D. *How is Cultural Competence Integrated in Education?* Center for Effective Collaboration and Practice. Available at: http://cecp.air.org/cultural/Q_integrated.htm

46. Ladson-Billings, G. *Crossing Over to Canaan: The Journey of New Teachers in Diverse Classrooms.* San Francisco, CA: Jossey-Bass; 2001

47. American Academy of Child and Adolescent Psychiatry. Practice parameters for the assessment and treatment of children and adolescents with Posttraumatic Stress Disorder. *J Am Acad Child Adolesc Psychol.* 1998;37 (Suppl 10):4S–26S

48. Brock S, Lazarus P, Jimerson S. *Best Practices in School Crisis Prevention and Intervention.* Bethesda, MD: National Association of School Psychologists; 2002

49. Hoagwood K, Erwin HD. Effectiveness of school-based mental health services for children: a 10-year research review. *J Child Fam Studies.* 1997;6:435–451

50. Minke K, Bear G, eds. *Preventing School Problems—Promoting School Success.* Washington, DC: National Association of School Psychologists; 2000

51. Nader K, Pynoos R. School disaster: planning and initial interventions. *J Social Behav Personal.* 1993;8:299–320

52. National Institute of Mental Health. Helping Children and Adolescents Cope With Violence and Disasters. Bethesda, MD: National Institute of Mental Health; 2001. NIH Publication No. 01-3518

53. Pfefferbaum B, Call JA, Sconzo GM. Mental health services for children in the first two years after the 1995 Oklahoma City terrorist bombing. *Psychiatr Serv.* 1999;50:956–958

54. Poland S, Pitcher G, Lazarus P. Best practices in crisis intervention. In: Thomas A, Grimes J, eds. *Best Practices in School Psychology-III.* Bethesda, MD: National Association of School Psychologists; 1995:445–458

55. Poland S, McCormick JS. *Coping with Crisis: Lessons Learned—A Resource for Schools, Parents, and Communities.* Longmont, CO: Sopris West; 1999:182–198

56. Garrity C, Jens K, Porter W, Sager N, Short-Cammilli C. *Bully Proofing Your School: A Comprehensive Approach for Elementary Schools.* 2nd ed. Longmont, CO: Sopris West; 2000

57. Nansel TR, Overpeck M, Pilla RS, Ruan WJ, Simons-Morton B, Scheidt P. Bullying behaviors among US youth: prevalence and association with psychosocial adjustment. *JAMA.* 2001;285:2094–2100

58. Newman DA, Horne AM, Bartolomucci CL. *Bully Busters. A Teacher's Manual for Helping Bullies, Victims, and Bystanders.* Champaign, IL: Research Press; 2000

59. Olweus D. Bullying at school: basic facts and effects of a school based intervention program. *J Child Psychol Psychiatry.* 1994;35:1171–1190

60. Pearce JB, Thompson AE. Practical approaches to reduce the impact of bullying. *Arch Dis Child.* 1998;79:528–531

61. Schmidt T. *Building Trust, Making Friends.* Minneapolis, MN: Johnson Institute; 1996

62. Twemlow, SW, Fonagy P, Sacco FC, Gies ML, Evans R, Ewbank R. Creating a peaceful school learning environment: a controlled study of an elementary school intervention to reduce violence. *Am J Psychiatry.* 2001;158:808–810

63. American Academy of Pediatrics, Committee on School Health. Corporal punishment in schools. *Pediatrics.* 2000;106:343

64. Centers for Disease Control and Prevention. Guidelines for school health programs to prevent tobacco use and addiction. *MMWR Recomm Rep.* 1994;43(No. RR-2):1–18

65. Children and Adults with Attention-Deficit/Hyperactivity Disorder. *Where We Stand: School Discipline.* Landover, MD: Children and Adults with Attention-Deficit/Hyperactivity Disorder; 2001. Available at: http://www.chadd.org/pdfs/school_discipline.pdf

66. Cotton K. *Schoolwide and Classroom Discipline.* School Improvement Research Series. Portland, OR: Northwest Regional Educational Library; 2001. Available at: http://www.nwrel.org/scpd/sirs/5/cu9.html

67. National Association of School Nurses. *Position Statement: Corporal Punishment in Schools.* Scarborough, ME: National Association of School Nurses, 1996. Available at: http://www.nasn.org/positions/positions.htm

68. Centers for Disease Control and Prevention. Guidelines for school and community programs to promote lifelong physical activity among young people. *MMWR Morb Mortal Wkly Rep.* 1997;46(RR-6):12

69. Messina SA. *A Youth Leader's Guide to Building Cultural Competence.* Washington, DC: Advocates for Youth; 1994. Available at: http://www.advocatesforyouth.org/publications/guide.pdf

70. Salmivalli C. Participant role approach to school bullying: implications for interventions. *J Adolesc.* 1999;22:453–459

71. Spivak H, Prothrow-Stith D. The need to address bullying: an important component of violence prevention (editorial). *JAMA.* 2001;285:2131–2132

72. UCLA Center for Mental Health in Schools. *What Schools Can Do to Welcome and Meet the Needs of All Students and Families.* Los Angeles, CA: Center for Mental Health in Schools; 1997

73. White House Council on Youth Violence. *Helping Your Children Navigate Their Teenage Years.* Washington, DC: White House Council on Youth Violence; 2000

74. Zins JE. *Helping Students Succeed in the Regular Classroom: A Guide for Developing Intervention Assistance Programs.* San Francisco, CA: Jossey-Bass; 1988

CHAPTER-RELATED LINKS

American Association for Suicide Prevention
http://www.afsp.org
Research, education, and statistics regarding suicide.

American Association of Suicidology
http://www.suicidology.org
Research, prevention, and a list of crisis centers.

Center for Effective Collaboration and Practice
http://cecp.air.org/
Supports and promotes a reoriented national
preparedness to foster the development and
the adjustment of children with or at risk of
developing serious emotional disturbance.

Center for Mental Health in Schools
http://smhp.psych.ucla.edu/
Resources, technical assistance, and continuing
education on topics related to mental health
in schools, with a focus on barriers to learning
and promotion of healthy development.

Center for School Mental Health Assistance
http://csmha.umaryland.edu/
Supports schools and communities in the development
of programs and provides leadership and technical
assistance to advance effective interdisciplinary
school-based mental health programs.

Children's Safety Network
http://www.childrenssafetynetwork.org
Resources on child safety in school and on
employed youth.

Collaborative for Academic, Social, and
Emotional Learning
http://www.casel.org
Resources include evidence-based social and
emotional learning programs.

Colorado Anti-Bullying Project
http://www.no-bully.com/
Part of the Center for the Study and Prevention of
Violence. Provides information for teachers,
parents and students to prevent bullying, including
resources, links, and a bullying quiz.

Connect for Kids
http://www.connectforkids.org/
Resources for teachers and parents with advice from
mental health professionals.

Keep Schools Safe
http://www.keepschoolssafe.org
Information on violence and unintentional injury
prevention in schools.

National Association of School Psychologists
http://www.nasponline.org
Includes resources for safe schools.

National Educational Service
http://www.nes.org/
For educators and other youth professionals to help
foster environments where all youth succeed.

National Institute of Mental Health
http://www.nimh.nih.gov/
Click "For the Public" to retrieve publication materials
relating to mental health for children and
adolescents, including materials on violence
and suicide, including surgeon general reports.

National Mental Health Information Center
http://www.mentalhealth.org/
A Web site for the United States Department of Health
and Human Services' Substance Abuse and Mental
Health Services Administration (SAMHSA); Links
to the National Strategy for Suicide Prevention and
other mental health resources.

National Resource Center for Safe Schools
http://www.safetyzone.org

Safe USA
http://www.safeusa.org/school/safescho.htm
Resources for safety on playgrounds and in sports
and for violence prevention.

Students Against Destructive Decisions
http://www.saddonline.com
Peer leadership organization to promote health and safety.

Students Pledge Against Gun Violence
http://www.pledge.org/

Suicide Awareness: Voices of Education
http://www.save.org
Educates public on suicide prevention.

Suicide Prevention Resource Center
http://www.sprc.org/
Technical assistance, training, and information designed
to strengthen suicide prevention, network, and
advance the national strategy for suicide prevention.

US Department of Education
http://www.ed.gov/

US Department of Education—Office of Safe and
Drug-Free Schools
http://www.ed.gov/about/offices/list/osdfs/index.html

US Department of Education—Individuals with
Disabilities Education Act (IDEA) Web site
http://www.ed.gov/offices/OSERS/Policy/IDEA/

US Department of Justice, Office of Juvenile Justice
and Delinquency Prevention
http://ojjdp.ncjrs.org/
Information and resources (conferences, funding
opportunities, publications) about juvenile justice,
delinquency, and combating youth crime.

US Surgeon General Reports
http://sgreports.nlm.nih.gov/NN/
Reports available with the following titles related to
social environment:
- Closing the Gap: A National Blueprint to
Improve the Health of Persons with Mental
Retardation (2002)
- Mental Health: A Report of the Surgeon
General (1999)
- Mental Health: Culture, Race, and Ethnicity:
A Supplement to Mental Health: A Report of
the Surgeon General (2001)
- Report of the Surgeon General's Working Meeting
on the Integration of Mental Health Services and
Primary Health Care (2001)
- Report of the Surgeon General's Conference
on Children's Mental Health: A National
Action Agenda (2001)
- Youth Violence: A Report of the Surgeon General
(January 2001)

◀ Staff Health and Safety ▶

8-01—STAFF SAFETY AND INJURY PREVENTION[1-14]

Provide working conditions that promote health and safety and that reduce the likelihood of unintentional and intentional physical injuries. Develop and clearly communicate plans for steps to be taken when injuries and threat of injuries occur.

▶ RATIONALE

Adoption of safety policies at school is essential to prevent injuries. Staff knowledge of safety policies is essential for compliance. When staff understand the essential components of preventing injuries in the school environment, they will model safe behaviors.

▶ COMMENTARY

Schools have a responsibility to minimize staff exposure to environmental hazards (eg, communicable diseases, toxins, allergens), to physical dangers (eg, violence, traffic hazards on campus), and injuries that can be incurred from supervising sports, science experiments, art, and industrial art classes, food preparation, and off-campus school activities. Teach staff about violence prevention strategies (Guideline 7-05). Educate staff about proper ergonomic precautions, such as proper desk set-ups for school secretaries or proper lifting techniques for staff who assist with the lifting and transferring of students with special needs. Teach proper handling of needles and syringes for those providing health services and universal precautions for anyone who may have contact with human tissue and fluids. Provide staff with adequate safety equipment (eg, laboratory goggles and other safety gear, communication devices, Hoya lifts) and educate them on how to use the equipment properly. Inform all staff of safety and involve them in the development and revision of these policies. Inspections by the US Occupational Safety and Health Administration (OSHA) (http://www.osha.gov) may be considered in order to verify compliance with meeting safety standards for staff. As staff also serve as role models for students, staff safety practices (eg, use of safety belts) can ultimately benefit more people.

Be certain that staff know how to reach immediate help and how to report the injury when an employment-related injury occurs. Provide financial and medical support for injured staff members. Many school districts achieve this by providing workers' compensation programs—programs that are often required by state law.

▶ RELATED GUIDELINES

5-02, 6-02, 6-05, 6-13, 6-16, 7-05

▶ RELATED LINKS

http://www.ashrae.org
http://www.astm.org
http://www.thecatalyst.org
http://www.epa.gov
http://www.nist.gov
http://www.safetyzone.org
http://www.nsc.org

8-02–HEPATITIS B IMMUNIZATION FOR STAFF[15,16]

Recommend that all school personnel at risk of exposure to bloodborne pathogens have current hepatitis B immunization.

▶ RATIONALE

Many employees are at risk of having contact with someone else's blood or other body tissues and fluids. To protect those employees and the students they serve, immunization is a cost-effective measure and is required by the US Occupational Safety and Health Administration (OSHA [http://www.osha.gov]).

▶ COMMENTARY

Employee education on means to protect oneself and others from bloodborne pathogens and the provision of hepatitis B vaccination to those employees at risk of contact is a requirement of OSHA (http://www.osha.gov). Those at risk of exposure to blood include school nurses, health assistants, custodians, athletic trainers, physical education and special education teachers, first responders (for first aid), coaches of contact sports, and playground aides. A worksheet has been developed to assist school district employees as they determine their level of risk and relative need for the vaccine.[15]

Because it is a legal requirement for the employer to provide this immunization to those at risk, employee health insurers are likely to shift the cost of vaccination programs to school districts, unless the vaccine is negotiated by the district to be covered as part of employees' health benefits. There are various ways immunization of staff can be organized. School districts may offer the vaccine on school sites, refer eligible employees to their personal physicians, arrange immunization programs with the local health department, or refer eligible employees to a contractual health care agency.

▶ RELATED GUIDELINES

0-02, 6-15

▶ RELATED LINKS

http://www.osha.gov

8-03—PROVISION OF WELLNESS PROGRAMS FOR STAFF[17-21]

Provide staff wellness and health promotion programs for school staff based on an assessment of their needs and interests.

▶ RATIONALE

Employees' mental health and physical health are essential to the success of a school system. The promotion of staff members' own health helps them to become positive role models for students and increases their commitment to promoting student health and safety. Staff who are fit and healthy may be expected to have fewer absences and have more energy.

▶ COMMENTARY

Work site health promotion (staff wellness) is not institutionalized in many school settings. School-site health promotion programs for staff may not only impact the health of school faculty and staff, but also have effects on students, their families, and community members. Examples of health promotion programs for school staff include: health screenings, physical activity and fitness programs, nutrition education, weight management, smoking cessation, and stress management. Aside from local school programs, school district and state offices (eg, departments of health and education) can develop health promotion programs that involve school staff.

Once wellness and health promotion programs are available, encourage staff to participate in these programs. Examples of promotion ideas include introducing wellness programs to new staff at their orientation sessions, presenting information at regular staff meetings, including flyers and brochures with paychecks, putting information into newsletter articles and e-mail messages, and offering health insurance discounts for participants.

▶ RELATED GUIDELINES

0-01, 0-03, 0-08, 0-10, 0-13

8-04—INSURANCE COVERAGE FOR STAFF [22]

Provide health, disability, long-term care, and life insurance to all employees. This includes coverage for health promotion programs; medical, dental and vision coverage; and coverage for their dependents.

▶ *RATIONALE*

The provision of health insurance benefits for staff members and their families increases their accessibility to preventive health services. Preventive health care and early detection and management of health problems will reduce employee absence and reduce staff turnover, resulting in potential cost savings to the district, ultimately benefiting students. Generous and comprehensive benefit packages are excellent ways to attract and retain the most outstanding employees.

▶ *COMMENTARY*

School districts can be role models for other employers on their policies toward employee benefits. In many cases, the level of insurance coverage is determined by collective bargaining agreements. At a minimum, health insurance should provide access to a health plan that is affordable with respect to staff salaries. Health plan options should provide coverage that is broad enough to protect the employee and the employee's family from economic hardship. Districts' benefits offices should be staffed to meet all health and disability insurance information needs of its employees.

Many school districts provide financial and medical support for injured staff members through provision of workers' compensation programs—programs that are often required by state law.

8-05–EMPLOYEE ASSISTANCE PROGRAMS[23-25]

Provide employees with a work-site environment that encourages them to express their feelings, fears, and anxieties and to rehabilitate during times of personal crisis, personal loss, and school crisis. Provide employee assistance programs that help address these crises as well as mental disorders and drug- and alcohol-dependence.

▶ RATIONALE

Adults need assistance with stressful life situations or these situations can adversely affect job performance and/or conduct. Employee assistance programs can restore employees to levels of full productivity. Staff are more likely to be effective helping students deal with similar issues once their own issues are addressed.

▶ COMMENTARY

At some time, many employees face mental and emotional problems, difficult family responsibilities, financial burdens, legal difficulties, or dependent care needs. Provide free, confidential, short-term counseling to help employees identify and deal with stressful problems. Often, school districts require referral arrangements with outside organizations in order to assist with the full range of problems that can confront a staff member. Programs offered should include comprehensive counseling, help for employees to achieve a balance between work and family and other personal responsibilities, and drug/alcohol rehabilitation.

The social environment of the work-site should encourage members of the school staff to discuss stressful situations with their supervisors and other staff. Managers and supervisors must become familiar with employee assistance programs and know how and when to make referrals and/or recommendations to employees who seek help. It is the employee's decision to participate and to follow through with any referral.

During a school crisis (such as a natural disaster, loss, or other trauma), adult staff will need assistance with their own trauma and grief reactions if they are to be helpful to students. Teachers and other staff should receive current information about the crisis, be invited to participate in planning and implementing school-wide interventions, and receive the emotional support they need to work through the stressful situation.

▶ RELATED GUIDELINES

0-01, 4-11, 6-12, 7-02

▶ RELATED LINKS

http://www.FEMA.gov
http://www.neahin.org

8-06—INTERPROFESSIONAL COLLABORATION, STAFF MENTORING[17,19,26–28]

Arrange for and encourage staff members to have opportunities to consult with and exchange information with other staff members across various disciplines. Arrange for peer mentoring.

▶ RATIONALE

Consultation and open exchanges across disciplines enhance school staff members' understanding and ability to manage program-related and student-related issues. Mentoring programs can be helpful to all school professionals (eg, teachers, school nurses, school counselors), whether they are beginners or veterans in new assignments or in need of remedial aid to improve their skills.

▶ COMMENTARY

Include health, mental health, teaching, and other staff members in student assistance teams. Interprofessional activity should go beyond problem-oriented models of dealing with educational challenges of students or student behavior. The National Education Association (NEA) (http://www.nea.org/health) has resources on its Internet site to help staff members engage in multidisciplinary exchanges that help to promote wellness, individual interventions, and systems change.

Mentoring is an essential part of staff development and a part of envisioning schools as professional learning communities. The Internet site of the NEA Foundation (http://www.nfie.org) has various publications that describe how schools can create mentoring programs and set up professional developmental centers led by the professionals themselves. Such resources can be used to help schools create a climate for mentoring, select training materials, protect the confidentiality of those who are mentored, and evaluate their mentoring program. Although directed primarily toward mentoring of teachers, concepts and planning tools on this Internet site apply very well to the development of mentoring programs for other school staff, including health and mental health professionals.

▶ RELATED GUIDELINES

0-07, 4-01, 6-20, 7-02

▶ RELATED LINKS

http://www.nea.org/health
http://www.nfie.org

8-07–ACCOMMODATING STAFF WITH DISABILITIES[29-31]

Accommodate staff with disabilities and other health and safety concerns, as required by federal and state laws.

▶ RATIONALE

The provision of access to employment for all eligible applicants and all current employees promotes a fair and inclusive environment. For most schools, this is also necessary to comply with federal laws and many state laws.

▶ COMMENTARY

As outlined in the Americans with Disabilities Act (ADA),[29] prohibit discrimination in regard to job application procedures, hiring, advancement, employee discharge, employee compensation, and job training. ADA also protects individuals who have a relationship or association with a person who has a disability. School districts are not required to hire an individual if that individual, with or without an accommodation, is incapable of doing the essential functions of the job. Establish written essential functions for each potential employment position in the school district. Determine what, if any, accommodation can be made to allow a disabled individual to perform those functions.

ADA requires public school districts with 50 or more employees to name an ADA coordinator to deal with questions and complaints about ADA compliance and accommodations and to establish a grievance procedure for the resolution of disputes under ADA. It is recommended that all schools, including private schools and others that are exempt under ADA, establish the same procedures.

A federal law known as the Family and Medical Leave Act (FMLA) (http://www.dol.gov/elaws/fmla.htm) provides for a total of 12 weeks (not necessarily consecutive) in each 12-month period for any combination of the following reasons: (1) the birth, adoption, or foster care of a child; (2) the employee's own serious health condition; and (3) to care for a parent, spouse, or dependent who has a serious health condition. Generally, for parental leave purposes, the FMLA leave would also have to be taken in consecutive weeks and is only available for 12 months after the birth or adoption of the child.

▶ RELATED GUIDELINES

0-02, 0-03, 6-01, 7-06

▶ RELATED LINKS

http://www.ada.gov
http://www.dol.gov/elaws/fmla.htm

CHAPTER REFERENCES

1. American Chemical Society, Committee on Chemical Safety. *Safety in Academic Chemistry Laboratories.* Washington, DC: American Chemical Society; 1995

2. American Public Health Association. Creating healthier school facilities. *Am J Public Health.* 2001;91:494–495

3. Bernacki EJ, Guidera JA, Schaefer JA, Lavin RA, Tsai SP. An ergonomics program designed to reduce the incidence of upper extremity work related musculoskeletal disorders. *J Occup Environ Med.* 1999;41:1032–1041

4. Centers for Disease Control and Prevention. School health guidelines to prevent unintentional injuries and violence. *MMWR Recomm Rep.* 2001;50(RR-22):1–73

5. Friedland LR. Universal precautions and safety devices which reduce the risk of occupational exposure to blood-borne pathogens: a review for emergency health care workers. *Pediatr Emerg Care.* 1991;7:356–362

6. Institute of Medicine, Committee on the Assessment of Asthma and Indoor Air. *Clearing the Air: Asthma and Indoor Air Exposures.* Washington, DC; National Academy Press; 2000

7. Knight S, Junkins EP Jr, Lightfoot AC, Cazier CF, Olson LM. Injuries sustained in shop class. *Pediatrics.* 2000;106:10–13

8. Laflamme L, Eilert-Petersson E. School-injury patterns: a tool for safety planning at the school and community levels. *Accid Anal Prev.* 1998; 30:277–283

9. McCann M. *Art Safety Procedures: A Health and Safety Manual for Art Schools and Art Departments.* New York, NY: Center for Safety in the Arts; 1992

10. National Science Teachers Association. *Guidelines for Responsible Use of Animals in the Classroom.* Arlington, VA: National Science Teachers Association; 1991. Available at: http://www.nsta.org/position#list

11. National Science Teachers Association. *Safety in the Elementary Science Classroom.* Arlington, VA: National Science Teachers Association; 1997

12. Posner M. *Preventing School Injuries: A Comprehensive Guide for School Administrators, Teachers, and Staff.* New Brunswick, NJ: Rutgers University Press; 2000

13. Smedje G, Norback D. Irritants and allergens at school in relation to furnishings and cleaning. *Indoor Air.* 2001;11:127–133

14. US Environmental Protection Agency. *IAQ Tools for School Kits.* Washington, DC: US Environmental Protection Agency; 2000. Available at: http://www.epa.gov/iaq/schools/pubs.html

15. Taras HL. The hepatitis B occupational risk worksheet. *J Sch Health.* 1994;64:122

16. Centers for Disease Control and Prevention. Hepatitis B virus: a comprehensive strategy for eliminating transmission in the United States through universal childhood vaccination: recommendations of the Immunization Practices Advisory Committee (ACIP). *MMWR Morb Mortal Wkly Rep.* 1991;40(RR-13):1–25

17. Allegrante JP. School-site health promotion for staff. In: Marx E, Wooley SF, eds. *Health is Academic: A Guide to Coordinated School Health Programs.* New York, NY: Teacher's College Press; 1998

18. Henderson AC. *Healthy Schools, Healthy Futures: The Case for Improving School Environment.* Santa Cruz, CA: ETR Associates; 1993

19. Institute of Medicine. *Schools and Health: Our Nation's Investment.* Washington, DC: National Academy Press; 1997

20. Marx E, Wooley SF, eds. *Health is Academic: A Guide to Coordinated School Health Programs.* New York, NY: Teachers College Press; 1998

21. Centers for Disease Control and Prevention. Module 7: health promotion for staff. In: *School Health Index for Physical Activity and Healthy Eating: A Self-Assessment and Planning Guide.* Middle School/High School Version. Atlanta, GA: Centers for Disease Control and Prevention; 2000. Available at: http://www.cdc.gov/nccdphp/dash/SHI/index.htm

22. Haynes G, Dunnagan T. Comparing changes in health risk factors and medical costs over time. *Am J Health Promot.* 2002;17:112–121

23. Figley CR, Bride BE, Mazza N, eds. *Death and Trauma: The Traumatology of Grieving.* New York, NY: Taylor & Francis; 1997

24. National Education Association, Health Information Network. *Violence in Communities and Schools: A Stress Reduction Guide for Teachers and Other School Staff.* Washington, DC: National Education Association; 2000

25. Vulpitta RT. *On-site Emergency Response Planning Guide.* Itasca, IL: National Safety Council; 2002

26. Holland RW. Mentoring as a career development tool. *CUPA J.* 1994;45:41–44

27. Hooper K, Lawson HA. *Serving Children, Youth, and Families Through Interprofessional Collaboration and Service Integration: A Framework for Action.* Oxford, OH: The Danforth Foundation and the Institute for Educational Renewal at Miami University; 1994

28. Rosenfield SA, Gravois TA. *Instructional Consultation Teams: Collaborating for Change.* New York, NY: Guilford; 1996
29. Americans With Disabilities Act of 1990. Pub L No. 101-336 (1990). Available at: http://www.usdoj.gov/crt/ada/pubs/ada.txt
30. Abraham JD, Strom DJ, Sloan M, McElroy L. *A Guide to the Family & Medical Leave Act.* Washington, DC: American Federation of Teachers, 1998
31. Bettenhausen S. *Avoid Potential Liability: The Americans with Disabilities Act and the Public Schools.* Washington, DC: Educational Resources Information Center (ERIC), US Department of Education; 2001. ED461966

CHAPTER-RELATED LINKS

American Society of Heating, Refrigeration, and Air-Conditioning Engineers
http://www.ashrae.org

ASTM International (formerly known as American Society for Testing and Materials)
http://www.astm.org/
Provides consensus standards and related technical information in order to promote public health and safety as well as contribute to the reliability of materials, products, systems, and services. This includes anything from art materials and sports equipment to construction supplies and playground equipment/surfaces.

The Catalyst
http://www.thecatalyst.org/
A site developed for secondary school teachers as a resource for finding relevant information for teaching chemistry. Includes safety measures to be taken in biology, chemistry, and physics classes.

Environmental Protection Agency
http://www.epa.gov/

Federal Emergency Management Agency
http://www.FEMA.gov/

National Education Association
http://www.nea.org/health/
"School employee health" link shares resources to help staff focus on their own health and lifestyle concerns while they continue to take care of others.

National Education Association, Health Information Network
http://www.neahin.org/
Nonprofit health affiliate of NEA, provides health information on topics of concern to educators and students.

National Institute of Standards and Technology
http://www.nist.gov

National Resource Center for Safe Schools
http://www.safetyzone.org

National Safety Council
http://www.nsc.org
Includes pages on ergonomic safety.

NEA Foundation
http://www.nfie.org/
Resources for educators to become agents for change to improve teaching and learning.

Occupational Safety and Health Administration
http://www.osha.gov/

Safe USA
http://www.safeusa.org/school/safescho.htm
Resources for safety on playgrounds and in sports and for violence prevention.

US Department of Justice, Americans with Disabilities Act
http://www.ada.gov/
Information and technical assistance on compliance with the Americans with Disabilities Act.

US Department of Labor, Family and Medical Leave Act
http://www.dol.gov/elaws/fmla.htm
Information about employee eligibility, employee/employer notification responsibilities, and employee rights and benefits.

◀ **Appendices** ▶

APPENDIX A. HEALTHY PEOPLE 2010 OBJECTIVES DIRECTLY RELATED TO SCHOOLS

1. Increase the proportion of children and youth with disabilities who spend at least 80% of their time in regular education programs. (Objective 6-9)

2. Reduce the proportion of people with disabilities reporting environmental barriers to participation in home, school, work, or community activities. (Objective 6-12)

3. Increase high school completion. (Objective 7-1)

4. Increase the proportion of middle, junior high, and senior high schools that provide school health education to prevent health problems in the following areas: unintentional injury; violence; suicide; tobacco use and addiction; alcohol or other drug use; unintended pregnancy, HIV/AIDS, and STD infection; unhealthy dietary patterns; inadequate physical activity; and environmental health. (Objective 7-2)

5. Increase the proportion of the Nation's elementary, middle, junior high, and senior high schools that have a nurse-to-student ratio of at least 1:750. (Objective 7-4)

6. Increase the proportion of the Nation's primary and secondary schools that have official school policies ensuring the safety of students and staff from environmental hazards, such as chemicals in special classrooms, poor indoor air quality, asbestos, and exposure to pesticides. (Objective 8-20)

7. Increase the proportion of young adults who have received formal instruction before turning age 18 years on reproductive health issues, including all of the following topics: birth control methods, safer sex to prevent HIV, prevention of sexually transmitted diseases, and abstinence. (Objective 9-11)

8. Maintain vaccination coverage levels for children in licensed day care facilities and children in kindergarten through the first grade. (Objective 14-23)

9. Increase routine vaccination coverage levels for adolescents. (Objective 14-27)

10. Increase the proportion of public and private schools that require use of appropriate head, face, eye, and mouth protection for students participating in school-sponsored physical activities. (Objective 15-31)

11. Reduce physical fighting among adolescents. (Objective 15-38)

12. Reduce weapon carrying by adolescents on school property. (Objective 15-39)

13. Increase the proportion of children and adolescents aged 6 to 19 years whose intake of meals and snacks at schools contributes to good overall dietary quality. (Objective 19-15)

14. Increase the proportion of school-based health centers with an oral health component. (Objective 21-13)

15. Increase the proportion of the Nation's public and private schools that require daily physical education for all students. (Objective 22-8)

16. Increase the proportion of adolescents who participate in daily school physical education. (Objective 22-9)

17. Increase the proportion of adolescents who spend at least 50 percent of school physical education class time being physically active. (Objective 22-10)

18. Increase the proportion of the Nation's public and private schools that provide access to their physical activity spaces and facilities for all persons outside of normal school hours (that is, before and after the school day, on weekends, and during summer and other vacations). (Objective 22-12)

19. Reduce the number of school or work days missed by persons with asthma due to asthma. (Objective 24-5)

20. Increase smoke-free and tobacco-free environments in schools, including all school facilities, property, vehicles, and school events. (Objective 27-11)

APPENDIX B. TIPS ON CULTURAL COMPETENCY FOR SCHOOL STAFF

There are 5 essential elements that contribute to a school's ability to become more culturally competent. The educational system must: (1) value diversity; (2) have the capacity for cultural self-assessment; (3) be conscious of the "dynamics" inherent when cultures interact; (4) institutionalize cultural knowledge; and (5) adapt curricula, teaching strategies, and support services (including school health services) to reflect diversity between and within cultures. This should be reflected in attitudes, structures, policies, and services.

To achieve cultural competence, staff must be aware of what constitutes "culture." For example, family relationships, faith, and health beliefs are components of culture. Staff must learn about their own culture through a process of self-assessment (eg, examining the assumptions and values of one's own culture as well as one's own personal perspectives on these values and assumptions). Staff must also learn about individual students in their school and, as much as possible, about important aspects of their cultural backgrounds.

Resources are available for individual staff members who wish to improve their cultural competence as well as for school-wide staff development. Advocates for Youth has published a resource called *A Youth Leader's Guide to Building Cultural Competence*. Descriptions of various cultural components are followed by questions that prompt school staff to think more about each component. A process of self-assessment is designed to help each staff member examine his or her own cultural background, values, and assumptions. The manuscript includes tips for learning about individual students, for continuing a process of learning about students' cultural backgrounds, and for providing effective multicultural education. This resource has 2 additional special focuses. One is how various cultures (especially black and some Hispanic communities) regard human immunodeficiency virus/acquired immunodeficiency syndrome (HIV/AIDS) prevention messages, and another is working with gay, lesbian, and bisexual youth of all races and ethnicities.

REFERENCES

King MA, Sims A, Osher D. *How is Cultural Competence Integrated in Education?* Washington, DC: Center for Effective Collaboration and Practice. Available at: http://cecp.air.org/cultural/Q_integrated.htm

Messina SA. *A Youth Leader's Guide to Building Cultural Competence.* Washington, DC: Advocates for Youth; 1994. Available at: http://www.advocatesforyouth.org/publications/guide.pdf/

Ladson-Billings G. *Crossing Over to Canaan: The Journey of New Teachers in Diverse Classrooms.* San Francisco, CA: Jossey-Bass; 2001

Sobocinski MR. Ethical principles in the counseling of gay and lesbian adolescents: issues of autonomy, competence, and confidentiality. *Prof Psychol.* 1990;21:240-247

National Education Association. *Report of the NEA Task Force on Sexual Orientation.* Washington, DC: National Education Association; 2002. Available at: http://www.nea.org/nr/02taskforce.html

Parents, Families and Friends of Lesbians and Gays. *From Our House to the School House: A Brochure for Educators.* Washington, DC: Parents, Families and Friends of Lesbians and Gays; 2002. Available at: http://www.pflag.org/publications/schools.pdf

APPENDIX C. INTERNET SITES FOR SCHOOL HEALTH- AND SAFETY-RELATED PROFESSIONS

NATIONAL SOURCES OF INFORMATION ON CREDENTIALS, LICENSING, CERTIFICATION, AND CONTINUING EDUCATION OF SCHOOL HEALTH AND HEALTH-RELATED PROFESSIONALS

Note: Licensure occurs through the state of residence. School administrators wishing to investigate whether licenses are available for a profession (and if available, the requirements of that professional licensure) are encouraged to contact their state professional licensing boards.

Certification and credentialing are often, but not exclusively, achieved through a national body. These national organizations listed below either credential or certify professionals or can provide information on professional qualifications.

Athletic Trainer
National Athletic Trainers' Association (NATA)
http://www.nata.org

Audiologist, Audiology Assistant
American Speech-Language-Hearing Association
http://www.asha.org

Coach (High School)
National High School Coaches Association
http://www.nhsca.com

Counselor (School)
American School Counselor Association
http://www.schoolcounselor.org

Dietitian
American Dietetic Association—
Commission on Dietetic Registration
http://www.eatright.org

Dental Hygienist
American Dental Hygienists' Association
http://www.adha.org

Dentist
American Dental Association—
National Dental Board Examinations
http://www.ada.org

Food Service Director
American School Food Service Association
http://www.asfsa.org

Health Educator
National Commission for Health Education Credentialing
http://www.nchec.org

Nurse (School) and Nurse Practitioners
National Association of School Nurses
http://www.nasn.org

National Association of Pediatric Nurse Practitioners
http://www.napnap.org

National Council of State Boards of Nursing
http://www.ncsbn.org

Occupational Therapist; Occupational Therapy Assistant
National Board for Certification in Occupational Therapy
http://www.nbcot.org

Pediatrician
American Academy of Pediatrics
http://www.aap.org

American Board of Pediatrics
http://www.abp.org

Physical Educator
National Association for Sport and Physical Education
http://www.aahperd.org/naspe

National Council on Accreditation of Teacher Education
http://www.ncate.org

Physical Therapist; Physical Therapy Assistant

American Physical Therapy Association

http://www.apta.org

Psychiatrist—Child and Adolescent Psychiatry

American Academy of Child and Adolescent Psychiatry

http://www.aacap.org

American Board of Psychiatry and Neurology

http://www.abpn.com

Psychologist (School)

National Association of School Psychologists

http://www.nasponline.org/index2.html

Social Worker (School)

School Social Work Association of America

http://www.sswaa.org

Speech Pathologist

American Speech-Language-Hearing Association

http://www.asha.org

APPENDIX D. STRATEGIES TEACHERS USE TO TEACH HEALTH AND SAFETY

Teachers should select strategies with an instructional purpose that lead to the acquisition of functional knowledge or essential skills that avoid gimmicks and go beyond entertainment. Strategies often used in health and safety courses include:

- Brainstorming
- Role playing
- Simulations
- Cooperative learning groups
- Whole-class discussion
- Small-group discussion
- Reports
- Projects
- Experiments
- "Angel on the shoulder"
- Forced-choice exercises
- Puppetry
- Values voting
- Debates
- Drama
- Poetry
- Songs
- Art work
- Creating media spots or videos
- Using technology such as the Internet or CDs
- Surveys
- Games
- Peer education
- Skill demonstration and practice with corrective feedback
- Lectures enhanced with slides or presentation software
- Out-of-class assignments that might include a service project or interviewing an adult family member

APPENDIX E. OUTDOOR SAFETY IN EXTREME WEATHER CONDITIONS

RECOMMENDATIONS FOR EXTREME HEAT

- Wear light-colored, porous, reflective materials.
- Keep fluids at the site of the activity (electrolyte solutions, water, or diluted fruit juice, not caffeine-containing beverages).
- Provide water breaks every 15 minutes, encouraging drinking beyond thirst level (8 oz for high school athletes), before exercise during physical activities.
- Allow 5 to 6 practice periods for students to acclimate to heat.
- Schedule frequent rest periods in shade.
- Consider weighing athletes before and after activity to identify a greater than 3% loss of body weight.
- Limit sun exposure and provide sunscreen for all sunny conditions. Reschedule strenuous activities for early morning and late afternoon.

RECOMMENDATIONS FOR EXTREME COLD

- Wear warm, layered clothing to conserve body heat.
- Use a "buddy system" to check for frostbite (pain, prickly sensations, white skin, peeling, blistering, itching, mottling, swelling, or hardness in the affected area) in extreme cold and wind conditions, at least on exposed areas such as cheeks, nose, and fingers.
- Provide supervision by persons trained to recognize the early signs of frostbite and hypothermia (shivering, tiredness, slurred speech, clumsiness).
- Stay dry.

RECOMMENDATIONS FOR SUN EXPOSURE

- Avoid the mid-day sun.
- Provide shaded spaces or indoor facilities for physical activity.
- Encourage students and staff to use protective hats, clothing, sunglasses, and sunscreen when in sunlight.

RECOMMENDATIONS FOR DAYS OF HIGH OZONE LEVELS

Ozone is a commonly measured air pollutant. It is always present in the air, but is not a health problem at low levels. High levels can cause breathing problems and be irritating to eyes and nose. Ozone levels are commonly announced in newspapers, by broadcast media, and on the Internet, especially in geographic regions susceptible to high levels and during seasons of high ozone. On days when ozone levels are high (as defined by the Environmental Protection Agency), recommendations are to:
- Ask children to report any symptoms that might be related to ozone, such as shortness of breath, coughing, wheezing, and eye and nose irritation.
- Monitor students for symptoms, especially those with asthma and other respiratory problems.
- Reduce intensity of physical activities by:
  a. Exchanging players off the field more frequently
  b. Alternating endurance activities with skills development
  c. Focusing on skill development versus endurance training
  d. Taking frequent rest and water breaks and shortening length of practices

- Move some activities indoors, whenever possible.
- Reschedule some activities to hours of the day when ozone is not as high (ozone is lower in early morning and early evening than it is at mid-day).
- Refer to the Environmental Protection Agency Web site (http://www.epa.gov/airnow) for local information and for updates on general recommendations.

REFERENCES

American Academy of Pediatrics, Committee on Sports Medicine and Fitness. Climatic heat stress and the exercising child and adolescent. *Pediatrics*. 2000;106:158–59

Centers for Disease Control and Prevention. Guidelines for school programs to prevent skin cancer. *MMWR Recomm Rep.* 2002;51(RR-4):1–20

APPENDIX F. SUICIDE AND VIOLENCE

FACTORS THAT MIGHT INCREASE RISK OF SUICIDE AND/OR VIOLENT BEHAVIOR

One or a combination of mental disorders (major depression, schizophrenia, alcoholism, substance abuse or dependence, conduct disorders) and possibly other conditions, such as mobility impairment, learning disability, or attention-deficit/hyperactivity disorder

- Carrying a weapon
- Access to firearms
- Exposure to violence in the community or family
- Recent loss
- Sexual identity issues
- Isolation, rejection, hopelessness
- Social withdrawal
- Sudden changes in behavior
- Victim of bullying
- Poor academic performance or low school interest
- Previous suicide attempts; inferred threats (eg, suicide drawings), or threats with a plan
- Recent exposure to a suicide (ie, friend, family member, acquaintance, or classmate)
- Uncontrolled anger, impulsive and chronic hitting or intimidating, bullying
- Serious threats of violence
- Abuse of animals

EXAMPLES OF STRATEGIES THAT SCHOOLS CAN TAKE

- Staff training related to at-risk behaviors associated with violent or suicidal behaviors
- Providing a protocol for staff to follow if they have identified students at risk of violent behavior and/or suicide
- Formation of a school mental health team that evaluates students referred by teachers
- Providing access to needed services for identified students
- Ensuring there are supports for students who have been identified
- Ensuring that staff know of referral resources and procedures
- Development of a partnership with the student, school, home, and community
- Integrating violence prevention and anti-bullying curriculum into school curricula
- Adopting effective suicide prevention programs
- Offering support groups, mentoring programs
- Tutoring students with academic difficulties
- Providing parent training and support (including a focus on teenage parents in school)
- Monitoring follow-up of referred students

DATA COLLECTION AND PROGRAM EVALUATION OF VIOLENCE AND SUICIDE PREVENTION PROGRAMS IN SCHOOLS

Tracking cases involves:
- Establishing clear definitions for all forms of verbal and physical violence.
- Establishing a system responsible for collecting, storing, and analyzing data on violence and suicide incidents.
- Developing brief, user-friendly procedures for reporting and recording incidents.

- Ensuring that reporting incidents does not have negative consequences.
- Ensuring that all school staff, students, and parents are involved in the reporting process.

Feedback involves:
- Developing a communication process that transmits results of data analysis to key members of the school community.
- Developing regularly scheduled reports.
- Identifying school and community stakeholders who review data reports and provide leadership in responding to changes or lack of changes in suicide and violent incident trends.

Program evaluation includes:
- Documenting program implementation.
- Linking program implementation to an ongoing case/incident tracking system.
- Utilizing information to change and/or modify program activities in response to data.

REFERENCES

Centers for Disease Control and Prevention. School health guidelines to prevent unintentional injuries and violence. *MMWR Recomm Rep.* 2001;50(RR-22):1–73

King RA, Schwab-Stone M, Flisher AJ, Greenwald S, Kramer RA, Goodman SH, Lahey BB, Shaffer D, Gould MS. Psychosocial and risk behavior correlates of youth suicide attempts and suicidal ideation. *J Am Acad Child Adolesc Psychiatr.* 2001;40:837–846

National Institute of Justice. *Conflict Resolution for School Personnel: An Interactive School Safety Training Tool* (CD-ROM). Washington, DC: US Department of Justice, Office of Justice Programs; 2002

Shaffer D, Craft L. Methods of adolescent suicide prevention. *J Clin Psychiatr.* 1999;60(Suppl 2):70-76, 113–116

◀ **Glossary** ▶

> ## A

ACTION RESEARCH
A systematic process that teachers and others can use to carefully study their actions and problems. Systematic self-reflection can guide, correct, and evaluate future professional decisions and actions. In essence, professionals research their own practice in their professional setting. (0-16)

ALLERGEN
Any substance, such as pollen, that can cause an allergy. (6-13, 8-01)

ANABOLIC STEROID
A synthetic hormone that promotes storage of protein in the body and promotes growth of tissues. Sometimes used by athletes to increase muscle size and strength. (3-09)

ANOREXIA NERVOSA
A psychiatric and physiological disorder characterized by an abnormal fear of becoming obese, a distorted self-image, a persistent unwillingness to eat, and severe weight loss. It is often accompanied by self-induced vomiting, excessive exercise, malnutrition, loss of regular menstrual periods, and other physiological changes. (3-09)

ANTICIPATORY GUIDANCE
Explanations to parents, older children and adolescents about the changes likely to occur in a child's behaviors, exposures, and risks as growth and development proceed. (4-27)

AUTOMATED EXTERNAL DEFRIBRILLATOR (AED)
A device that administers an electric shock through the chest wall to the heart to treat those having a cardiac arrest. Built-in computers assess the patient's heart rhythm, judge whether defibrillation is needed, and then administer the shock. (4-07, 6-22)

> ## B

BIOAEROSOLS
An airborne dispersion of particles, where the particles contain bacteria, viruses, dust mites, fungi (spores or hyphae), or other biological entities or parts of biological entities. (6-14)

BLOODBORNE PATHOGEN
Any organism (bacteria, virus, etc) that can cause disease is a pathogen. Bloodborne pathogens are those found in blood itself as well as on blood-soiled bandages, needles, and other items that contain blood. (6-15, 8-02)

BUILDING COMMISSIONING
Putting a building through a trial run before opening it for occupants. (6-03)

BULIMIA
An eating disorder characterized by self-induced vomiting after eating. (3-09)

▶ C

CARDIAC DISORDER

Disorders that pertain to the heart. Cardiac disorders of school-aged children are often structural abnormalities of the heart that have existed from birth. (3-03)

CASE MANAGEMENT

Also referred to as "care coordination" or "care management," case management is the process of helping an individual or family explore options and services based on a review of a person's or family's needs, then helping the family or individual plan and implement care. A case manager plans, implements, coordinates, monitors, and/or evaluates the provision of all the selected services. (4-03)

CERVICAL SPINE

The part of the spine at the level of an individual's neck. Injuries to the cervical spine are rare but catastrophic if mishandled. Protection of the cervical spine after an injury requires trained individuals to immobilize head and neck before moving the injured person. (4-07)

CHRONIC CONDITIONS

An illness or medical condition that lasts over a long period and sometimes causes a long-term change in the body. (4-16)

CLINICAL LABORATORY IMPROVEMENT AMENDMENT (CLIA)

All laboratory testing (except research) performed on humans in the United States, including those done in outpatient settings, such as school-based health centers, is regulated through the Clinical Laboratory Improvement Amendments (CLIA). The objective of CLIA is to ensure quality laboratory testing. (4-32)

COMMUNICABLE DISEASE

A disease that is able to be passed from one person, animal, or organism to another. (4-22, 4-24, 6-02, 6-16, 8-01)

CONDUCT DISORDER

A psychiatric diagnosis for a repetitive and persistent pattern of behavior in which a child either violates basic rights of others or violates age-appropriate societal norms. The onset is before age 18 and behaviors include (a) aggressive conduct that threatens physical harm to people or animals; (b) nonaggressive conduct that causes property damage; (c) deceitfulness or theft; and (d) serious violations of rules. (7-04)

CREATINE

A compound made by the body and used to store energy in cells of muscle tissue. Internal creatine supplies energy for muscle contraction. It is available as a dietary supplement (animal sources). There is scientific evidence to support creatine's ability to somewhat enhance muscular performance, with claims escalated well beyond science. Safety of long-term creatine supplementation among youth remains unknown. (3-09)

CRYPTOCOCCOSIS

A fungal infection that can occur when people inhale the spores usually introduced into the air via contaminated bird droppings. Infection with *Cryptococcus* species results in inflammation of the brain and sometimes the lungs, kidneys, prostate gland, bones, skin, or liver. (6-14)

CYSTIC FIBROSIS
A hereditary disease of the exocrine glands (glands that secrete), characterized by the production of abnormally viscous (thick and sticky) mucus by the affected glands and frequent respiratory infections and impaired digestion. It usually develops during early childhood and affects mainly the pancreas (digestive system), respiratory system, and sweat glands. (3-03)

D

DENTAL HOME
A primary dental care provider system that is accessible, continuous, comprehensive, family centered, coordinated, compassionate, and culturally effective. (1-03, 4-29)

DENTAL SEALANTS
A plastic coating placed in the pits and grooves of molar teeth found to reduce dental cavities by 60%. (4-12)

DIURETIC
A substance or drug that increases volume of urination and can cause dehydration. Such substances are sometimes abused by athletes to modify weight. (3-09)

DOWN SYNDROME
A congenital disorder, caused by the presence of an extra 21st chromosome. The affected person has mild to moderate mental retardation, short stature, and a flattened facial profile. Also called trisomy 21. (3-03)

E

EPINEPHRINE
A hormone secreted as a response to physical or mental stress. Sometimes administered as a medication to stimulate heart action and increase blood pressure, often used to treat severe allergic reactions (anaphylactic shock). Also called adrenaline. (4-21, 6-22)

F

FAMILY RESOURCE CENTER
A location that provides primary prevention services for families, such as parent education, information and referral to local health and social services, and collaborative work with community development initiatives. Some also provide home visiting, early childhood services, parent/child play groups, and opportunities for personal and family development. (1-04, 1-05)

FLUORIDE RINSE
A solution used to prevent dental caries. A person places some of the solution in the mouth, swishes, and spits the solution into the sink. (4-12)

FLUORIDE VARNISH
A compound containing high concentrations of fluoride that dental care providers apply to teeth and leave for hours, releasing fluoride into the smooth surface areas of the teeth until it is brushed off after a few hours. Found to be very protective against cavities. (4-12)

FOODS OF MINIMAL NUTRITIONAL VALUE (FMNV)

As stated in the National School Lunch Program, a list of foods published by the US Department of Agriculture that have few nutrients. Carbonated sodas, chewing gum, hard candies, licorice candy, and marshmallows are examples of items on this list. (5-09)

FROSTBITE

An injury to the skin that results from prolonged exposure to moderate cold or brief exposure to extreme cold. When skin is exposed to the cold, blood vessels in the skin clamp down. The decreased blood flow to the skin causes fluid in and around skin cells to develop ice crystals. Areas of the body most prone to frostbite are fingers, toes, hands, feet, nose, ears, and cheeks.

▶ G

GASTROSTOMY TUBE

A feeding tube inserted into a permanent opening in a person's abdominal wall and stomach. The gastrostomy or permanent opening is created surgically for persons whose intake of food by mouth is not possible or is inadequate to support a healthy weight. (4-21)

GLUCAGON

A hormone produced by the pancreas that stimulates an increase in blood sugar levels. As a medication for a person with diabetes, it is injected to rapidly and safely increase blood sugar in urgent situations due to too much insulin. (4-21, 6-22)

▶ H

HANTAVIRUS

Any of a group of viruses carried by rodents that cause fever, accompanied by internal bleeding, low blood pressure, shock, and severe respiratory infections in humans. (6-14)

HEIMLICH MANEUVER

An emergency technique used to eject an object, such as food, from the trachea of a choking person. The technique employs a firm upward thrust just below the rib cage to force air from the lungs. (4-07)

HEPATITIS B

An infection of the liver that is caused by a virus transmitted by contaminated blood or blood products, by sexual contact with an infected person, or by the use of contaminated needles and instruments. Also called serum hepatitis. (8-02)

HISTOPLASMOSIS

A fungal infection that can occur when people inhale spores usually introduced into the air via contaminated bird droppings. Infection with *Histoplasma* species is often accompanied by no symptoms or some mild respiratory symptoms, such as a cough, fever, and/or tiredness. (6-14)

HOYA LIFTS

A small crane with a swing-like cloth seat used to transfer heavy students with disabilities who are not able to stand/walk (eg, can be used to transfer a student from a chair to a changing table, onto buses, or into pools). (8-01)

HYPOALLERGENIC

Having a decreased tendency to provoke an allergic reaction. Substances unlikely to cause an allergic reaction. (6-03)

HYPOTHERMIA

A condition when the body cannot generate sufficient heat to maintain its functions; defined as a body temperature of less than 35°C or 95°F.

I

INDIVIDUALIZED EDUCATION PROGRAM (IEP)

A written document that describes the educational plan for a student with a disability. (4-20)

INDIVIDUAL FAMILY SERVICE PLAN (IFSP)

Similar to an individualized education program (see above) but applies to students with disabilities who are infants or toddlers and defines the family, not only the student, as the recipient of services. All medical and health services that a student requires are to be defined in the IFSP, even if provision of one or more of these service falls outside of the school district's obligations (IDEA law; Sec. 303.344(e)). (4-20)

INDIVIDUAL HEALTH SERVICE PLAN (IHSP)

A written plan that outlines the safe delivery of health services by a school or school district to the student. Students whose health status requires professional nursing observation or intervention, administration of procedures, or the use of a health device need an IHSP. (4-20)

INSULIN PUMP

A portable device for people with diabetes that injects insulin at programmed intervals in order to regulate blood sugar levels. (4-19)

INTEGRATED PEST MANAGEMENT (IPM)

Pest and environmental information and pest control methods intended to prevent pest damage economically and with little hazard to people, property, and the environment. (6-13)

L

LEGIONELLOSIS

A bacterial pneumonia caused by *Legionella pneumophila* distributed in aerosols from water sources such as cooling towers, evaporative condensers, whirlpools, shower heads, faucets, and hot water tanks. (6-14)

LETHARGY

A condition of indifference with abnormal drowsiness or stupor. (4-22)

LOCKDOWN

Students and staff are secured in place, and access to and from the building is denied. (4-11, 6-23)

▶ M

MALARIA
An infectious disease caused by a protozoan infection of red blood cells characterized by cycles of chills, fever, and sweating. The protozoan is transmitted to humans by the bite of an infected female anopheles mosquito. (6-14)

MALOCCLUSION
Faulty contact between the upper and lower teeth when the jaw is closed. (4-12)

MEDICAL HOME
A medical care system for infants, children, and adolescents and their families that is accessible, continuous, comprehensive, family centered, coordinated, compassionate, and culturally effective. Well-trained physicians who provide primary care deliver care directly or indirectly by and help to manage and facilitate essentially all aspects of pediatric care. (1-03)

MEDICALLY FRAGILE
A condition when a student's medical condition is unstable and, as a result, requires ongoing or frequent observation by persons skilled to recognize sudden changes in condition and/or who are skilled to respond to that change. A student whose airway is prone to sudden blockage or who requires oxygen would usually be considered medically fragile. (4-03)

METERED-DOSE INHALER
One of many inhalation devices used to inhale medication—often for asthma. Metered-dose inhalers are compact, portable devices that deliver consistent doses. Alternate popular and portable ways to deliver inhaled medications are through dry powdered inhalers (devices that break a capsule, releasing a dry powder that is then inhaled). (4-21)

▶ N

NEBULIZER
Electrically powered machines that convert a liquid medication to a fine spray used to deliver inhaled asthma medications. Portable devices are available, but none are compact. (4-21)

NITRIL OR NITRILE (GLOVES)
A tested material for gloves that is less likely than latex to cause allergic reactions and has been found to be superior to neoprene or vinyl gloves for medical purposes. (6-13, 6-15)

▶ P

PARAPROFESSIONALS
Workers who are academically trained in a given profession to assist a trained professional in providing certain services. (4-05, 4-10)

PEAK FLOW METER
A simple device to measure airway restriction. It can be used at home or school to help predict asthma episode, often before symptoms appear. Peak flow values of 50% to 80% of an individual's personal best indicate a moderate asthma attack, and values below 50% indicate a severe attack. (4-21)

PEER MEDIATION

A process in which 2 or more people involved in a dispute meet with another student who is trained in the role of mediator to work out a mutually acceptable solution to their problem. Many communities have mediation centers that provide this training. (7-05)

PERIODONTAL DISEASE

Disease of the gums, the tissues encasing teeth. (4-12)

PERTUSSIS

The medical term for whooping cough. (4-14)

POSITIVE PREDICTIVE VALUE

(For screening tests), the proportion of individuals with a positive screening result who actually have the disease. (4-18)

POSITIVE YOUTH DEVELOPMENT

An approach toward all youth that builds on their assets and their potential and helps to counter problems that may affect them. Examples of key elements include providing youth with safe and supportive environments, providing opportunities for youth to pursue their interests, and providing opportunities for youth to show they care about others and their society.

POSTURAL DRAINAGE

Facilitation of the flow of secretions from various parts of the lung into the airways and throat so that they can be cleared and expelled from the lungs more easily by individuals as they assume various positions. Often required by students with cystic fibrosis and other lung diseases. Requires expertise and training to perform. (4-21)

PROCESS EVALUATION

An investigation of the all the processes that occurred when delivering a program or service. It includes documentation and assessment of what actually occurred compared to a plan. (0-13)

▶ Q

QUALITY ASSURANCE

A process of monitoring and improving the quality of health services through enforcement of health and safety standards, technical assistance, and dissemination of new technology and methodologies. (0-13, 4-32)

▶ R

RISK COMMUNICATION

Interaction with the public regarding a potential health or safety risk. Communication is bidirectional: the public needs to understand the science behind the risk, and information is often needed from the community to assess the risk. (6-02)

RUBELLA

The medical term for German measles. (4-14)

▶ S

SALMONELLA

Bacteria that cause food poisoning, typhoid fever, and other diseases in humans and domestic animals. (6-14)

SCHIZOPHRENIA

A psychotic disorder marked by disconnection between thoughts, feelings, and actions (as in hallucinations and delusions); characterized by loss of contact with the environment and by noticeable deterioration in the level of functioning in everyday life. (7-04)

SECTION 504 PLAN

A written plan that describes accommodations to be made by a school or district for a student with a disabling condition that substantially limits a major life activity. It is an individualized plan that ensures each student has access to his/her education. The title refers to Section 504 of the Rehabilitation Act of 1973. (4-20)

SEIZURE DISORDER

Predisposition to sudden disruptions of the brain's normal electrical activity accompanied by altered consciousness or other neurological and behavioral manifestations. Also known as epilepsy.

SENSITIVITY

(For a screening tests), the ability of a test to identify correctly all screened individuals who actually have the disease. (4-18)

SERVICE LEARNING

Programs that incorporate citizenship values into education by requiring students to perform community service. In some school districts, community service is a mandatory requirement for graduation. (2-08)

SOURCE CONTROL MEASURES

Actions that eliminate or reduce the release of contamination from a known source. (6-03, 6-13)

SPACER

A chamber placed between metered dose inhalers (see definition, above) of inhaled medication and the patient's mouth. Useful for children with asthma who cannot coordinate timing of their inhalation with the spray of the medication. As droplets of medication slow down and evaporate, spacers also allow for less direct impact of the medication on the lining of the mouth, minimizing some side effects. (4-19)

SPECIFICITY

(For health screening tests), the ability of a test to correctly identify only nondiseased individuals of all those who actually do not have the disease. (4-18)

STREP THROAT

An infection of the throat accompanied by fever and pain, caused by streptococcal bacteria. (4-22)

SYNTHESIS RESEARCH

The study of numerous existing research reports in order to arrive at conclusions drawn from a combination of studies. (0-11)

▶ **T**

TOXOPLASMOSIS
A disease caused by a sporozoan *Toxoplasma* when acquired after birth, characterized by fever, swollen lymph nodes, and lesions in the liver, heart, lungs, and brain. Can also affect the unborn child. (4-21, 6-14)

TRACHEOSTOMY SUCTIONING
Removal of natural fluids that are secreted in the windpipe using a small vacuum-suctioned tube. A tracheostomy is the surgical formation of an opening through the neck and into the windpipe that allows the passage of air for people who cannot breathe adequately or at all through the nose and mouth. (4-07)

TYPE 2 DIABETES
The inability of cells to respond normally to insulin; once called adult-onset diabetes, it is increasingly prevalent in children and youth because of rising rates of obesity. (4-18)

▶ **U**

UNIVERSAL PRECAUTIONS
The practice of treating the blood and body fluids of every patient as if they were infected with human immunodeficiency virus, hepatits B, or another bloodborne pathogen. Recommended precautions include using barriers, such as nonporous gloves, goggles, and face shields, and careful handling and disposal of sharp medical instruments such as needles. (8-01)

URINARY TRACT CATHETERIZATION
Passage of a catheter (thin flexible tube) into the bladder. Required at regular intervals for individuals who cannot urinate normally. (4-21)

▶ **V**

VARICELLA
The medical term for chicken pox. (4-14)

▶ **W**

WEST NILE VIRUS
A relatively newly emergent virus that primarily affects birds but can be transmitted to humans through infected mosquitoes; causes no symptoms in most individuals, flu-like symptoms in others, and serious brain inflammation on rare occasions. (6-14)

◀ **Subject Index** ▶